To Rescue
the
Constitution

TO RESCUE THE CONSTITUTION

GEORGE WASHINGTON
AND THE FRAGILE AMERICAN EXPERIMENT

BRET BAIER

with CATHERINE WHITNEY

MARINER BOOKS
New York   Boston

The Mariner flag design is a registered trademark of HarperCollins Publishers LLC.

HarperCollins books may be purchased for educational, business, or sales promotional use. For information, please email the Special Markets Department at SPsales@harpercollins.com.

A hardcover edition of this book was published in 2023 by Mariner Books.

FIRST MARINER BOOKS PAPERBACK EDITION PUBLISHED 2024.

Title page illustration © Hulton Archive/Stringer/Getty Images

Library of Congress Cataloging-in-Publication Data has been applied for.

ISBN 978-0-06-303960-5

24 25 26 27 28 LBC 5 4 3 2 1

For all who seek common ground
in the unifying principles in this book that have made
our country great from the beginning.

CONTENTS

A Note About the Text

In many instances, the spelling, punctuation, and grammar in correspondence and documents have been modernized to reflect current practices. These minor edits are designed to make the text more accessible, while reflecting the original intent.

INTRODUCTION

Our Common Ground

In the Assembly Room at Independence Hall in Philadelphia, the ghosts of the Framers spring to life from 1787. Their presence is in the woodwork. While I was writing this book, immersing myself in the life of George Washington and the work of the Constitutional Convention, I visited the scene, feeling like a time traveler from the future. I couldn't resist wondering what I and my fellows from the twenty-first century would have had to say, had we been there to join the constitutional debate. I wondered what we could have told them as they grappled with the fundamental constitutional issues. How might we have improved upon what they created?

The Constitution and the levers of government were ever present for me during the year 2022, reminding me of our purpose and rituals as a nation. I thought again of the Framers on June 13, as I stood on the floor of the US Senate, preparing for an important debate. One hundred desks were arrayed in tiers before me. The gallery above was filled with spectators. The chamber, with its vibrant color scheme of red and blue, was lit up.

Yet the setting, so familiar to television viewers, was off limits to journalists. In truth, I wasn't on the *actual* Senate floor that day. I was standing in an exact replica of the Senate chamber at the Edward M. Kennedy Institute in Boston. I was there to host a debate between two senators, both of whom assured me that the replica was so exact that it felt like home. The senators, political and ideological rivals Bernie Sanders and Lindsey Graham, had agreed to debate the economy at the invitation of the Senate Project, a coalition of the Bipartisan Policy Center, the Orrin G. Hatch Foundation, and the Edward M. Kennedy Institute for the United States Senate.

I was miked up and ready to go. The intro music could be heard over the speakers, and animated graphics for the special presentation filled the TV screens on either side of the chamber. The red light on the camera facing me flicked on, and the floor director quickly pointed to me to start. "Good afternoon from the Edward M. Kennedy Institute in Boston," I began. "We are joined today by a live audience inside the institute's full-size replica of the United States Senate, some four hundred fifty miles north of the nation's capital, for a special debate. I'm Bret Baier."

It was to be the first in a series of Oxford-style debates designed to see if agreement could be found among even the most entrenched partisans—to try to rekindle the Senate's tradition of collegial debate. The goal was to foster a discussion based on principles, not politics, much like the example of bipartisan bridge-building set by Massachusetts Democratic senator Ted Kennedy and Utah Republican senator Orrin Hatch. Their relationship was the model. In the 1990s and early 2000s, the staunchly conservative Mormon Orrin Hatch and the freewheeling liberal Edward (Ted) Kennedy—sometimes referred to as "the odd couple" and "strange bedfellows"—rose above their extensive differences when they found issues they could agree on. Together they ushered in the Americans with Disabilities Act, the Children's Health Insurance Program, and other important legislation. And though they could face off in fiery debate on the Senate floor, their close friendship endured.

The timing of the Sanders–Graham debate was meaningful for me. I was in the process of completing this book, and my mind was filled with stories of the debates at the Constitutional Convention, with Washington seated in the president's chair. Washington's purpose, the new country having won the Revolutionary War, was to create a road map for the peace. Throughout our history, Americans have looked to Washington to guide us toward meaningful civic dialogue.

The Sanders–Graham debate also had significance for the current times. The country was driven by a deep sense of division, as if a physical chasm had opened between political sides. Every idea, every word seemed to be loaded. Polls showed that a majority of Americans believed that our democracy was in jeopardy. Depending on their politics, people differed about the reasons for this, but the anxiety was clear. As a journalist traveling across twenty-first-century America covering these divisions, I heard the question everywhere: Is our system of government failing? At the same time, I could see that people were hungry for bipartisanship so that our government could get things done, and my decision to moderate the bipartisan debate was a response to the hope that this could happen.

I continued: "For the next hour, we'll try to find common ground through the constructive disagreement and search for bipartisan compromise that have been the hallmark of the US Senate for more than two centuries."

I was a journalist, but I was also an author, finishing this book about George Washington and the internal conflicts of an emerging nation. I felt as if I was straddling two eras, in which the upheavals and rhetoric sounded different in presentation but were very similar in substance.

For example, imagine this scene. In the weeks after the Constitutional Convention concluded in September 1787, as copies of the Constitution were circulated and published in local newspapers, a furor arose. Two sides formed. On one side, the Constitution was instantly considered a sacred document beyond criticism. Its opponents were said to deserve nothing better than tar and feathers. On the other side, the claws were out, tearing into the document with fevered energy. Many of the dissenters charged that the new form of government was a monarchy in disguise. Our nation, hardly born, was dangerously divided, on the brink of collapse before it even got started. And yet, by June 21, 1788, nine of the thirteen states had ratified the Constitution, making it the law of the land. The remaining four states followed. What had seemed to be insurmountable differences were resolved.

Observing this result, Washington, soon to be elected the country's first president, spoke of "a new phenomenon in the political and moral world"—referring to the powerful sight of citizens in opposition nevertheless reaching a consensus without resorting to violence.

He was right. Ratification of the Constitution was something of a miracle. Yet again and again throughout our history, such clashes of principles and ideals have occurred. And despite Washington's early optimism, there has been violence—though we've always, as a country, pulled ourselves back from the brink.

Writing about the early days of our nation, I couldn't help thinking: of course there were divisions! This was not a monarchy. This was not a dictatorship. It was a free country where the most valued principle was the open exchange of ideas. Dissent was baked into the cake. But so was union.

"And now, without further ado, let's get started," I announced to the audience. "Please welcome Vermont senator Bernie Sanders and South Carolina senator Lindsey Graham." Applause filled the chamber as the senators walked in from opposite sides of the room, smiling, waving, and eventually shaking each other's hands. I walked up and shook each man's hand as well.

I found the modern-day matchup between Sanders and Graham telling. Glimmers of age-old face-offs could be seen. Sanders, a classic Northeast liberal/socialist, carried shades of the radical Sam Adams and of Elbridge Gerry, one of three Framers who refused to sign the new Constitution. Graham, a conservative in the mold of Southern Framers like Charles Pinckney, echoed some of the same debates that occurred 235 years ago on the subject of states' rights and the power of the national government.

Senator Sanders won the coin toss and strode to the lectern for his opening remarks. In his distinctive voice, he began, "Well, let me thank the Kennedy Institute for hosting the event, Fox News for broadcasting it, and my colleague Lindsey Graham for being here with me."

After a four-minute opener, largely about the challenges facing the working and middle class in America, it was Senator Graham's turn. In his thick South Carolina drawl, he said, "This place is awesome! If you get to Boston, come see this place. We're here to honor Ted and Orrin. Ted Kennedy and Orrin Hatch, who were great friends. They fought like tigers, but they could work together. And I have a different take on things than Bernie, but I like Bernie."

Graham's four minutes were largely filled with examples of why Americans were not better off than they were two years earlier (when President Biden took office) and how socialism is not the answer to all of our problems.

The Sanders–Graham debate wasn't exactly an ode to common ground, but there were moments of agreement, most surprisingly over gun-control legislation that was then being considered in the Senate. The takeaway for me was that even when common ground was lacking on individual issues, there were positive signs for our republic. The debate got hot at moments (as the Hatch–Kennedy debates used to), but it was largely cordial and serious. The two men were willing to go beyond political posturing and delve into policy in ways the public does not often see. It was heartening—an unusually civil and civic-minded occasion at a time when our nation seems hopelessly fractured and our adherence to the Constitution has seemed insecure. In 2023 I would moderate another debate between Iowa Republican Senator Joni Ernst and New Hampshire Democratic Senator Jeanne Shaheen. It began with a hug and then became a forceful debate involving sharp differences and areas of common ground.

This is the fifth book in my presidential series. The first three books focused on America at the critical period from before World War II until the end of the Cold War. *Three Days at the Brink: FDR's Daring Gamble to Win World War II* took readers inside the Tehran conference, where President Franklin Delano Roosevelt, Winston Churchill, and Josef Stalin laid plans for D-Day, which ushered in the end of World War II; but their meeting also marked the beginning of the Cold War. *Three Days in January: Dwight Eisenhower's Final Mission* explored the dangerous early days of the Cold War, with Stalin breaking the promises he'd made to Roosevelt and Churchill, and showed Eisenhower leading during a treacherous era, when fear of a nuclear catastrophe was ever-present. *Three Days in Moscow: Ronald Reagan and the Fall of the Soviet Empire* focused on the end of the Cold War, when Reagan deployed a masterful diplomatic strategy with his Soviet counterpart Mikhail Gorbachev.

After the *Three Days* series, I went back to another dangerous turning point of our nation with *To Rescue the Republic: Ulysses S. Grant, the Fragile Union, and the Crisis of 1876*. That book examined the extraordinary efforts by President Grant to hold the country together and prevent it from falling into a second civil war.

The four books focused on leadership and moments in time that history has largely overlooked or taken for granted in the telling of our American story. In this book we return to the beginning, the founding of our nation, to report on the amazing efforts of delegates to the Constitutional Convention and beyond. It showcases the leadership of many who toiled to make the new nation work—none harder than George Washington, our first president. Time and again, Washington accepted the mantle of service to the country. By twice unanimously electing him president, the people's electors acknowledged his critical role in rescuing and elevating our system of government.

In recent years, the US Constitution has been under attack from both sides of the ideological spectrum. Is it still relevant? Does it need to be changed for our times? In a recent piece for *Chicago Policy Review*, the journal's executive editor, Sidhant Wadhera, writes, "New circumstances require new institutions to handle the situations of the day. In the United States we are told to revere our Constitution and its Framers. The fact of the matter is that a flawed 18th century document cannot rise to the challenges of our time." Others strenuously disagree, and the debate is essential to our nature as a nation.

This book tells the story of the Framers and their great leader—and how close they came to not getting a constitution at all. It describes how the Constitution became what many have called the greatest legal writing ever penned to paper and the one piece of paper protecting us from tyranny. It shows the formation of a nation based on ideals.

"Senator Sanders, Senator Graham, we'll have to leave it at that. Thank you very much." The crowd applauded and the music started again, marking the end of the program, as I made my way to the stage to shake the senators' hands. "This was fun!" said Graham. "Yeah, it was," agreed Sanders. One step closer to common ground.

Bret Baier, October 2023

TO RESCUE
THE
CONSTITUTION

PROLOGUE

Where Are the Delegates?

On May 14, 1787, a disgruntled George Washington sat in the Pennsylvania State House (later Independence Hall), fuming. Outside the rain was pouring down, and the nearly empty Assembly Room felt desolate and chilly. Washington wasn't feeling well—he suffered from severe rheumatoid arthritis, and his shoulder, which had been bothering him for weeks, throbbed. Even so, he'd made the journey of 150 miles from Mount Vernon in Virginia to Philadelphia, setting off on May 9 despite inclement weather, and had arrived on time for the scheduled start of the Constitutional Convention on May 14. Yet on that day, only he and the delegates from Pennsylvania and Virginia were present, and not even all of them. Where was his neighbor and colleague George Mason, with whom he had spent long hours planning for this day? Where were the delegates from the other states? As the days dragged on, and only a few others arrived, Washington brooded. It was, he complained, "highly vexacious to those who are idly, and expensively spending their time here."

James Madison, the scrappy Virginia legislator who, despite being socially shy, was a dogged federalist and a leading force behind the convention, joined Washington, having arrived in Philadelphia a full eleven days early from his office in New York City. He reassured him: The others were coming. Terrible weather had slowed their progress. Don't worry! Washington might have observed that the weather had been no impediment to *him*—though his carriage had slogged through rain and mud, the bumpy ride painfully firing up his shoulder.

Madison and Washington were not longtime friends, but in the previous year they had come to a common frame of mind about the desperate need for action. As Washington wrote to Madison in late 1786, a new constitution was needed, and "the superstructure we have been seven years raising at the expense of much blood and treasure must fall. We are fast verging on anarchy and confusion."

Soon after the end of the War of Independence, the fragile union began cracking apart. Starkly put, the state of the new nation was a terrible mess. Having won the eight-year battle with Great Britain, it now faced self-destruction. Washington had shepherded a ragtag, undisciplined army through the horrors of war and on to victory. He now faced the unsettling prospect that the unity derived from battling a common foe would be destroyed by peacetime quarrels.

Like the dog who caught the carriage, the American patriots had no solid plan for what would happen once independence was secured. The Articles of Confederation passed by the thirteen states in 1777 described little more than a loosely joined arrangement—hardly a union worthy of the title "United States of America." The states basically did as they pleased, and what pleased one state often created trouble for another. A central government that might settle disputes, particularly over trade and tariffs, was nonexistent.

The war had left an enormous debt in its wake, to both foreign and domestic creditors, and as the bill came due in the states, people were shocked by a crushing reality check. Individual states took it on themselves to collect taxes and raise tariffs, pitting some states against others in conducting commerce. Relations became so bitter that there was talk of civil war in a nation barely formed.

Watching with alarm from Virginia, Washington wrote to Madison in November 1785, "We are either a united people, or we are not. If the former, let us, in all matters of general concern act as a nation, which have national objects to promote, and a national character to support—If we are not, let us no longer act a farce by pretending to it."

Matters came to a head in western Massachusetts in 1786, when Daniel Shays, who had served as an officer in the war, led an uprising of farmers—most of them veterans—against tax and debt collectors. The farmers, and the citizenry at large, were outraged at being asked to pay taxes higher than those they'd paid to Great Britain, and felt they were being held hostage to unreasonable loan repayment terms. A spate of farm foreclosures and even arrests stirred the smoldering embers of revolutionary fervor.

In a morose letter to John Jay, a friend and ally, in May 1786, Washington wrote, "From the high ground on which we stood—from the plain path which invited our footsteps, to be so fallen!—so lost! is really mortifying." The only hope was to take dramatic action: "That it is necessary to revise and amend the Articles of Confederation I entertain *no* doubt. But what may be the consequences of such an attempt *is* doubtful."

Although Shays' Rebellion was ultimately quelled by a hastily formed army directed by the governor of Massachusetts, the incident underscored the weakness of the Articles of Confederation in providing a governing blueprint. Prompted by a rising sense of urgency, on February 21, Congress passed a declaration calling for a convention of state delegates in Philadelphia on the second Monday in May "for the sole and express purpose of revising the Articles of Confederation."

As delegations from the states began to take shape, Washington, contentedly retired at Mount Vernon, let it be known that he probably would not attend. After the war he had vowed to retire from public life—to let others carry the banner of the new nation. When the war ended, in 1783, he'd sent a message to the states, bidding a formal farewell. He made his intentions crystal clear, leaving no opening for anything but a certain retirement: "The great object, for which I had the honor to hold an appointment in the service of my country being accomplished, I am now preparing to resign it into the hands of Congress, and to return to that domestic retirement; which it is well known I left with the greatest reluctance, a retirement for which I have never ceased to sigh through a long and painful absence, and in which (remote from the noise and trouble of the world) I meditate to pass the remainder of life, in a state of undisturbed repose."

He went on to offer a lengthy treatise on the new nation, including this dire warning: "It appears to me there is an option still left to the United States of America; that it is in their choice and depends upon their conduct, whether they will be respectable and prosperous or contemptible and miserable as a nation."

It was just such misery weighing down the country that created the need for a constitutional convention. Washington, however, continued to resist involvement. He was beset by concerns: Would the convention attract sober delegates who could meet the challenge, or would it devolve into a chaotic airing of hostilities? Would his reputation be tarnished by such bedlam—or conversely, would his reputation suffer from his unwillingness to participate? Did he have a moral obligation to be there? On a personal level, would his absence be fair to Martha and his family? Was he physically up to it?

He grumbled in a letter to Henry Knox, a senior general in the Continental Army and his former chief of artillery during the war:

"This journey (of more than one hundred miles) in the disordered state of my body will, I am persuaded, unfit me for the intended trip to Philadelphia, and assuredly prevent me from offering that tribute of respect to my compatriots in arms which result from affection and gratitude for their attachment to, and support of me upon so many trying occasions."

But he couldn't turn away from what was happening, and the actions of his compatriots were gnawing away at his resolve to stay home.

He was disturbed that his fellow Virginian, Patrick Henry—whose "Give me liberty or give me death!" speech to the Virginia legislature in 1775 had roused the people to fight—now opposed the Constitutional Convention and refused the governor's invitation to serve as a delegate. Henry believed that the convention would be a subversion of democracy and the first step to creating a monarchy. Already there were rumors that Rhode Island would decline to participate at all, amid similar concerns.

A pragmatist, Washington recognized that the view of firebrands like Henry was misguided. The task of the convention was challenging but straightforward: to write a script that the nation could follow in all its business. Washington rejected the binary choice set up by critics: monarchy or chaos. And as the convention date approached, he finally gave in to the urging of his colleagues. He would attend the convention. Perhaps his change of heart came from accepting the simple truth that he held a singular place in the hearts of his countrymen. For this sacrifice he won the praise of Madison: "To forsake the honorable retreat to which he had retired and risk the reputation he had so deservedly acquired, manifested a zeal for the public interest. . . ."

Now Washington had to break the news to his wife. Their happy private life was about to be interrupted. There is no record of that conversation, but it couldn't have been easy. Martha had believed with all her heart that her husband's public service was over. Having made the sacrifice of eight long years at war, as well as devoted service beforehand to the emerging Continental Congress, he had earned his retirement, and she had earned the right to have him by her side. This new commitment would not feel like a one-off to her. She knew how much people relied on George, and she had to believe that his involvement in the convention would be the beginning of a new public chapter.

George and Martha had been invited by Robert Morris to stay at his grand Philadelphia house, two blocks from the State House, for the duration of the convention. Morris, an English-born Philadelphia merchant, had become an indispensable financial organizer during the war, superintendent of finance of the nascent United States, and a Pennsylvania delegate to the Continental Congress. He and Washington were close friends; their wives were also close. Morris would be serving as a delegate to the convention, and he and his wife, Mary, were excited about the prospect of having the Washingtons stay in their home. "We will give you as little trouble as possible," he wrote, "and endeavor to make it agreeable, it will be a charming season for traveling, and Mrs. Washington as well as yourself will find benefit from the journey, change of air, etc."

Washington was grateful for the invitation, which spared him having to look for lodging at public houses. He wrote back to Morris, apologizing that Martha would be absent, as she was too busy looking after two grandchildren who lived with them. "Mrs. Washington is become too domestic, and too attentive to two little grandchildren to leave home." He'd be coming alone, regretfully.

Although his greatest wish was "to glide gently down the stream of life in tranquil retirement," in truth, Washington's life at Mount Vernon was hardly a gentle glide into oblivion. His home was a constantly bustling enterprise, frequented by tourists, who thought nothing of arriving unannounced to gawk at the famous general, and by friends and family clamoring for attention: children and grandchildren, nieces and nephews. So he might have been looking forward to getting away to Morris's quieter abode.

He knew one thing: it would be a difficult journey, one he wasn't looking forward to. Then, shortly before his scheduled date of departure, Washington received an urgent message summoning him to Fredericksburg, forty miles away. His mother, suffering from breast cancer, had taken a turn for the worse, and his sister Betty, who was caring for her, was in a state of exhaustion. (The mother of eleven, Betty was stressed on an ordinary day. Caring for her dying mother added to her burden.) Moreover, the whole family had been shaken by the recent unexpected death of George's younger brother John Augustine, known to be his favorite sibling. Thinking that his mother was dying, he immediately set off. He wrote to Henry Knox, "I am summoned by an express who assures me not a moment is to be lost, to see a mother, and *only* sister (who are supposed to be in the agonies of death) expire; and I am hastening to obey this melancholy call, after having just bid an eternal farewell to a much loved brother who was the intimate companion of my youth and the most affectionate friend of my ripened age."

When Washington arrived in Fredericksburg, his arthritic arm dangling in a sling, he found things better than he'd expected. In fact, his mother would live two more years. He returned home, where he rested for a few days before setting out for Philadelphia.

As his carriage traveled into Chester, south of Philadelphia, Washington peered out through the haze and downpour at the sodden blanket of earth ahead. He spotted a rain-soaked gathering at the side of the road. As his carriage approached, people called out to him with eager voices. A familiar figure, as if from a flashback, rode toward him, and as the rider drew near, Washington recognized his wartime aide-de-camp, Colonel David Humphreys. Behind him, among others, was General Henry Knox. The welcoming committee—which totaled three generals, two colonels, and two majors—rode with him into Philadelphia.

There, Washington found that bad weather had not dampened the spirits of the citizenry. Hearing that he was coming, people had gathered along his route, cheering as if he was sweeping into town after a military victory rather than arriving humbly in the cloak of a working legislator. Scores of mounted civilians greeted him, along with the Light Horse Troop of Philadelphia, which had fought in the battles of Trenton, Princeton, Brandywine, and Germantown. Newspapers headlined his arrival with great excitement, the *Pennsylvania Evening Herald* reporting the spectacle and applauding Washington's devotion to the nation: "This great patriot will never think his duty performed, while any thing remains to be done."

The enthusiastic welcome touched Washington deeply, reminding him of the gravity of the mission. Dropping his bags at Morris's mansion, he immediately set off toward Third Street to pay his respects to Benjamin Franklin, the nominal host of the convention by virtue of being a revered elder and the leader of the Pennsylvania delegation.

When Washington arrived, he admired Franklin's newly renovated property, only a block from the State House and charmingly situated around a tranquil courtyard. Franklin was obviously quite proud of the renovation, although he'd been in London for most of its construction.

The two men hadn't seen one another since 1776. As they enjoyed a drink by the fire, Washington regarded his aging colleague with affection. Though stooped, Franklin was mentally sharp and still impossibly active at eighty-one, eager to start this fresh adventure. He was unfailingly cheerful, with a robust personality, even though plagued by some common trials of age—gout, kidney stones, and physical weakness, as well as being overweight. He chatted with Washington in high spirits about the marvelous features of his new home, which included a vast library of more than four thousand books and an elegant dining room table that seated twenty-four. He had plans to transform a large ground-floor area into a working print shop and bindery for his grandson Benjamin Franklin Bache.

In Franklin's presence, Washington was reminded of the inevitability of aging. Despite his own stiff bones and aching joints, he still managed an erect posture, but he knew he showed his years. The delegations would represent a fair split between young and old. Eighteen delegates were under forty, among them Alexander Hamilton (thirty) and James Madison (thirty-six). The youngest delegate, Jonathon Dayton of New Jersey, was twenty-six. Twenty-three men were in their forties, with the remainder in the elder tier. At fifty-five, Washington fit into that category. Franklin, of course, was the oldest.

On the morning of May 14, Washington and Madison walked together to the State House, where the proceedings were scheduled to begin that day. They would gather in the large Assembly Room, forty by forty feet with high ceilings and wide windows. The room was so bright that it shimmered. Later, in the heat of a particularly brutal summer, slatted blinds would be drawn over the windows to reduce the sun's glare, but even so there was plenty of light. In this room the Declaration of Independence had been signed. Neither man had been present on that occasion: Washington was with the Continental Army in New York, and Madison, just twenty-five in 1776 and not yet on the national stage, was serving in the Virginia legislature.

They were met by members of the Pennsylvania and Virginia delegations. No other states were represented on what was supposed to be the convention's opening day. Nor did anyone arrive on May 15.

On the 16th, with only those two states yet in attendance, Washington joined a few of the men for dinner in Franklin's expansive dining room. Franklin described the evening as "what the French call *une assemblée des notables*, a convention composed of some of the principal people from the several states of our confederation." Franklin had procured a cask of porter, a delicious dark beer, which was greatly appreciated. The event was a sweet respite, and the conversation around the table was high-minded and even important, but Washington was itching to get started with the convention.

But the wait continued through the following days, with delegates drifting in. Once all of the Virginia delegates were present, they began to hold meetings with the Pennsylvania delegation every day at 3:00 p.m. for several hours, hoping to get a head start on proceedings. Their purpose was "to grow into some acquaintance with each other."

Day by day, state delegates continued to trickle in, and by May 20, Washington was running out of patience. He wrote to his neighbor Arthur Lee, "Not more than four states were represented yesterday. If any are come in since it is unknown to me. These delays greatly impede public measures, and serve to sour the temper of the punctual members who do not like to idle away their time." The only good news was that his shoulder was feeling better.

At last, on May 25, a quorum of seven states was reached, with twenty-nine delegates present. Ultimately twelve states and a total of fifty-five delegates (out of seventy chosen) would take part. The exception was Rhode Island, which didn't send delegates at all, boycotting the convention to protest centralized government. (The famously even-tempered Washington was disgusted with Rhode Island's decision, writing at one point during the proceedings, "Rhode Island . . . still perseveres in that impolitic, unjust, and one might add without much impropriety, scandalous conduct, which seems to have marked all her public councils of late.")

Finally the convention was convened. The first order of business was to elect a president. Franklin had wanted to nominate Washington but was ill and not in attendance that day. With Franklin absent, Morris had the honor of nominating his friend. Elected unanimously, Washington was ushered to a polished, high-backed chair at the front of the hall, where he would oversee the proceedings. Made by a local craftsman in 1779 for the speaker of the Pennsylvania legislature, the chair was replete with symbols. Carved into its crest rail was a liberty pole with cap, symbolizing freedom, along with a semicircular sun.

Looking out on the gathering, Washington expressed his respect for the solemnity of the occasion. He thanked his fellows for the honor they had given him, lamented his lack of qualifications for the position, and asked them to forgive him in advance for any errors his inexperience would cause. This wasn't false humility. He was sincere. But other delegates might have chuckled or rolled their eyes at the thought that a man so central to the creation of the nation, both in war and in peace, would consider himself inexperienced.

Washington's demeanor was grave. He was not optimistic about the convention's prospects. As he wrote to Thomas Jefferson, who was abroad serving as ambassador to France, "Much is expected by some—but little by others—and nothing by a few. That something is necessary, all will agree; for the situation of the general government (if it can be called a government) is shaken to its foundation. . . . In a word, it is at an end, and unless a remedy is soon applied, anarchy and confusion will inevitably ensue."

More than a decade earlier, Jefferson had fathered the nation's fundamental statement of purpose—the declaration of what these men were about and what they were about to do. It was followed by the Articles of Confederation, hammered out by the Second Continental Congress as the war that would secure independence raged on. With heartfelt intention and the sacrifice of lives and treasure, the Founders had formed a union. Now it was time to fully realize its promise with a document that would stand the test of the ages.

PART ONE

THE MAKING OF WASHINGTON

CHAPTER ONE

A STROKE OF DESTINY

Two days before Christmas of 1777, on a desolate plateau north of Philadelphia, George Washington, commander in chief of the Continental Army, surveyed his troops with dismay. He had just sent an urgent message to Henry Laurens, president of the Continental Congress—in exile in York, Pennsylvania. Philadelphia, the center of the new government, had been captured by the British in September, and now only Washington's beleaguered troops stood in the way of utter defeat. But the condition of the soldiers under his command was desperate—men without shoes trailing bloody footprints on the ground, their uniforms shredded with wear. Starved and dirty, they were unfit to fight.

For Washington, this season at Valley Forge was a low point in the war, well into its third year. "I am now convinced beyond a doubt," he wrote to Laurens, "that unless some great and capital change suddenly takes place in that line this Army must inevitably be reduced to one or other of these three things. Starve—dissolve—or disperse. . . ." He was not exaggerating, he told Laurens, detailing the many indignities and the poor conditions his men were enduring.

For now General Washington would wait, steeling himself against the chill and deprivation, executing the small daily acts of care and leadership that were within his power. He was aware of a chorus of dissatisfaction in the colonies, including a prominent group that had formed for the sole purpose of replacing him as commander. He shot back at his critics in the same letter to Laurens: "I can assure those gentlemen that it is a much easier and less distressing thing to draw remonstrances in a comfortable room by a good fireside than to occupy a cold, bleak hill and sleep under frost and snow without clothes or blankets."

A year earlier nearly to the day, the Continental Army under his leadership had scored the most decisive victory of the war so far, when he crossed the icy Delaware River to attack the British at Trenton, New Jersey. That glorious victory had propelled them on, giving the troops an extra measure of endurance. This moment at Valley Forge, Washington believed, was the final crucible, which would determine whether they were capable of victory.

Their purpose for fighting and struggling and dying was writ large in the Declaration of Independence, produced the preceding year. The declaration was not a legal document but a force of inspiration. Its chief author and Washington's fellow Virginian, Thomas Jefferson, knew how to make the poetry of independence resonate: "We hold these truths to be self-evident, that all men are created equal, that they are endowed by their Creator with certain unalienable Rights, that among these are Life, Liberty and the pursuit of Happiness."

Those high aspirations, standing against the oppressive rule of the British monarchy, had brought them to this grim outpost of Pennsylvania to endure the trials of a long winter. The emerging nation was battling for its life.

In this new land, where fighting and governing were not separate occupations but part of a continuum of service, it would be Washington's destiny to play a seminal role in both war and peace. "America . . . has ever had, and I trust she ever will have, my honest exertions to promote her interest," he wrote to Patrick Henry, at the height of the war. "I cannot hope that my services have been the best—but my heart tells me they have been the best that I could render." He fulfilled that aim throughout his lifetime of public service.

The forty-five-year-old commander of the Continental Army looked the part: tall, erect, strong, and solemn in his demeanor. He revealed little of his inner life, and much about his true nature remains a mystery, subject to frequent embellishments over the centuries.

Washington wasn't scholarly and elitist like Thomas Jefferson or an intellectual powerhouse like John Adams. He lacked Ben Franklin's genius and charisma. He showed little of Alexander Hamilton's fiery passion or James Madison's analytical rigor.

He was even-tempered (most of the time), thoughtful, humble, and circumspect. Aristocratic in bearing, he was also good-natured, with a sweet and affectionate side. He was a good husband to Martha, a warm stepfather to her two children, a doting grandfather, and a lover of dogs.

Americans think they know George Washington nearly as well as their own fathers. In the chiseled cut of his face as it appears in illustrations and on statues, they divine his character: strong, steady, solemn. As our first military general and first president, he became the exemplar of leadership.

But he wasn't made of stone. He had flaws and unfulfilled passions. He had family difficulties, just like anyone else.

The people hadn't yet formulated what they wanted from a chief executive, but clearly Washington's role as chief commander in the decisive war spoke to them of leadership. For nearly 250 years since then, George Washington has been the vessel into which Americans pour many of their hopes and dreams. He is not just one of the Founders; in the minds of many he is the first Founder.

Some historians have noted that he was exactly the model the Framers of the Constitution had in mind when they designed the role of president—an idea borne out by the electors' unanimous selection of him as the first to hold that office.

But who was he?

In a nineteenth-century treatise, Henry Cabot Lodge perfectly captured the dilemma of defining Washington: "In the progress of time Washington has become in the popular imagination largely mythical. . . . Thus we have today in our minds a Washington grand, solemn, and impressive. In this guise he appears as a man of lofty intellect, vast moral force, supremely successful and fortunate, and wholly apart from and above his fellow men." In other words, godlike.

Biography is often the process of finding the extraordinary in ordinary lives. But the opposing impulse can be found too. As the popular nineteenth-century author Wayne Whipple pointed out, "Nearly every recent biographer has announced that he was now taking down the wooden image called 'Washington' from its high pedestal."

That image, and the pedestal upon which it sits, has survived mostly unchanged, although modern historians are more inclined to point out Washington's flaws, including the big one—his status as a slave owner. But his contribution to our constitutional system is without parallel.

In his life, Washington was more instrumental than any other person in the creation of the American ideal of leadership. He not only helped write its blueprint; he lived it. As president, the choices he made set the standard for how that role would be defined. He had no models to look to. No one left a note in his desk when he took office as president. He was the only president who did not receive the torch from another. He was the torch.

The birth of our republic did not happen in a dream but through a bloody and contentious battle over the course of many years. It was a human drama, just as the Constitution is a human document. It was not handed down from any mountaintop but was hammered out on the ground.

Many patriots were made in those tumultuous years, and George Washington was first among them. Who was this man who reached such elevated standing—chosen as the nation's commander, both in war and in peace?

George Washington—no middle name—was born on February 22, 1732, on a farm at Pope's Creek, a tributary that feeds into the Potomac River. It was a lush corner of Virginia's Westmoreland County, and George's father, Augustine, was a moderately prosperous tobacco farmer.

Augustine's American lineage dated back to the mid-1600s, when his tobacco merchant grandfather, John, made a tumultuous arrival. His merchant ship traveling from England sank, stranding him in Virginia. He didn't mind staying, though. He appreciated the advantages of distance from British oversight. John settled in the fertile area between the Rappahannock and Potomac Rivers. A well-to-do plantation owner named Nathaniel Pope (for whom Pope's Creek was named) befriended John, who became enamored of Pope's daughter Anne. George and Martha married and became prominent citizens of the thriving colony of Virginia.

Over the course of more than a century, the thirteen colonies were established by British settlers. Virginia was the first of them—established in 1607 and named Jamestown—and Georgia the last, founded in 1732. They were distributed into three general regions: The Northeast included Massachusetts, New Hampshire, Rhode Island, and Connecticut. The middle states were New York, New Jersey, Maryland, Pennsylvania, and Delaware. The southern tier comprised Virginia, North Carolina, South Carolina, and Georgia.

The colonies were by no means monolithic. Settlements were formed for various reasons and took on their own cultural identities, depending on where the settlers originated and the nature of the geography of the terrain. All were colonies of England, but they developed different systems of local government. In Virginia's case, it was a commonwealth.

One thing the colonies had in common was the attraction of freedom. Long before a government was established on principles of religious and political freedom, the quest for these was essential to the nature of the emerging society. With freedom came the promise of self-realization and opportunity that did not exist in Europe. Still, the colonies' ties to the motherland were strong, and America was considered rough around the edges. For example, young men whose families could afford it were still educated in England.

As the first colony, Virginia was socially the most developed. Alexander Spotswood, who served as lieutenant governor for twelve years in the early eighteenth century, noted that it was the most pleasing place he'd ever been, with "less swearing, less profaneness, less drunkenness and debauchery, less uncharitable feuds and animosities, and less knavery and villainy than in any part of the world." This air of civility was Virginia's claim to fame, and the Washingtons were emblematic of that society.

George Washington arrived in this new world as the first child of Augustine and Mary Ball Washington. It was Augustine's second marriage. His first wife, Jane, had died tragically at age twenty-nine, leaving Augustine with three children—Lawrence, age eleven at the time; Augustine Jr., ten; and Jane, seven. Only the two boys would live to adulthood; Jane died when she was twelve. In 1731, Augustine, then thirty-seven, married the twenty-three-year-old Mary Ball, who brought to the marriage some independent resources. They would have five surviving children: George, born in 1732; Elizabeth (Betty), 1733; Samuel, 1734; John Augustine, 1736; and Charles, 1738. A sixth child, Mildred, born in 1737, died when she was three. It was quite a brood.

When George was six, the family moved to a 280-acre property on a hill overlooking the Rappahannock River, across from Fredericksburg. It boasted a one-and-a-half-story clapboard structure, with four rooms below and four above a center hall, and a large basement. There Augustine farmed corn, wheat, and tobacco, with the aid of enslaved labor. He owned twenty-five slaves. The family called the property the Home Farm. Much later, after the Washingtons no longer owned the place, it became known as Ferry Farm, for the ferry that crossed the Rappahannock there.

Ferry Farm was not left standing for posterity. During the Civil War, Union soldiers encamped at Ferry Farm were well aware of its historical importance, even sending cherry pits home to family as souvenirs. However, that didn't stop them from tearing down the house, plank by plank, to use as fuel and as timber for their headquarters.

A frustrating vagueness surrounds Washington's early life. It is so barren of anecdotes that it's no wonder the famous cherry tree story was invented. That story—for generations the only thing schoolchildren learned about George's childhood—was the brainchild of an early Washington biographer named Mason Locke Weems, who embellished the dry account of his life with details meant to show his virtuous character—therefore, "I cannot tell a lie."

What is well established is that a striking event completely changed George's life when he was eleven years old—the death of his father at the age of forty-nine. Augustine's passing, on April 12, 1743, abruptly put an end to George's normal comforts and expected future.

It must have been a confusing and demoralizing time for George. Certain dreams and ambitions died along with Augustine. Growing up, George had been fully aware of the advantages he was owed, including an opportunity to receive a classical education in Great Britain, like his two older half-brothers. This education, he'd been told, separated men of promise from ordinary farmers, and though Augustine was not as rich as some of his neighbors, he was full of ambition to stand toe to toe with them.

George's half-brother Lawrence, fourteen years his senior, had served in the British army in the West Indies, fighting against the Spaniards. Returning home shortly before his father's death, he found himself suddenly responsible for the family business and property. He soon married, making a favorable match: Anne Fairfax was the daughter of Colonel William Fairfax, the cousin of Lord Fairfax who was influential and wealthy, with massive property holdings in Virginia. It was a family connection that would prove beneficial to George. The William Fairfaxes lived in a beautiful brick mansion called Belvoir on the Potomac River. Lawrence began building a home three miles away on his inherited land— what would later become Mount Vernon. George would often visit his brother, and he became close friends with Anne Fairfax's young brother, George William.

No longer able to attend school in England, George had to make do with a cobbled-together education from tutors and self-study. He learned the basics but also discovered an interest in mathematics, particularly geometry and trigonometry, that would come in handy later.

An important part of George's education was instruction on being a good person, which his mother urged upon him. He was encouraged to read and copy out each of the 110 rules outlined in a sixteenth-century etiquette book titled *Rules of Civility and Decent Behavior in Company and Conversation*. The idea was that, by copying them in slow and careful penmanship, he would internalize them and make them his own.

Many of the rules were purely matters of etiquette. For example:

- If You Cough, Sneeze, Sigh, or Yawn, do it not Loud but Privately; and Speak not in your Yawning, but put Your handkercheif [sic] or Hand before your face and turn aside.

- Bedew no man's face with your Spittle, by approaching too near him [when] you Speak.

- Play not the Peacock, looking everywhere about you, to See if you be well decked, if your Shoes fit well if your Stockings sit neatly, and Cloths handsomely.

Others were more of a moral code or code of character:

- Show not yourself glad at the Misfortune of another though he were your enemy.

- When a man does all he can though it Succeeds not well blame not him that did it.

- Be not hasty to believe flying Reports to the Disparagement of any.

- Associate yourself with Men of good Quality if you Esteem your own Reputation; for 'tis better to be alone than in bad Company.

- Labour to keep alive in your Breast that Little Spark of Celestial fire Called Conscience.

We can imagine young George copying each of these dictates carefully into his school notebook. By all accounts, he was that kind of boy. According to his contemporary biographer, David Ramsay, writing in 1807, Washington's friends described him as "grave, silent, and thoughtful; diligent and methodical in business, dignified in his appearance, and strictly honorable in his deportment." Alas, Ramsay notes, these friends were unable to summon a single illustrative anecdote.

If the characterization is true, these qualities were instilled largely by his mother, who was a dominating force in his life. Henry Cabot Lodge described Mary Ball Washington this way: "She was an imperious woman, of strong will, ruling her kingdom alone."

After his father's death, George saw the strength of his mother in a new light. Having lost both of her own parents at an early age—her father when she was three and her mother when she was thirteen—she had learned to be self-sufficient. But she could be tough on those around her.

George chafed under her controlling grip, resenting the fact that her word was law. Mary was startled one day to learn of a plan being hatched by Colonel Fairfax and Lawrence to enlist George into the Royal Navy. He was only fourteen! For his part, George was thrilled by the idea of embarking on a life at sea, but Mary absolutely forbade it. Her judgment was not solely or even primarily based on her son's tender years. She had consulted with her half-brother Joseph in England, and he had assured her that a naval career was a nonstarter for George. He lacked the connections and the education to rise through the ranks and make something of himself. That verdict stung and reinforced his diminished status since his father's death. Whatever her true concerns, Mary put her foot down and refused to let him go.

Much about Mary lives in the realm of legend, word of mouth and speculation repeated by writers and historians. Little is known for certain about her character. Depending on the source, she is presented as tart-tongued, demanding, difficult, and a bane on her famous son's existence. Historian Bonnie Angelo brutally judged her effect on George, calling her "a woman of small intelligence and great complaints, [who] gave him a hard time all her long life."

But another perspective shows her as a strong woman fiercely devoted to her children. Although she was only thirty-five when her husband died and might have had suitors, she chose not to remarry, and she raised her family on her own. Her husband's will gave George ownership of the Home Farm when he turned twenty-one, so, like many women of the time, she ran a farm that did not belong to her and relied on the benevolence of her son. She didn't always think he treated her as well as he should. Later, George would buy Mary a house in Fredericksburg, near his sister Betty and her husband, but Mary would continue to complain that her needs were unmet.

Decades later, George Washington Parke Custis, the son of Washington's stepson Jacky, offered a romanticized view of Mary's strong hand in the development of her son's character.

> The matron held in reserve an authority, which never departed from her; not even when her son had become the most illustrious of men. It seemed to say, "I am your mother, the being who gave you life, the guide who directed your steps when they needed the guidance of age and wisdom . . . ; whatever may be your success, whatever your renown, next to your God you owe them most to me."

Well, not quite. Washington loved his mother, but as an adult he had little patience for her. There is no record of his expressing pure affection, and he appeared to tire of her difficult nature.

Because Washington has been so admired and even worshipped, his treatment of his mother may seem troubling and inconsistent. And where were Mary's other children? In their defense, George assured a friend that his mother "has not a child that would not divide the last sixpence to relieve her from real distress. This she has been repeatedly assured of by me; and all of us, I am certain, would feel much hurt, at having our mother a pensioner, while we had the means of supporting her; but in fact she has an ample income of her own."

But all that angst came later. The young George, now fatherless, was focused on who he would become. He was strong, athletic, and well-behaved—a good son and brother. But he was longing to escape.

During this uncertain period, George spent as much time as he could at Mount Vernon and was also a frequent guest of the Fairfaxes at Belvoir. Colonel Fairfax liked the boy and decided to take him under his wing.

Two years after his effort to launch a naval career for George, Colonel Fairfax had another idea—to set him up with a job as a surveyor. Surveyors were much in demand in the developing colonies surrounded by a vast, unmapped frontier. Every year the population was growing as people flocked westward to those fertile lands, and surveyors defined the territory. In many respects, they held the fortunes of the eager arrivals in their hands. George's math skills made him a good candidate for the work. So did his youth and adventurous spirit. He thought surveying might become his profession.

Lord Fairfax had a massive land grant of more than five million acres in Virginia, inherited through his mother's family, and the sale of parcels would become a lucrative venture. In 1748, Fairfax hired his son George William and George to take part in a survey party. The two boys were mostly there to observe more practiced surveyors and learn what was involved. The assignment was also meant to see how the youths would hold up in rugged conditions. As biographer Douglas Southall Freeman described it, George emerged from his initiation with fresh skills and a deeper appreciation of the territory: "He had seen with his own eyes the fine western lands. He had felt the frontier."

Afterward, Colonel Fairfax used his influence to get Washington a position as county surveyor for the new Virginia county of Culpeper, then on the edge of the western frontier. He worked for Culpeper for a year before going out on his own for two years, primarily in Frederick County.

Washington was good at the job of surveyor because he was robust, curious, and energetic. He loved the life, which was such a departure from his staid upbringing. He recorded his experiences in "A Journal of My Journey over the Mountains," including details of the harsh weather, a friendly encounter with Indians, and the uncomfortable sleeping conditions—in one situation, "nothing but a little straw, matted together without sheets or anything else but only one threadbare blanket with double its weight of vermin such as lice and fleas."

He seemed to be growing into an outdoorsman, at ease with nature. Outdoor living brought its own challenges, both from animals and from humans. There is an intriguing tale from that time, which the staff of Mount Vernon discovered buried in court records. While he was bathing in the Rappahannock River the summer of his nineteenth year, Washington's clothing was stolen from the riverbank. There is no record of what happened as he emerged from the water quite naked. But two women, Ann Carrol and Mary McDaniel, were arrested and stood trial in December 1751. When Carrol turned state's evidence, the charges against her were dropped, but McDaniel was found guilty of petty larceny and sentenced to fifteen lashes on her bare back. This seems like a harsh sentence for a crime of so little import, but it was typical of the times.

Washington wasn't around to witness the trial and its outcome. That September he had sailed for Barbados with Lawrence. For some time, Lawrence had been suffering from a lung ailment that was finally diagnosed as tuberculosis. His doctor recommended that he spend the winter in the tropics, but he was worried about leaving his dear wife, Anne, who had endured the loss of three babies, and could not imagine risking the safety of their one surviving child on such a dangerous journey.

Nevertheless, Lawrence was told he must make the journey for his survival. George offered to accompany him, and they set sail on September 28, 1751, on a small trading ship named the *Success*. It took six weeks to travel the "fickle and merciless ocean," as George called it in his journal.

On the island, a physician told Lawrence that his condition could be cured, and he felt a new sense of optimism. George loved Barbados, writing that he was "perfectly ravished" by its beauty. People were very kind to him and Lawrence, and he enjoyed the hospitality. But on November 17, he began to feel ill. Within days, spots that turned into blisters appeared on his skin. The diagnosis was smallpox, which, George noted in his journal, had "strongly attacked" him.

He was sick for three weeks, but he was young and strong, and when his fever broke he began to recover. Lawrence, however, was not doing so well. The treatments weren't working. He wrote home expressing his disappointment that "this climate has not afforded the relief I expected from it, so that I have almost determined to try the Bermudas." In the end, he decided to send George home and go on alone. On December 21, George set sail for Virginia. It is notable that this was his only trip abroad during his lifetime.

In the Caribbean, Lawrence continued to wage his health battle, but by the summer of 1752, he came to accept that he was dying. All he wanted now was to be home in the embrace of his family when he passed. When he arrived in July, his frailty and gaunt face showed the truth: he had come home to die. He was only thirty-four years old.

Lawrence's death forced George into manhood in a new and jarring way. He became the executor of his brother's estate and caretaker of his widow and her daughter, Sarah, who died in 1754. When Anne remarried, George leased Mount Vernon from her, finally becoming its owner upon her death in 1761.

His last obligation to his beloved brother, who had been a father figure in his life, was to organize a funeral and arrange for a burial vault. He would have given anything to have Lawrence back—but his brother's death was soon to open a new avenue of opportunity for him.

CHAPTER TWO

THE KING'S UNIFORM

Lawrence's death affected Washington in many ways, but perhaps the most significant was that it initiated him into the military life. He took Lawrence's place in the Virginia militia, which was part of the British Royal Militia. His service began at a critical point when Britain and France were jousting for control of land to the west, in the Ohio Valley, home to a sophisticated network of American Indian tribes but unclaimed by European powers.

The verdant promise of the vast open lands westward of the colonies was bound to cause conflict—between the colonial powers as well as with the native inhabitants. Did England or France have a right to it, or neither? It had not yet occurred to colonists that they might have an independent right, because of course they were not yet independent. By the early decades of the eighteenth century, in any case, colonial America had become a British jewel in a new world that others, particularly France, were trying to lay claim to. This gave rise to what was known as the Seven Years' War (1756–63) between Great Britain and France, which began when the British North American colonies asserted themselves in areas claimed by France.

The center of attention was an area west of the Appalachian Mountains on the Ohio River, where the acreage was large and valuable. The French had been making incursions here, traveling from Canada and collaborating with Indian tribes. They had built a fort—Fort LeBoeuf—on the land to stake their claim.

The young Major Washington's first assignment from Lieutenant Governor Robert Dinwiddie of Virginia was to deliver a message to the French forces at Fort LeBoeuf, ordering them to leave. (Today, the Fort LeBoeuf French and Indian War Museum in Waterford, Pennsylvania, features the only statue in existence of George Washington wearing the uniform of the British colonial militia.)

Inexperienced and naive, Washington nonetheless had one quality that set him apart—his time as a surveyor in untrampled lands. He eagerly set off on his mission, reveling in the remembered experience of the western forests. He was accompanied by a French interpreter, several woodsmen, and a prominent surveyor, Christopher Gist, who would serve as a scout, messenger, and translator with the tribes.

Washington's first task was to befriend local tribes and learn as much as possible from them about the French plans. He also hoped that he could win the tribes over, at least to the extent that they would serve as escorts when he approached the French fort.

Washington met with the Seneca leader Tanacharison, known by Europeans as the Half King. The Half King had signed a treaty with the British and was opposed to French settlement, but Washington quickly discerned that the Native leader was mostly self-interested. He considered the British a bit more trustworthy as trading partners, but that could always change.

The Half King allowed Washington to address his council, and in the end Washington was given four Seneca escorts for his journey. They set off in a miserable rain, sloshing through water and mud toward Fort LeBoeuf for five days. Along the way, they encountered a party of overly friendly French soldiers who shared food and drink with them—to the point where Washington's Indian escorts became drunk and could not go on. It was a clever ruse on the part of the French, and Washington hadn't seen it coming.

Recovery took a few days, but finally they set off again, now contending with an early snowfall. Finally, Washington stood before the French commander, Captain Jacques Legardeur de Saint-Pierre. He delivered Dinwiddie's letter and was told to wait for a reply.

Saint-Pierre made Washington cool his heels for several days as he crafted a response to the British request. Eventually Washington was given a formal document to deliver to Dinwiddie, along with two canoes to begin the return trip. As a last ploy, the French tried to bribe the Half King and his men to stay, without success.

The journey home was slow and tortuous, through a harsh December snow. At times Washington and Gist were almost done in when they rode a meager raft through icy waters. They finally arrived in Williamsburg on January 16, 1754, and Washington gave Dinwiddie the letter. Saint-Pierre's reply was a complete rejection of the Virginia official's demand.

Although the result wasn't what he wanted, Dinwiddie was pleased with Washington and promoted him to lieutenant colonel. He then gave him a mission of great importance—one that would seem to require more experience and skill than the young officer had. Washington was only twenty-two, had no military training, and had yet to encounter combat. He'd had no leadership or mentoring. He hadn't learned how to judge the nuances of a fraught situation, to make informed decisions about when to withdraw and when to fire. And for this reason, Washington is sometimes blamed for accidentally starting the French and Indian War, which would become a theater in the larger Seven Years' War.

Here's what happened. Dinwiddie gave Washington command over about 160 members of the Virginia militia and sent them back into the Ohio Valley in March 1754. His men were just as inexperienced as he was, many of them previously unemployed. Some had just been released from jail.

Their mission was vague. They were to head to the Ohio River and see what was up. They weren't expected to attack the French, if they found them, but Washington could use his judgment to kill or take prisoners if circumstances warranted it.

As Washington began his march, he was under the misimpression that other forces would be coming to back him up. This colored his behavior. It's one thing to think that you're the leader of a band of misfits with no experience. It's another to see yourself as the advance team of a larger army.

In an open field called the Great Meadows (located in what is now Fayette County in southwestern Pennsylvania), Washington built a makeshift fort dubbed Fort Necessity. The Half King alerted Washington to the presence of a French encampment of about fifty soldiers in a ravine fifteen miles away. Washington believed (without evidence) that they were planning an attack, and he decided to beat them to it. It was a tragic miscalculation.

In the driving rain of a May night, Washington and forty of his party, along with the Half King and twelve of his warriors, rode to the French camp. The first shot was fired at dawn, catching the French off guard. They had not come there to attack the British but to launch a diplomatic mission under the command of Joseph Coulon de Villiers, Sieur de Jumonville, and they were not prepared to engage in battle. Blindsided, the French fired back, and Jumonville and others were killed before the French surrendered.

Washington described the scene of his first battle in a letter to his brother John Augustine (Jack): "I fortunately escaped without any wound, though the right wing, where I stood, was exposed to and received all the enemy's fire and was the part where the man was killed and the rest wounded. . . . I heard bullets whistle, and, believe me there was something charming in the sound."

It was an unfortunate description. For the French, it was a scene of horror. Later reports said that the Indians scalped the French dead and displayed the scalps as trophies.

The French would have their revenge. Five weeks later, six hundred French troops led by Jumonville's half-brother, Louis Coulon de Villiers, attacked Washington's position at Fort Necessity, overwhelming his meager force. They fought through a hard rain, and Washington's men suffered many casualties before he surrendered. The terms of the surrender were generous: Washington and his men were allowed to return to Virginia. But Fort Necessity was burned to the ground.

Egged on by the Half King, Washington had erred with deadly results. Washington's reputation barely survived the ordeal. Had he stayed in the military he would have faced a demotion. Instead, he chose to resign, but his civilian period was short-lived. In early 1755, he returned to service as a volunteer aide-de-camp to General Edward Braddock, the commander of British forces in North America. Braddock's immediate goal was to take out the French who were camped in the Forks of the Ohio.

But on July 9 as they made their way to their destination, Braddock's forces were surprised by French forces and their Indian allies near the Monongahela River (near modern-day Pittsburgh). Outgunned, Braddock fought hard as his troops fell around him. As he was issuing an order to retreat, the general was struck by a bullet that entered through his right arm and reached his lung. He fell to the ground, still conscious but helpless to act. Washington rapidly stepped into the breach and led the retreat, as Braddock had ordered.

Lying on the ground, Braddock refused Washington's aid until his remaining troops had been gathered. Washington was able to summon a force of about two hundred men. Braddock asked him to find Colonel Thomas Dunbar, the next in command, who was seven miles away with their extra supplies and more troops. By the time Washington reached Dunbar's camp, he was exhausted and could barely summon the strength to dismount his horse. But the next morning, he returned to Braddock and moved the commander and the rest of the forces to Dunbar's camp. Despite his injuries, Braddock continued to give orders until he turned over command to Dunbar. He died a day after arriving at Dunbar's camp.

Washington took it upon himself to bury Braddock in the road-bed, hiding the site well enough that it would not be discovered by the French. It stayed undiscovered until 1804, when workmen uncovered the hasty grave. Braddock's remains were moved to a monument in Virginia on what is now Braddock Road.

The Battle of Monongahela propelled Washington to a degree of fame, even in Great Britain. His celebrity was deserved. He was emerging as a genuine military figure, seasoned by war in the harshest terrain.

At the same time, Washington's friends were encouraging him to run for office as a member of the House of Burgesses, Virginia's legislative body, representing Frederick County. They wanted him to leave his post and come home to campaign, which he refused to do. Even so, he still beat the other three contenders by a large margin. He resigned from the militia in 1758, and looked forward to life as a farmer and legislator.

How easily Washington laid down the weapons of war and picked up the planter's tools. War had plucked him out of the confines and predictability of colonial Virginia life. For the first time, people were taking note of him and looking at him with admiration. Grateful to have survived, he thanked divine providence for "his Mercies," after the war becoming a regular at his Anglican church.

The widow Martha Dandridge Custis could light up a room. Petite, vivacious, intelligent, wealthy, and by most accounts "agreeable," she was heartily courted by many suitors. A biographer described her as a "pocket Venus," a British term used to describe someone small and beautiful. That she was, standing only five feet tall, with delicate features, hazel eyes, and sparkling white teeth. Martha had the special advantage of having inherited her rich husband's estate, White House, on the Pamunkey River. She lived there with her two surviving children and had full control over the estate's activities.

Born in 1731, the eldest of ten children, Martha was eight months older than Washington and had lived a comfortable life. Her late husband, Daniel Parke Custis, had been a bachelor of thirty-seven when he'd fallen in love with eighteen-year-old Martha Dandridge in 1749. Although Martha's family was upscale, the Custis fortune placed Martha in a different stratum.

Martha had charm, but early in her relationship with Custis she also demonstrated a spine of steel. Daniel's father was apoplectic when he learned of his son's intention to marry a woman who was not his equal in class or wealth. When Daniel argued, John threatened to disinherit him if he didn't drop the idea.

Martha decided to act boldly. She rode to Williamsburg and paid a visit to John Custis, who must have been shocked to find the diminutive object of his son's desire sitting calmly in his parlor. They sat together talking, Martha stating her case with quiet persuasion. There is no record of what was said in that conversation, but after

Martha departed, Custis called his lawyer, James Power, and asked him to send Daniel a message:

> I am empowered by your father to let you know that he heartily and willingly consents to your marriage with Miss Dandridge—that he has so good a character of her, that he had rather you should have her than any lady in Virginia—nay, if possible, he is as much enamored with her character as you are with her person, and this is owing chiefly to a prudent speech of her own.

He added the strong suggestion that Daniel hurry home in case his father should change his mind.

Daniel and Martha were married on May 15, 1750, settling at White House. By all accounts, they had a good marriage, and what it might have lacked in romance it more than made up for in mutual respect and kindness and the welcome arrival of children—all of it bolstered by wealth and comfort.

In the next six years, Martha would bear four children, two boys and two girls, with only a boy, John (called "Jacky"), and a girl, Martha (called "Patsy"), surviving.

Their comfortable existence was short-lived. On July 8, 1757, Daniel Custis died at the age of forty-five. In a sign of his strong regard for his wife, he made sure that Martha was not trapped in the usual property arrangement that rendered wives subordinate to their children or other male heirs. He purposely died without a will, allowing Martha to receive "dower share"—a third of his substantial wealth, the rest going in trust to their surviving children. She took on the challenge of running the estate and showed herself to be quite capable.

By the time she caught Washington's eye, Martha had come into her own as a businesswoman and property manager. It is unclear whether he set his sights on Martha and arranged a meeting or circumstances brought them together. Whichever the case, the attraction was immediate.

Whether theirs was a passionate love affair isn't entirely clear, as Martha burned all but two of their letters, in which they might have expressed their feelings. It's widely believed that these two extraordinary people were drawn to each other, that their union was a combination of attraction and mutual benefit that matured into a deep love.

She most certainly found his appearance pleasing. At six-foot-two, Washington was taller than average and muscular, with wide shoulders and an erect posture. His brown hair was tied with a ribbon. He sometimes lightly powdered it but never wore a wig, as was the British custom. His blue-gray eyes were calm and friendly. For his part, Washington was drawn to the lively young widow's sunny personality and sheer joy in life. He felt understood and lavished with care in a way he'd never experienced.

Before meeting Martha, Washington had been in love more than once and was suitably dashed when his approaches were rejected. An early heartbreak triggered the composition of an overwrought poem:

> O, ye gods, why should my poor resistless heart
> Stand to oppose thy might and power
> At last to surrender to Cupid's feather'd dart
> And now lays bleeding every hour
> For her that's pitiless of my grief and woes
> And will not on me pity take

By all accounts, the single Washington eventually achieved an active social life, and he certainly had other love interests. One often reported relationship was with Sally Fairfax, the wife of his great friend George William. A particularly suggestive letter has intrigued historians for centuries, though is hardly evidence of an affair. More likely its teasing intimacy was a feature of a close but not sexual relationship.

They were married on January 6, 1759, at White House. A large gathering of friends and family managed the trip along snow-covered roads to attend. Martha's biographer Helen Bryan paints the scene: "Advance preparations must have involved making up endless sleeping pallets; preparing bedding; stocking up with fire-wood, extra soap, and candles; and an orgy of roasting, smoking, and baking; not to mention provisioning with cordials, brewing of beer, and ordering plenty of wine, Madeira, port, rum, brandy, and whiskey. Colonials were a notoriously hard-drinking lot. And in keeping with the custom of the time, Martha probably decorated White House with pine boughs, holly, mistletoe, and ivy." A good time was undoubtedly had by all. Both George and Martha loved a party.

Soon after the wedding, Martha lovingly agreed to leave White House and live in Washington's less elaborate home, which he was furiously working to upgrade. Over the years Washington would transform Mount Vernon into a stunning property, worthy of his growing stature and his wife's pleasure.

By all accounts, Washington was happy living with Martha and enjoying the life of a planter. He acknowledged later in life that "more permanent and genuine happiness is to be found in the sequestered walks of connubial life, than in the giddy rounds of promiscuous pleasure, or the more tumultuous and imposing scenes of successful ambition."

Although Washington would never have children of his own, he embraced four-year-old Jacky and two-year-old Patsy wholeheart-edly and enjoyed showering them with presents, attention, and fatherly advice.

Within a year, Washington wrote to a business associate, "I am now I believe fixed at this seat [Mount Vernon] with an agreeable consort for life, and hope to find more happiness in retirement than I ever experienced amidst a wide and bustling world." By "retirement" he meant from military adventures. Little did he know.

Unquestionably, the most disappointing and incongruous fact about the men who would become the Founding Fathers was that many of them were slaveholders, Washington among them. Although his attitude about slavery evolved over his lifetime, he was, like others of his generation, born into a status quo that made the horrific practice of enslaving other human beings seem normal and even desirable. That's not a justification, simply the way it was. Washington inherited a dozen slaves from his father and a smaller number from Lawrence. But Martha came to the marriage with eighty-four. Even as Washington grew uncomfortable with the idea of slavery, he nonetheless could not imagine Mount Vernon without these workers—indeed, their unpaid labor was essential to the operation of the estate. He was said to have treated them relatively well, yet the very act of "owning" another human being remains morally unsupportable.

At some level the Framers of the Constitution knew this. Although slavery would be debated at the Constitutional Convention, the word "slave" does not appear in the Constitution—only a vague reference to imported "persons," who were judged for population purposes to count as three-fifths of a person. The sad irony of the patriots' cause was their insisting on a God-given right to freedom while denying some people that right.

People often experience a change of heart about deeply formed attitudes when a personal experience challenges their views. This began to happen for Washington as a result of his relationship with his Black valet William Lee, called Billy. Washington purchased sixteen-year-old Billy and his younger brother, Frank, in 1768, and Billy was by his side for twenty years. During the Revolutionary War, Billy became so close to him that Washington began to change his beliefs about slavery. He vowed to cease all sales and purchases of slaves and to cease the practice of separating their families. In his will he wrote that all of the enslaved at Mount Vernon would be freed upon his wife's death, and he freed Billy outright at the time of his death. More about this later.

Washington entered his forties a very satisfied man, content with his farm life, a happy family, and the opportunity to engage in local government for the commonwealth he loved. By the early 1770s, however, it was growing clear that a peaceful rural existence, interspersed with sessions in the legislature and family events, was not to be. Like a weed in the underbrush, which reveals itself only when it grows and proliferates, a sense of discontent was spreading across the colonies.

On the surface, things didn't seem too serious. It was a time of relative peace and prosperity, with war in the rearview mirror. When we look back at the beginnings of our nation and the birth of a new system of government, we tend to identify the impetus for these events as a deep and urgent longing for freedom and independence—a desire so constant and overwhelming that it inevitably led to war. The truth was more complicated.

The spark that lit the fuse of revolution was struck in Boston, and not unlike in our day, people who lived in Virginia and other Southern states weren't all that impressed by their hotheaded neighbors to the north. It might be said that the nation's first example of open dissent was the internal debate that went on in the 1760s and '70s about whether to seek independence or to continue working for change from within.

The French and Indian War had changed America. As colonists watched England and France do battle over which would have free rein to settle the vast frontier, most had been on the side of England, considering themselves British subjects. But now England was turning to the colonies to help settle its large war debt while planning to claim for itself the riches of exploring the frontier. This did not sit well with the colonies.

Another factor was that the British had a new king. George III (whose father had died in 1751) succeeded his grandfather when George II died in 1760. He was only twenty-two but unusually well educated. He was also unmarried when he ascended the throne. A bride was hastily procured—Princess Charlotte, the daughter of royalty of a northern German duchy. She was just seventeen when they met on the day of their wedding; they would have a long and productive marriage, with fifteen children.

From the start, King George took a hard line with the colonies, and his inflexibility and imperiousness no doubt hastened the revolution. He never stopped thinking of America as completely under his royal control, the way a child is ruled by his parents. He thought the colonists should do as they were told and be glad to have such a strong benefactor. And he couldn't bear to be challenged, once stating, "Everyone who does not agree with me is a traitor and a scoundrel." Much has been made of the supposed madness of King George, who is often portrayed as the raving lunatic who lost America. Historians agree that the king's mental illness was probably bipolar disorder, and it only worsened later in his life.

During the troubled 1760s, Washington often found himself sitting with his neighbor, the wealthy planter George Mason, discussing the issues of the day: Great Britain, taxes, and the facade of representation across an ocean.

Stocky and quiet but intense, Mason had inherited Gunston Hall, a striking brick home near Mount Vernon. The two men easily became friends when Washington moved there. Both were sons of Virginia whose ancestors had carved out a comfortable place for them. Neither was well educated in a formal way, but they were intellectually curious, with probing minds and avid appetites for study. And both men were seasoned by experience.

A widower with eleven children, Mason cared little for fame and fortune. Grief over his wife's early death had taught him that the most important things in life were its private joys, yet he did not shrink from his public duty. He gave his sons this advice:

> I recommend to my sons, from my own experience in life, to prefer the happiness of independence and a private station to the troubles and vexations of public business; but if either their own inclination or the necessity of the times should engage them in public affairs, I charge them, on a father's blessing, never to let the motives of private interest or ambition to induce them to betray, nor the terrors of poverty and disgrace, or the fear of danger of death deter them from asserting the liberty of their country, and endeavoring to transmit to their posterity those sacred rights to which themselves were born.

On this Mason and Washington were of common mind: if colonists were expected to pay taxes like citizens, they should have the rights of citizens, including the right to elect their own governors.

CHAPTER THREE

BREAKING POINT

For most of his forty-three years Samuel Adams had struggled to gain a foothold. Born to a successful Boston brewing family, he had inherited his father's passion for public service and his deeply felt Puritan values but not his business acumen.

After bankrupting the brewery business left to him by his father, Adams threw his passions into leading a political movement of dissent. He was well educated and able to articulate the spirit of the times. Standing six-foot-three, he had a strong physical presence and outstanding oratorical skills. A man of both golden voice and golden pen, he was, as his second cousin, John Adams (no slouch in that department), declared, "a born rebel." He was suited for the moment that presented itself to him in his native town.

An undercurrent of opposition to the crown had been growing stronger since the end of the French and Indian War. Many colonists were simply tired of being "owned," and this sentiment was most prevalent in places like Boston, where the temperament was a little hotter and the character of individualism more pronounced than in other colonies to the south. When it came to edicts governing the colonies, the British government was by turns paternalistic and punitive. Many colonists who had been loyal to British interests—fighting their wars, educating children in England, and forming lucrative trade partnerships—felt demeaned by the poor treatment and lack of respect they received.

A turning point came in 1765 after the British Parliament passed the Stamp Act—basically a scheme to tax every piece of paper that passed over a colonial desk, whether it be a legal document, a property deed, a license, or a newspaper. Its reach was so extensive and its effect so patently unfair that even some members of Parliament objected to the bill's passage.

The issue wasn't just taxes; it was self-determination. Although the colonies had well-developed systems of local governance, they had no say in taxation policies. As Sam Adams coined the term, they occupied a state of "taxation without representation."

In Boston, reaction to the Stamp Act was explosive. More than a thousand protesters surged into the streets. Andrew Oliver, the Stamp Act commissioner, was hung in effigy from a massive elm in the South End of the city—later dubbed the Liberty Tree. This hapless official happened to be the brother-in-law of Lieutenant Governor Thomas Hutchinson, a figure reviled by the protesters. Hutchinson, known as "the Wicked Statesman," was considered to be a royal bootlicker who profited greatly from his loyalty to England, receiving a high salary and many perks. Biographers have since challenged the fairness of this depiction—he opposed the Stamp Act, for one thing—but at the time he was the face of British authoritarianism, a convenient and convincing villain.

The crowd's anger only grew as the protest continued, and a day later they were no longer content to stand around the Liberty Tree. Protesters surged from the area carrying the effigy, parading it past the stamp office, which was destroyed, and then on to Hutchinson's home.

Hutchinson described what happened next:

> In the evening whilst I was at supper and my children round
> me somebody ran in and said the mob were coming. I directed
> my children to fly to a secure place and shut up my house . . .
> and withdrew . . . to a neighboring house where I had been but
> a few minutes before the hellish crew fell upon my house with
> the rage of devils and in a moment with axes split down the
> door and entered. . . . Some ran immediately as high as the top
> of the house others filled the rooms below and cellars and oth-
> ers remained without the house to be employed there. . . . I was
> obliged to retire through yards and gardens to a house more
> remote where I remained until 4 o'clock by which time one of
> the best finished houses in the Province had nothing remaining
> but the bare walls and floors.

Historians quibble about just how responsible Sam Adams was
for firing up the mob, but it's clear that his leadership in the Massachusetts protest movement was significant. His melodramatic prose
fit the mood. In an article published in the *Boston Gazette*, Adams
called the rioters the "Sons of Liberty," who, "animated with a zeal
for their country then upon the brink of destruction . . . resolved,
at once to save her, or like Samson, to perish in the ruins." He
concluded, "The People shouted; and their shout was heard to the
distant end of this Continent."

For the time being, though, the rioters were outliers. Soon afterward, when Sam Adams was elected to the Massachusetts legislature, he moderated his position and signed on to a statement
that, while condemning the Stamp Act, offered reassurance that
the people retained "the strongest affection for his Majesty, under
whose happy government they have felt all the blessings of liberty."

Given the protest rhetoric, it was hard to imagine having it both ways.

The seeds of a radical language were beginning to crop up in the writings of Adams and others. References to "inalienable rights" and "God-given rights" entered the popular rhetoric of the day, as the would-be revolutionaries began to craft terms describing a nation they did not yet imagine. At the time, no one was talking about independence or separation. They were just looking for concessions and a say.

John Adams, a thoughtful, somewhat pretentious, but rigorously fair Massachusetts lawyer, previously inclined to moderation, found himself aligned with the dissenters, whose argument he could not challenge on moral or intellectual grounds. As the year came to an end, he wrote in his diary: "The year 1765 has been the most remarkable year of my life. The enormous engine fabricated by the British Parliament for battering down all the rights and liberties of America, I mean the Stamp Act, has raised and spread through the whole continent a spirit that will be recorded to our honor, with all future generations."

The cousins were not that much alike, yet John, in his typical high-minded prose, gave his cousin more than his due, describing Sam as "born and tempered a wedge of steel to split the knot of lignum vitae" (the strongest known wood) that bound America to Great Britain.

Dissatisfaction with the Stamp Act lingered, and by the end of 1765, the signs of rebellion had spread to other colonies. Meanwhile, in London, Benjamin Franklin tried to cool the upheavals from afar. He had been in London since 1757 representing the interests of Pennsylvania. His main plan was to get along with Britain—he was a fervent royalist—while gaining a few concessions for his people back home. But he was then far away from the sensibilities of the colonies he purported to represent, and when his moderate position reached them, they didn't take it well.

Franklin's consummate biographer, Walter Isaacson, wrote that Franklin's reluctance to speak out against the Stamp Act "was due in part to his temperament, his love of Britain, and his dreams of a harmonious empire. It was in his nature to be a smooth operator rather than a revolutionary. He liked witty discussion over Madeira, and he hated disorder and mob behavior."

The problem for Franklin at home was that his fellow Pennsylvanians had given him their trust, and he wasn't coming through for them. In September 1765, a mob gathered at a Philadelphia coffeehouse, and the target of their fury was Franklin. He was beyond their reach, but his wife, Deborah, was at home nearby. Her friends begged her to take refuge elsewhere. She refused. As she wrote to her husband, "I said when I was advised to remove that I was very sure you had done nothing to hurt anybody, nor had I given any offense to any person at all. Nor would I be made uneasy by anybody. Nor would I stir."

Deborah was effectively the head of the Franklin household during her husband's long forays abroad. Although their bond was strong, Deborah did not begrudge Franklin his work, which he loved. She knew the man she'd married. If she was upset with him over his Stamp Act position, she kept it to herself. But Franklin seemed rattled by the reality check of the September event and quickly began to reassess his position. By the end of the year, he was strongly speaking out against the Stamp Act. In January 1766, he testified before the House of Commons, answering 174 questions over four hours. His sharp retorts show how much his mind had been changed:

Question: "Do you think the people of America would submit to pay the stamp duty, if it was moderated?"

Answer: "No, never, unless compelled by force of arms."

Question: "Have not you heard of the resolutions of this House, and of the House of Lords, asserting the right of Parliament relating to America, including a power to tax the people there? What will be the opinion on the Americans on those resolutions?"

Answer: "They will think them unconstitutional and unjust."

Franklin concluded by stating that Americans could do without the products they were receiving from England. They were luxuries and "conveniences," not necessities. With some extra effort, they could make their own. As an example, he claimed that the pride of the Americans was once "to indulge in the fashions and manufactures of Great Britain." And now? "To wear their old clothes over again, till they can make new ones."

In March, Parliament repealed the Stamp Act, but it was a hollow victory. Along with the repeal came the publication of the Declaratory Act, affirming the British government's full authority to pass laws that would be binding on the colonies.

In the years following this signature uprising, the temperature only increased. The Townshend Acts of 1767, which imposed taxes on a variety of essential goods, including china, glass, lead, paper, and tea, increased colonial discontent, and protests became a regular thing on the streets of Boston. If the king had once thought that the rabble-rousing colonists would cool down and tire of protest, he now realized that sterner action would have to be taken. He dispatched one thousand British troops to keep the peace in Boston, and suddenly the city was overrun with redcoats. Locals maligned and taunted the soldiers, calling them "lobsters" and "bloody backs" for their red uniforms.

On March 5, a large crowd of Bostonians gathered outside the Custom House to sling insults, snowballs, and other objects. The commander of the post, Captain Thomas Preston, felt threatened. He ordered his soldiers to stand ready, and they lined up and faced the crowd as objects continued to fly. One hit a young private, who accidentally fired his weapon, setting off a barrage of shots from the other troops. In the bedlam, five protesters were killed and three injured in what became known as the Boston Massacre.

Captain Preston and eight of his soldiers were arrested and set for trial, and thirty-four-year-old John Adams was approached about defending them. It was the kind of request that many would have refused out of consideration for their reputation and safety, but Adams's principles would not allow him to decline. If his position was that every man had the right to counsel, this had to mean British soldiers as well. Naturally, he was immediately assaulted with scorn and derision, but he held firm.

In his closing argument to the jury, Adams, looking calm but weary, told them, "Facts are stubborn things; and whatever may be your wishes, our inclinations, or the dictums of our passions, they cannot alter the state of facts and evidence." His evidence and argument won the case, and Captain Preston and six of his men were acquitted. Two were found guilty of manslaughter and punished by having their right thumbs branded with an *M*.

Adams received some criticism from the hard-liners, but he mostly won the respect of the population. The trial burnished his reputation for justice and fairness, and he was elected to the Massachusetts legislature in 1770—quite a vindication. Later, he wrote of how much it meant to him to represent those soldiers. In its selflessness, it changed him:

> The part I took in defense of Captain Preston and the soldiers, procured me anxiety. . . . It was, however, one of the most

gallant, generous, manly and disinterested actions of my whole life, and one of the best pieces of service I ever rendered my country. Judgment of death against those soldiers would have been as foul a stain upon this country as the executions of the Quakers or witches, anciently.

For the first time in his life, Adams was achieving real prominence and success, which were welcome, as his family was growing. He confided only to his diary his political dissatisfaction and his longing for freedom and equality, which were in short supply under colonial rule. His public obligation, however, was to his wife, Abigail, and his children, although the strong-willed Abigail was not shy about voicing her own political opinions about the monarchy.

John's cousin Sam had lost none of his zeal. He was on a mission, and clearly in his mind it was a divine mission. A devout man, he frequently characterized the will of the people as being sanctioned by the Almighty as "God's Law." He often wrote treatises for the *Boston Gazette* using a pseudonym. In one, published on December 19, 1768, he wrote that "government is an ordinance of Heaven, designed by the all-benevolent Creator, for the general happiness of his rational creature, man."

He didn't always hit the right note with his religious entreaties— for one thing, he slandered Catholics for their "popery"—but the basic notion of God's law bestowing happiness and freedom was a theme that would carry into the new nation.

In Virginia, George Washington and George Mason continued to study the question of what could be done to stand against the constricting British onslaught of taxes and authoritarianism. They were sober revolutionaries, more temperate than the Northern rebels but every bit as decisive and focused in their approach. They agreed, however, that a scheme originating in Boston to starve the British merchants of American business was a good one.

On April 5, 1769, Washington wrote to Mason:

At a time when our lordly Masters in Great Britain will be satisfied with nothing less than the deprivation of American freedom, it seems highly necessary that something should be done to avert the stroke and maintain the liberty which we have derived from our ancestors; but the manner of doing it to answer the purpose effectually is the point in question.

He suggested that they try to adopt a similar plan in Virginia. Perhaps they could come up with some ideas he could take to the next meeting of the Virginia General Assembly in Williamsburg. Washington also sent Mason copies of similar agreements drawn up in Philadelphia, which could serve as models.

Mason agreed. Over the next month, the two men quietly pieced together the elements of a proposal, and Mason sent the final draft version of a plan for a "nonimportation association" to Washington in late April.

Mason's resolutions involved the suspension of trade. The most significant item was the declaration that Virginia would no longer import goods that were being taxed by England in order to raise revenue in America. The list was long:

"Spirits, Wine, Cyder, Sherry, Beer, Ale, Malt, Barley, peas, Beef, Pork, Fish, Butter, Cheese, Tallow, Candles, Oil, Fruit, sugar, pickles, Confectionary, Pewter, Hoes, Axes, Watches, Clocks, Tables, Chairs, Looking-glasses, Carriages, Joiners & Cabinet work of all sorts, upholstery of all Sorts, Trinkets & Jewelry, plate, & Gold & Silver Smiths work of all sorts, Ribbon & Millinery of all sorts, Lace of all sorts, India Goods of all sorts (except Spices), Silks of all sorts (except sewing silk.) Cambric, Lawn, Muslin, Gauze except Boulting cloths, cotton or cotton stuffs of more than 2/ pr yd, Linens at more than 2/ pr yd, Woolen Worsted & Mixed Stuffs of all sorts at more than 1/6 pr yd, Broad Cloths of all kinds at more than (*mutilated*) pr yd, narrow Cloths of all kinds at more than 3/ pr y(d), Hats, Stockings, Shoes, & Boots, Saddles, & all manufactures of Leather & skins of all kinds until the late acts of Parliament imposing Duties on Tea, Paper, Glass, etc. . . . are repealed." The resolutions also threatened to withhold the export of tobacco, tar, pitch, turpentine, timber, lumber, skins, and furs if Parliament was unresponsive. By Mason's calculation, stopping exports of tobacco would wield a mighty blow "by which the revenue would lose fifty times more than all their oppression could raise here."

Washington arrived in Williamsburg for the Virginia Assembly meeting in May 1774 to discover that his fellow burgesses—Thomas Jefferson and Patrick Henry among them—were united in their desire to take action against the monarchy. They put together a unanimous resolution declaring that taxes were the sole domain of the House of Burgesses, that citizens had the right to petition the throne, and that citizens had the right to a trial in Virginia. No sooner had they agreed than a loud clamor arose at the back of the hall. The sergeant at arms called out, "Mr. Speaker, the Governor commands the immediate attendance of your House in the Council Chamber."

Speaker Peyton Randolph, a career public servant who had served in Virginia's House of Burgesses since 1748, led his members to the council chamber, where the governor, Lord Baron Botetourt, was waiting. Lord Botetourt was a pompous royalist who enjoyed the most elaborate trappings of imperial splendor. Opening the May assembly the preceding week, he'd arrived in an impressive coach drawn by six white horses, a gift from King George. Many in the assembly had contempt for him, but nevertheless he was strangely popular in the state.

Now he regarded the burgesses coldly. "Mr. Speaker and gentlemen of the House of Burgesses," he declared, "I have heard of your resolves, and augur ill of their effect. You have made it my duty to dissolve you, and you are dissolved accordingly."

Stunned, the burgesses left and walked down the street to the Raleigh Tavern, a favorite gathering place, named after Virginia's founder, Sir Walter Raleigh. There, in the Apollo Room, they reconvened in a semiformal manner, with Randolph as nominal leader. As they began agonizing over their options, Washington stepped forward, holding up Mason's draft. He could see the hope in their eyes. Randolph appointed him to a committee to present the next day a plan for forming a Virginia nonimportation association.

On May 18, ninety-six of the one hundred sixteen Virginia burgesses voted to adopt Mason's plan with few changes. As the burgesses returned to their homes across the colony and began to spread word of the document, their constituencies fell into line. In the election that year, there were no challengers to the sitting burgesses.

The next general assembly was called by Lord Botetourt for November 7. Washington did not relish the thought of entering that snake pit without reinforcements. He asked Martha and Patsy to accompany him, and Jacky wheedled an invitation to leave school and go along for part of the time.

When the governor opened the assembly, Washington noted curiously that he did not even mention having dissolved the body in May. Instead, the governor offered a hearty defense of Parliament's good intentions, noting that it planned to remove the duties on many products—though not tea. This took some of the wind out of the upstarts' sails. By the time the assembly adjourned in late December, everyone was eager to get back to their homes. In the coming year, the Virginians continued to debate among themselves whether a nonimportation association should even be formed. Finally they came up with a watered-down version—as Washington described it regretfully, "the best that the friends to the cause could obtain here." It confined the boycotted goods to luxury items and eliminated the condemnation of violators, instead emphasizing support for those who complied.

The Tea Act of 1773, issued by Parliament on May 10, was not, as people often suppose, an imposition of higher taxes on tea. That had already happened. Rather, the event that triggered the Boston Tea Party created a monopoly for one company, the British East India Tea Company, which would ship millions of pounds of surplus tea to the colonies, cutting off the opportunity for colonial merchants to buy on the open market or smuggle it in themselves (a big business).

Colonists saw it as an unfair power grab by Parliament and wondered where it would end. The outcry was immediate. This would be a test of the will of the people to stand up for their rights. At the opening of the Massachusetts legislative session, the activist pastor Charles Turner warned, "Unlimited power has generally been destructive of human happiness. Whether this people and all they enjoy shall be at the absolute disposal of a distant legislature is soon to be determined."

But during that period, Washington's attention was distracted by multiple crises at home. Around 1770, eleven-year-old Patsy, the stepdaughter whom he loved as his own child, had begun experiencing seizures, which gradually became worse and more frequent. Patsy was a delightful girl; she endured her ailment bravely and was often cheerful. But it made normal life very difficult.

The Washingtons embarked on a serious effort to find a cure. Countless remedies were recommended for epilepsy, including herbs like valerian to calm the nerves or purges and bleeding to rid the system of impurities. One dubious remedy they gamely tried involved an iron "cramp ring" placed on Patsy's finger to stop seizures. None of these methods worked.

Meanwhile, Patsy's older brother, Jacky, was away from home, studying in Annapolis with a tutor who thought so little of him that he wrote to Washington, "I never did in my life know a youth so exceedingly indolent, or so surprisingly voluptuous. One would suppose nature had intended him for some Asiatic prince." Washington was disappointed in his stepson. He had tried in every way to help him, and he wasn't sure what the young man's destiny would be without a decent education.

But Jacky accomplished one thing that made a huge difference to the family. In 1773, when he was eighteen, he courted a young lady named Nelly Calvert. Although she was only fifteen, Jacky announced that they wanted to be engaged. Martha was consumed at that time with Patsy's rapidly failing health, so Washington met with the Calverts and liked them, finding Nelly to be delightful. He finally approved the engagement in exchange for Jacky's promise to make one more attempt at formal education. He also suggested that Nelly pay a visit to Mount Vernon.

It's not known whether Washington issued the invitation with the idea that Nelly would be a cheering companion for his sick daughter, as they were close to the same age. Whatever the intention, Nelly became a source of comfort and happiness during Patsy's final days. Martha tearfully watched her daughter's face as she visited with Nelly, and she was grateful to the girl who could restore the light to her daughter's eyes.

Two days after Nelly's arrival, she and Patsy were chatting. Patsy was in high spirits, enjoying time with her new friend. Then she left the room to get a letter Jacky had written. Soon Nelly heard a disturbing noise and rushed to Patsy's room, where she found her on the floor in a severe epileptic seizure. Nelly called for the family, and they rushed into the room.

Washington gently placed Patsy on the bed and knelt beside her, tears coursing down his cheeks. Within minutes she slipped away "without uttering a word, a groan, or scarce a sigh," according to Washington.

The death of another child threw Martha into a state of intense grief and despair. Wanting to offer comfort, Nelly received her parents' permission to stay with Martha for a week. During that time, Martha clung to her future daughter-in-law, and they formed a connection that would permanently shape their relationship. Martha would always view Nelly not only as a daughter-in-law but as a *daughter*.

Distracted by this crushing family tragedy and by getting Jacky situated at school, Washington had nevertheless been following the building dissent throughout the colonies over the Tea Act. In mid-December, three ships appeared on the horizon beyond Boston Harbor—the *Dartmouth*, the *Eleanor*, and the *Beaver*. The cargo was 342 crates of tea from the East India Tea Company, which Bostonians had vowed to return to England without unloading. Samuel Adams was among thousands of protesters who gathered on the docks to take a stand: they would not be unloading the tea in Boston. Despite the rowdy crowd, Governor Hutchinson ordered the tea unloaded.

On the frigid night of December 16, lit by a glowing moon, a group of Bostonians dressed as Mohawk Indians and carrying small hatchets boldly boarded the three ships docked in the harbor. They did not act in secret or use the night as cover. Nor was it a maddened mob. The event, which would become known much later as the Boston Tea Party, was oddly decorous. As the intruders boarded the ships, they politely asked for the keys to the ship's hold, which were turned over on the promise that they would not harm the ships. In the next three hours, they pulled the 342 chests of tea onto the decks, split them open with their hatchets, and threw them overboard, the tea spilling out as the chests fell into the dark waters of Massachusetts Bay. True to their promise, the raiders did no harm to the ships and even swept the decks when they were done.

It didn't stop there, as one of the participants—a shoemaker's apprentice named George Hewes—recalled: "The next morning, after we had cleared the ships of the tea, it was discovered that very considerable quantities of it were floating upon the surface of the water; and to prevent the possibility of any of its being saved for use, a number of small boats were manned by sailors and citizens, who rowed them into those parts of the harbor wherever the tea was visible, and by beating it with oars and paddles so thoroughly drenched it as to render its entire destruction inevitable."

A century later, Dr. Oliver Wendell Holmes perfectly captured the mood of the night in his poem "A Ballad of the Boston Tea Party":

The mighty realms were troubled,
The storm broke loose, but first of all
The Boston tea-pot bubbled!
The evening party—only that,
No formal invitation,
No gold-laced coat, no stiff cravat,
No feast in expectation;
No silk-robed dames, no fiddling band,
No flowers, no songs, no dancing!
A tribe of Red men, axe in hand—
Behold the guests advancing!

It was far more than a tea protest. Revolutionary War historian Benjamin Woods Labaree judged the action to be "the catalyst that set off the revolt of the colonies. In three short hours on a cold December night in 1773, a small band of men started a chain reaction that led with little pause to the Declaration of Independence. Perhaps some other event might have had the same result. We will never know. But we do know that the Boston Tea Party had just those characteristics necessary to change the course of history."

John Adams found himself inspired by the Tea Party—legality be damned. He gave it a rave review in his diary: "There is a dignity, a majesty, a sublimity in this last effort of the Patriots I greatly admire. The people should never rise without doing something to be remembered—something notable. And striking. This destruction of the tea is so bold, so daring, so firm, intrepid and inflexible, and it must have so important consequences, and so lasting, that I cannot but consider it as an epocha in history."

Four hundred fifty miles away, George Washington was of two minds about the event. He supported the Bostonians and acknowledged that their ideals were American ideals, but he had difficulty squaring the act of vandalism with his own upright principles. He thought the East India Tea Company was due some compensation for the spoilage. Ever the patriot, ever the do-gooder, he expressed to George William Fairfax his view that "the cause of Boston . . . is and ever will be considered as the cause of America (not that we approve her conduct in destroying the tea)."

In London, Franklin was upset by the destruction of property. He didn't think it was a good way to win support for the cause. Whatever the colonists' issues with the government, private property was sacred, and he too thought the East India Tea Company should be compensated for the ruined tea. In a letter to the Massachusetts House of Representatives, Franklin warned, "I am truly concerned . . . that there should seem to any a necessity for carrying matters to such extremity, as . . . to destroy private property." He reminded them that "the India Tea Company . . . are not our adversaries."

But authorities in London were not thinking merely of compensation. They were set on issuing a punishment that would put the colonies in their place. Prime Minister Lord Frederick North, in office since 1770, decided they could not let such an egregious act go unanswered. He proposed a series of legislative measures, called the Coercive Acts, which Parliament passed in the spring of 1774. They were known in the colonies as the Intolerable Acts for good reason. The measures landed like an iron boot meant to crush the spirit of independence:

1. The Boston Port Act: This measure would close the port of Boston until compensation was paid for the destroyed tea.

2. The Massachusetts Government Act: This measure suspended representative government. The elected Massachusetts Council would now be appointed by the royal governor, who would have broad powers.

3. The Act for the Impartial Administration of Justice gave the royal governor full authority over trials, and eliminated the right to a trial by a jury of one's peers.

4. The Quartering Act: This measure ordered colonists to house (quarter) British troops whenever they required it, including in their private homes.

North assumed that the other colonies would stand back and allow Massachusetts to take the full brunt of these oppressive measures, as its citizens were directly responsible for the destruction of the tea. The British had always regarded Boston as a troublesome pest, a hotbed of rabble-rousers, and not at all reflective of the larger colonial mentality. Hundreds of miles and large cultural differences separated Boston from Virginia, the Carolinas, and Georgia, and even the middle colonies were much more moderate. But the British leaders miscalculated. A united sentiment was spreading, a recognition that what was befalling Boston could soon be their own fate. Washington made that clear when he wrote to Fairfax, "The cause of Boston . . . now is and ever will be the cause of America."

Public opinion was turning, as John Adams vividly described, looking back on those days many years later. It was 1774, Adams recalled, and "I stopped one night at a tavern in Shrewsbury about forty miles from Boston: and as I was cold and wet I sat down at a good fire in the bar room to dry my great coat and saddlebags; til a fire could be made in my chamber." As he sat there, half a dozen or so men from the neighborhood joined him by the fire, lighting their pipes and warming themselves as they engaged in a lively discussion of politics. None of them recognized Adams, and he listened in silence. One man laid out their circumstances in this way: "What would you say, if a fellow should come to your house and tell you he had come to take a list of your cattle that Parliament might tax you for them at so much a head? And how should you feel if he should break open your barn, to take down your oxen, cows, horses and sheep?"

Another replied, "What would I say? I would knock him in the head."

"Well," concluded another, "if Parliament can take away Mr. Hancock's wharf and Mr. Row's wharf, they can take away your barn and my house."

Finally, a man who had so far been silent interjected, "Well it is high time for us to rebel. We must rebel, some time or other and we had better rebel, now than at any time to come. If we put it off for ten or twenty years, and let them go on as they have begun, they will get a strong party among us, and plague us a great deal more than they can now. As yet they have but a small party on their side."

While such glib talk of rebellion disturbed Adams, he was struck by how the cry of independence was being raised among the common people, not just intellectuals and radicals. It was in the marrow of the public mood. Throughout the land, volunteer militias were forming, anticipating the possibility of a greater conflict. In Fairfax County, George Mason spearheaded the creation of a volunteer militia, and Washington agreed to be its commander.

The Fairfax Independent Company of Volunteers was formed not as a fighting force but as a training force. As Mason explained, its purpose was "to rouse the attention of the public, to introduce the use of arms and discipline, to infuse a martial spirit of emulation, and to provide a fund of officers; that in case of absolute necessity, the people might be the better enabled to act in defense of their invaded liberty."

The uniform, paid for by the members, was a "regular uniform of blue, turn'd up with buff . . . buff waist coat & breeches, & white stockings."

The citizenry was ready for action, but there was not yet a consensus about what form that action should take. Before Shays' Rebellion, Washington, Mason, and Madison had been engaged in serious deliberation about the need for a continental convention that would bring the states together. This idea gained urgency as the rebellion surged. It was time for united action and a plan of governance.

CHAPTER FOUR

THE COLONIES CONVENE

Carpenters' Hall is a beautiful structure on Chestnut Street between Third and Fourth streets in Philadelphia, next to the State House. It was designed and built in 1770 by master builder Robert Smith of the Carpenters' Company. The two-story building served as the headquarters of the architectural firm—one used by Ben Franklin and other Philadelphia notables—and had a grand hall on the ground floor. It was there that representatives of twelve of the colonies gathered on September 5, 1774, under the banner of the First Continental Congress. (Georgia was not represented, its legislature having been convinced by the royal governor not to attend.)

"At ten the delegates all met at the City Tavern, and walked to the Carpenters' Hall," John Adams told his diary, "where they took a view of the room, and of the chamber where is an excellent library. There is also a long entry, where gentlemen may walk, and a convenient chamber opposite to the library. The general cry was, that this was a good room, and the question was put, whether we were satisfied with this room, and it passed in the affirmative."

The first Continental Congress was a toe in the water for most of the delegates, who believed that some kind of agreement with Britain was still possible. These were educated men, many of them lawyers and most of them legislators, who were accustomed to negotiation. Certainly Washington favored that approach. "I am well satisfied, as I can be of my existence, that no such thing is desired by any thinking man in all North America; on the contrary, that it is the ardent wish of the warmest advocates of liberty that peace and tranquility, upon constitutional grounds, may be restored and the horrors of civil discord prevented."

A divide was emerging in the population between the "loyalists," who favored a version of the status quo, with American colonies remaining under British rule, and the "patriots," who favored rebellion and ultimately independence. Loyalists were typically members of the upper class—Anglicans of wealth and influence, whose ties to Great Britain were strong through commerce and tradition. The colonial governors and their political circles were part of this crowd. Patriots emerged primarily from the working class—laborers, farmers, some clergy and merchants—in general, those who experienced less prosperity under British rule.

Fifty-four men were present at the convention, and Peyton Randolph, Virginia's distinguished former speaker of the House of Burgesses, was elected president of the gathering.

Washington had been appointed as one of seven Virginia delegates by a committee of the burgesses. He arranged to ride to Philadelphia with Patrick Henry, another delegate. Henry, thirty-eight, a lawyer from Hanover County, was a stalwart patriot. He was known to be an electrifying speaker; one of his first public acts of protest, in 1765, was a speech before the House of Burgesses in which he compared George III to Julius Caesar: "Caesar had his Brutus; Charles the First his Cromwell; and George the Third may profit by their example." As the alarmed speaker shouted, "Treason!" Henry shouted back, "If this be treason, make the most of it."

Forty-six of the fifty-four delegates gathered on the first day, the others arriving over time. For the next fifty-two days, they wrangled over the most critical issues facing the colonies. It was slow going much of the time. Even establishing the rules of the convention was a laborious process, as all of them were used to the legislative processes of their individual states. They weren't accustomed to speaking as one voice. "Fifty gentlemen meeting together, all strangers, are not acquainted with each other's language, ideas, views, designs," John Adams wrote to Abigail. "They are therefore jealous of each other—fearful, timid, skittish."

Later, when Patrick Henry loudly declared, "I am not a Virginian, but an American," some of those present glared at him, not yet ready to go that far.

The central rules issue was one that would become a cornerstone of American debate, and remains so to this day: whether the larger colonies should receive more votes than the smaller colonies. The ultimate decision was one vote per colony.

They also argued about whether or not to start each session with a prayer. Thirty-year-old John Jay, a lawyer from New York who would become one of the most influential Founders, advised against it. The delegates represented a number of different religious faiths, he said, and to choose a chaplain of one faith over another to deliver an invocation would be an insult to many. But Sam Adams disagreed. He said that he didn't care about the religious practice of the chaplain—anyone would do. Adams won that argument and quickly produced a Philadelphia minister, Reverend Jacob Duché, who was the Anglican rector at Christ Church. He proved to be a good choice, opening the session with Psalm 35—"Plead my cause, O Lord, with them that strive with me: fight against them that fight against me." He then invoked the power of the "King of kings" to look favorably upon the body and guide its work.

On September 16, there was a flurry of activity when a Bostonian named Paul Revere arrived with a document, the Suffolk Resolves—a declaration by the leaders of Suffolk County, Massachusetts, made on September 9.

Revere, a silversmith by trade and the father of eight children, had increasingly abandoned normal domestic life to become an activist for the cause of rebellion. He worked as a courier, riding between Boston and New York to spread news through the colonies, and he had volunteered for this important delivery.

The Suffolk Resolves had come about at a meeting of representatives from Boston and other towns in Suffolk County to decide how to respond to the Coercive Acts. A series of resolutions was passed unanimously. They included a boycott of British goods and a halt to all trade with Britain, a refusal to pay taxes until the Massachusetts Government Act was repealed, a recommendation that citizens form a militia, and the creation of a colonial government independent of royal authority.

Randolph presented the Suffolk Resolves to the Continental Congress, which voted its support. The declaration might have gone further than the Congress was willing to go, but everyone agreed that the basis of their power rested in their ability to enforce commercial leverage. On September 22, the full congress gathered to vote on an extremely serious matter—whether to ask the governing bodies of the colonies to cease all trade with Great Britain.

They could not reach consensus or agree as a body about what rights they would define as essential or what actions they would recommend. They only broadly agreed on financial measures and were sharply divided on the question of whether to form a military, an act that would be considered treasonous by the British.

John Jay rose to present what he considered a realistic set of options. There were three: negotiation, suspension of commerce, or war. War should not be considered, he said, and negotiation was pointless. That left suspension of commerce. A vigorous debate followed.

Many delegates feared they had stepped to the brink of war, and few believed that the colonies could win a war with Great Britain. They worried that Massachusetts was going too far with its resolves. They didn't want to suffer for what some firebrands in Boston had set in motion.

The loyalists thought that if the colonies ended commerce with Britain, the powerful empire's response would be swift and brutal. Furthermore, Americans would suffer economically as well. Could the Congress in good faith propose actions that would leave farms and businesses bankrupt?

Joseph Galloway, a Pennsylvania lawyer known to be a staunch loyalist, gave a speech recommending that the colonies back off and try to resolve the dispute in a conciliatory manner. He said that the British Parliament was not being unreasonable when it taxed Americans. He even defended the Stamp Act as Parliament's right, adding that Parliament had always displayed "a generous tenderness" toward America. He insulted the colonies, calling them "inferior societies . . . disunited and unconnected" and in need of "supreme direction." Galloway proposed to establish a national colonial council that could unite the colonies and represent them to Parliament.

Although Galloway's speech inflamed some delegates, his plan, surprisingly, wasn't immediately disregarded. The delegates argued it thoroughly and in good faith. Though it never went anywhere, the dissenters didn't throw him out of the hall.

They were learning how to work together while still looking after their individual interests—the first step toward democracy.

When Edward Rutledge of South Carolina declared that it would crush South Carolina's economy to stop selling tobacco to Great Britain, adding that Virginia could easily replace its tobacco crops with wheat, the Virginia contingent was not happy. But such relatively minor issues as one colony misrepresenting another were simply growing pains.

The delegates not from Virginia learned a lot about George Washington during this first Continental Congress. Many were eager to meet him: his military exploits in the French and Indian War had made him famous, and they may have expected him to be a powerful orator and a riveting presence. Instead, they encountered a man whose face was as still as a glassy lake, whose demeanor was serious but humble. He did not showboat during the convention or feel compelled to present his views at every turn, as some did. He contributed where it mattered, and his fame enabled him to perform a valuable service behind the scenes. Nearly every evening he could be found dining at a different prominent home in the city, listening thoughtfully to the views expressed by his hosts and other guests. In this way he broadened his understanding of the issues at hand while gently bringing important supporters over to the cause.

Washington said little on the record during the convention, but the talk of boycotts and petitions and other halfway measures disturbed him. He was beginning to believe that they were in serious trouble. In a letter to Captain Robert McKenzie, a British officer he'd served with in the French and Indian War, he admitted his worry and pressured McKenzie to consider the consequences of further indignities. If the British forced the issue, he wrote, "more blood will be spilt on this occasion than history has ever yet furnished instances of in the annals of North America."

The First Continental Congress ended with a vote to reconvene in May 1775. No definitive actions were taken, but the process served one important purpose: to familiarize the colonies' leaders with the process of working through a representative body on behalf of all. Despite their unresolved disputes, they had spent fifty-two days in the process of seeking agreement.

They did produce a lengthy petition to King George III, a masterful appeal authored chiefly by Philadelphia solicitor John Dickinson. It was respectful to the point of obsequiousness, yet it hit the mark with a list of the familiar grievances the colonies begged the king to remedy. The list was followed by this supplication:

> To a sovereign, who "glories in the name of Briton," the bare recital of these acts must, we presume, justify the loyal subjects who fly to the foot of his throne and implore his clemency for protection against them. . . .
>
> In the magnanimity and justice of your majesty and Parliament, we confide for a redress of our other grievances, trusting that when the causes of our apprehensions are removed, our future conduct will prove us not unworthy of the regard we have been accustomed in our happier days to enjoy. For appealing to that Being who thoroughly searches the hearts of his creatures, we solemnly profess that our councils have been influenced by no other motive than a dread of impending destruction.
>
> We therefore most earnestly beseech your majesty that your royal authority and interposition may be used for our relief, and that a gracious answer may be given to this petition. . . .

The petition was sent to Benjamin Franklin in London, who solemnly arranged for its delivery to his majesty. Some British legislators thought that it might prove an opening for peace. Maybe England should accept the opportunity. The Anglo-Irish statesman and member of Parliament Edmund Burke gave a speech urging the king to seek reconciliation with the colonies:

> Let the colonies always keep the idea of their civil rights associated with your government—they will cling and grapple to you, and no force under heaven will be of power to tear them from their allegiance. But let it be once understood that your government may be one thing and their privileges another, that these two things may exist without any mutual relation—the cement is gone, the cohesion is loosened, and everything hastens to decay and dissolution.

But the king would not hear of it. "The die is now cast," he told Lord North, the prime minister, bitterly. "The colonies must either submit or triumph."

Patrick Henry was restless. Even before the Second Continental Congress convened in May 1775, he was convinced that the patriots could not delay action until another slow-moving gathering had concluded. He believed that Virginians must make hard decisions at their own convention in March.

The Virginia legislators gathered on March 20, not at the capital in Williamsburg but at a less prominent location—St. John's Episcopal Church in Richmond. They were trying to stay off the royal governor's radar. Lord Botetourt had died in 1770, but an equally royal-minded governor was now in office, John Murray, Fourth Earl of Dunmore.

The Virginia delegates could be divided into two camps. On one side were the conservatives, who favored reaching a reconciliation with Great Britain. These included Peyton Randolph, Richard Bland, Edmund Pendleton, Robert Carter Nicholas, and George Wythe. On the other were those who demanded immediate, radical action—Patrick Henry, Richard Henry Lee, and Francis Lightfoot

Lee. George Washington favored this side, but he initially stood apart, listening and weighing the arguments.

A new voice on the radical side was Thomas Jefferson, a member of the House of Burgesses and an aristocrat with a populist soul. Jefferson would quickly become a leader in creating a revolutionary narrative that touched hearts and minds.

The main conflict they needed to resolve was this: either there was a good faith opportunity for negotiation and reconciliation, or there wasn't. The conservatives agreed that the situation was dire, but they held on to the possibility that avenues for improvement still existed. For those demanding action, the situation was futile. They didn't believe there was any hope of reconciliation with their brethren across the ocean.

The activists pushed forward, urging the gathering to raise funds and prepare to organize a militia. War was inevitable, they argued, and George III was preparing to crush them if they continued their insubordination. The conservatives were horrified. It was too soon to be talking like that!

So it went—until Patrick Henry rose to his feet and began to speak with such emotional power that the room fell silent. He laid it all out in the starkest terms—the faithless cruelty of England's rulers, the indignities suffered by each and every one of them and those they loved, the urgent moment they faced. He concluded with the most galvanizing cri de coeur any of them had ever heard:

Gentlemen may cry, Peace, Peace—but there is no peace. The war is actually begun! The next gale that sweeps from the north will bring to our ears the clash of resounding arms! Our brethren are already in the field! Why stand we here idle? What is it that gentlemen wish? What would they have? Is life so dear, or peace so sweet, as to be purchased at the price of chains and slavery? Forbid it, Almighty God! I know not what course others may take; but as for me, give me liberty or give me death!

When he finished, there was dumbfounded silence as his countrymen came to terms with the truth of Henry's claims. Then some tried feebly to argue, but their hearts were no longer in it. Jefferson later called his words "impressive and sublime beyond what can be imagined." The Virginia delegates voted to put the colony "into a posture of defense." Though the first shots of the revolution had not yet been fired, the militias were organizing and most people believed there would be a war. As Henry put it symbolically, "the war is actually begun."

By the time they met again two months later, at the Second Continental Congress, it had.

As Washington packed for the Second Continental Congress, which would open in Philadelphia on May 10, he carefully folded the uniform of the Virginia militia into his bag. He did this grimly, feeling the full weight of his forty-three years. The colonial world was suddenly a place of greater uncertainty than ever before. The first musket fire had boomed in Concord, Massachusetts. Men had fallen.

On the night of April 18, Samuel Adams and John Hancock were in Lexington, preparing to set off on their own journey to Philadelphia. There the news reached them that British troops had been authorized to arrest them and other patriot leaders in Boston, under an edict that judged the provincial congress to be treasonous.

Dr. Joseph Warren, an activist and medical doctor who had been instrumental in the cause, contacted Paul Revere and, as Revere recounted, "begged that I would immediately set off for Lexington, where Messrs Hancock and Adams were, and acquaint them of the movement [of British troops] and that it was thought they were the objects."

Revere had arranged for a friend to set up a signal system at Christ Church in north Boston to warn about the British approach. If they were coming by land, one lantern would be lit; if by sea, two lanterns. As two lanterns appeared, Revere set out on his mission to Lexington to alert Adams and Hancock of the British advance. Riding with him was William Dawes. They were joined by a third man, Dr. Samuel Prescott. Unfortunately, they didn't complete the job: the three messengers were intercepted by the British. While Dawes and Prescott managed to escape, Revere was held for a long time before being released, and he lost his horse.

Before dawn, a thunderous din was heard outside Lexington as the boots of seven hundred British troops pounded the ground. A militia of five hundred was ready to meet them. "Throw down your arms!" cried a British officer. The militia, knowing they were outnumbered, began to back away, but then shots were fired, and the battle was on. It is not known which side fired first—the "shot heard round the world" as immortalized by the poet Ralph Waldo Emerson.

The battle that ensued left fifty colonists dead and thirty-nine wounded—a terrible toll, but it was worse for the British, who suffered losses of sixty-five dead, 180 wounded, and twenty-seven missing. "O! What a glorious morning is this!" an elated Sam Adams exclaimed to Hancock the next day. But as the news reached the other colonies, the sobering realization set in that the die really had been cast. There was no going back. Riding to Philadelphia, Adams and Hancock encountered many men vowing to fight. They entered Philadelphia with the aura of conquering heroes, even though they were far from that. In the heady thrill of the first battle, some lost sight of the ominous power imbalance.

War had started, in practice if not in declaration. As Washington rode through Maryland, Delaware, and Pennsylvania, he encountered crowds of men in loosely formed militias, gathering in expectation of fighting.

On May 10, the opening day of the Congress, Washington walked into the hall of the State House with a calm and steady gait. As the eyes of his fellow delegates turned to him, they were struck by his dress: the blue-and-buff uniform of the Fairfax Independent Company of Volunteers. Washington might have protested that his garb was symbolic and not meant to indicate his desire to lead an army. He would always say that it was the last thing he wanted. But he also meant business.

The path to war was not so obvious to everyone—and it was widely mocked by the loyalists throughout the land. A Tory handbill being circulated at the time made the call to arms seem frivolous: "Never did a people rebel with so little reason; therefore our conduct cannot be justified before God!" The treatise went on, "It is all the consequences of the arts of crafty knaves over weak minds and wild enthusiasts who, if we continue to follow, will lead us to inevitable ruin."

Ignoring the taunts, the delegates came to Philadelphia with a solemn sense of duty and respect for those who had shown bravery in the inaugural fight. John Hancock and Samuel Adams were treated with great deference: they were assigned to important committees and listened to with new regard. No longer the Boston rabble-rousers, they were now veterans and survivors. When Peyton Randolph was called back to Virginia, Hancock was elected president of the Congress.

This Second Continental Congress, which would become the essential governing body of the emerging nation for the next six years, was composed mainly of people from the first congress, with several important additions. Ben Franklin, the oldest at sixty-nine, had just returned from London to take his place as a delegate. Some of the others regarded Franklin with suspicion. He'd lived in the cradle of the monarchy for so long he might well have become one of them. He had spent years holding the middle ground, dedicated to the cause of reconciliation between Great Britain and America. He'd believed fully in his ability to bring the angry sides together, and he had failed thoroughly. Although demoralized by his failure, Franklin had no doubt about his loyalties, and his firm and eloquent presence dispelled any concerns of his fellow delegates.

Franklin's stalwart patriotism was even more notable given the personal, familial sacrifice it entailed. His beloved son William, forty-five, was the royal governor of New Jersey. Although illegitimate (his mother is unknown), William was raised by Franklin and his wife, Deborah, and the two men had become close. Franklin had arranged a military post for William during the French and Indian War, and William had gone on to study law in Britain. He had also accompanied his father to England, which strengthened his association with the British viewpoint, leading to his appointment as royal governor of New Jersey in 1763. Now, as William spoke out about loyalty to the king and his father advocated independence, a rift opened between them. It became deeper and more permanent as William continued to be a leader of the loyalists. He was eventually imprisoned during the war and exiled from America afterward. Franklin's participation in the founding of America had an undercurrent of sadness caused by the loss of his son.

On June 14, the Congress passed a critical resolution, establishing a Continental Army. It was with great reluctance that the members embarked on this course. "Unhappy it is . . . ," Washington wrote to George William Fairfax, "to reflect that a brother's sword has been sheathed in a brother's breast and that the once happy and peaceful plains of America are either to be drenched with blood or inhabited by slaves. Sad alternative! But can a virtuous man hesitate in his choice?"

So how was this army created? It did not just materialize by fiat. Loosely organized militias, composed of part-time soldiers, had been operating throughout the colonies for many years. But early in 1775, Massachusetts recognized the need for a more formal colonial army to respond to British aggression, and several other colonies followed suit. It wasn't a simple matter of gathering willing volunteers and handing them muskets. In Massachusetts, the leadership recognized that an army could exist only if there was a governing body to direct it. The patriot leader and pastor Joseph Warren wrote to Sam Adams, "We tremble at having an army, although consisting of our own countrymen, established here without a civil power to provide for and control it."

Chosen to lead the Massachusetts colonial army was forty-seven-year-old Artemas Ward. Though suffering from kidney stones, he had left his sickbed to fight the British at Lexington and Concord. Short and portly, wearing a powdered wig, Ward wasn't the picture of a noble leader, and he certainly had his critics, but in general the men trusted him.

In Rhode Island, the thousand-man "army of observation," a collection of farmers and laborers, was led by thirty-two-year-old Nathanael Greene, who set aside his great wealth and comfort to take on the task. Although he had never seen combat, Greene took it upon himself to whip the men into shape, physically and morally. As his biographer described it, "Greene ran his camp the way his Quaker father would have run his forge: no swearing; no card-playing; clothes would be cleaned and faces shaved."

With its resolution, the Continental Congress folded these colonial forces into a national army. The initial plan was to sign up recruits for one-year stints. Congress worried that longer enlistment periods would encourage slackers and the chronically unemployed to join. Another factor was the typical psychology at the start of a war: most imagined that it would be brief; few imagined the eight-year ordeal they would face.

Who would lead this army? As discussion began about naming a commander in chief, John Hancock's name came up almost as often as Washington's. The Massachusetts delegation pushed strongly for his appointment, but some thought it would be a mistake to cede war leadership to Massachusetts, lest the other colonies feel the stakes were not as high for them. And although Hancock was a dedicated patriot, he had no military experience. People needed to have confidence in their military leader, not just as a patriot but as a commander and a strategist. That favored Washington. His reputation remained strong, burnished by his steady leadership during the first Continental Congress and in the Virginia assembly. Many delegates privately told Washington that they would vote for him, but he was not interested in promoting himself and wanted to avoid being selected if he could. He knew that if he was chosen, a sense of honor would require him to accept, and he honestly didn't know if he was up to the job.

On June 15, after much informal discussion, John Adams rose to speak. The Massachusetts delegates were especially interested in what he had to say, assuming that he would endorse Boston's own John Hancock. But Adams surprised everyone.

There was only one man, he said, who was the right man for this job, and that man was George Washington.

Hearing his name, Washington bowed his head. Then he got up and left the hall.

The others remained debating the matter for the rest of the session and decided to continue the discussion the next day. Washington stayed out of it. He didn't want to hear what was being said, and it would be unseemly for him to participate in the debate.

But at the end of the second day, when he passed delegates coming out of the meeting, they addressed him as "General," and he knew.

The next day, he addressed Hancock with a heavy heart and a sober resolve. "Mr. President," he said, "Tho' I am truly sensible of the high honor done me in this appointment, yet I feel great distress, from the consciousness that my abilities and military experience may not be equal to the extensive and important trust. However, as the Congress desire it, I will enter upon the momentous duty, and exert every power I possess in their service and for the support of the glorious cause; I beg they will accept my most cordial thanks for this distinguished testimony of their approbation."

He took a breath and added in a quieter voice, "But lest some unlucky event should happen unfavorable to my reputation, I beg it may be remembered by every gentleman in the room, that I this day declare with the utmost sincerity, I do not think myself equal to the command I am honored with."

In the coming days, the delegates hammered out the details of the army's organization. Washington made preparations to leave as soon as possible for Boston, where he would begin the process of organizing his forces. He was saddened that he would not be returning to Mount Vernon, and he sat down to write a difficult letter to Martha (one of the rare letters to her that survive). Using her nickname, Patsy (the same one bestowed on her deceased daughter), he wrote:

My Dearest,

I am now set down to write to you on a subject which fills me with inexpressible concern—and this concern is greatly aggravated and increased when I reflect upon the uneasiness I know it will give you. It has been determined in Congress, that the whole army raised for the defense of the American cause shall be put under my care, and that it is necessary for me to proceed immediately to Boston to take upon me the command of it. You may believe me my dear Patsy, when I assure you in the most solemn manner, that, so far from seeking this appointment, I have used every endeavor in my power to avoid it, not only from my unwillingness to part with you and the family, but from a consciousness of its being a trust too great for my capacity and that I should enjoy more real happiness and felicity in one month with you, at home, than I have the most distant prospect of reaping abroad, if my stay was to be seven times seven years. But as it has been a kind of destiny, that has thrown me upon this service, I shall hope that my undertaking of it is designed to answer some good purpose.

He enclosed his last will and testament, a sobering token of the dangers ahead.

John Adams was pleased to see Washington prepare to take command, but he felt a bit melancholy, as his health would prevent him from joining the fight, leaving "others to wear laurels which I have sown, others to eat the bread which I have earned." Yet Adams's role was equally essential. The need for a strong governing body was just as important as the need for a fighting force. Congress was hardly idle during the war, directing the action, raising funds, and issuing the Declaration of Independence and the Articles of Confederation. This two-pronged attack—by musket and by pen—created the United States of America.

His letter sent, Washington prepared to set off, still wearing the blue-and-buff uniform, to take his place at the front in the new war. News from the north about a major battle was already reaching Philadelphia. Britain aimed to seize the first opportunity to truly show its might—the power and discipline of its army.

The American army was stitched together by sheer will and passion from militias of various colonies, whose members had not trained together and barely knew one another. And even though they outnumbered their enemy—there were sixteen thousand colonists to fewer than nine thousand redcoats—the British had the superior advantage of dominating the ocean and waterways.

Often referred to as the Battle of Bunker Hill, the combat actually focused on Breed's Hill—then in Charleston, now part of Boston. The Americans hunkered behind hills, while the British, infused with the hubris of men expecting victory, marched toward them in orderly fashion and were repeatedly mowed down. By the time the British took the hill, they had been bloodied, suffering more than a thousand casualties to four hundred for the Americans.

In spite of the result, Americans were elated by their performance and felt vindicated when the British retreated to regroup. Washington, learning the details as he headed north, scoffed at the idea it had been a victory. "A few more such victories would put an end to their army and the present contest," he observed. Yet the patriots' tenacity served as a warning that they would not be cowed by the mighty British army.

Among the American casualties was the patriot leader Joseph Warren, who would be labeled by some as the revolution's founding martyr. His death is memorialized in a John Trumbull painting titled *The Death of General Warren at the Battle of Bunker's Hill*. Warren never wavered in his willingness to sacrifice his life for his country. He set out to prove that the patriots were dead serious. They were not cowards or ne'er-do-wells, and to the charge that they would flee at the first attack, he responded, "I hope I shall die up to my knees in blood."

PART TWO

THE CALL OF
INDEPENDENCE

CHAPTER FIVE

THE COMMAND

"The liberties of America depend upon him, in a great degree," John Adams confided to Abigail after Washington had set off from the Second Continental Congress for Massachusetts. Many people felt a sense of confidence in the new commander, and even if suspicion of the military state lingered, most recognized that war was at hand. Abigail and the Adams children were near enough to smell the smoke from the musket fire.

Confidence in Washington's unproven leadership might have been exaggerated, and Washington himself agonized over his ability to meet the moment. "I am now embarked on a tempestuous ocean from whence, perhaps, no friendly harbor is to be found," he wrote to his brother-in-law Burwell Bassett, as he prepared to leave Philadelphia.

I have been called upon by the unanimous voice of the colonies to the Command of the Continental Army. It is an honor I by no means aspired to. It is an honor I wished to avoid, as well from an unwillingness to quit the peaceful enjoyment of

my family as from a thorough conviction of my own incapac-
ity and want of experience in the conduct of so momentous
a concern—but the partiality of the Congress added to some
political motives, left me without a choice. May God grant
therefore that my acceptance of it may be attended with some
good to the common cause and without injury (from want of
knowledge) to my own reputation. I can answer but for three
things, a firm belief of the justice of our cause, close attention
in the prosecution of it, and the strictest integrity.

Washington had reason to be nervous about how he would be
greeted in Boston. Its patriots considered their home the cradle of
liberty, far removed from the South. They were seasoned rebels,
lacking Washington's natural discipline, and they represented a
central challenge of the new army. While rabble-rousers had been
instrumental in lighting the flame, winning the war would require
organization and discipline.

And how did the Massachusetts army greet their commander?
Washington has been so glorified historically that it's necessary
to sort through varying accounts to find a semblance of reality.
For example, the writer Washington Irving described Washington
meeting the troops in Cambridge, Massachusetts, this way: "As
he entered the confines of the camp the shouts of the multitudes
and the thundering of artillery gave note to the enemy beleaguered
in Boston of his arrival." This scene never happened, not least
because it would have been unthinkable to waste gunpowder.
Another account described Washington greeting the troops by
reading from Psalm 101, which speaks of God's destruction of
the wicked. There is no definitive verdict on this story, but it, too,
appears to be fictionalized and doesn't seem characteristic of a
man of Washington's reserve.

Such stories were meant to build up Washington as an avenging angel sent to slay the enemy. More likely, the humble general, plagued by inner doubt about his ability to lead this army, spoke with calm and dignity to his men. Soon enough they would feel the heat of his disapproval. Rather than a moment of Psalmic inspiration, Washington's reaction to his first encounter with the troops was a gentleman's disdain. He privately called them "an exceedingly dirty and nasty people."

Most of the troops came from the ranks of the working class and unemployed and included African American slaves, who were offered freedom in exchange for their service. Most were amateurs, poorly dressed and undisciplined, with little notion of what it meant to operate as a cohesive army.

An exception was Nathanael Greene's orderly camp of Rhode Islanders, neatly housed in tents, a sight that immediately endeared Greene to Washington. He soon raised Greene to the rank of brigadier general.

Along with Greene, Washington also relied heavily on Henry Knox, a Boston bookseller and friend of John Adams, who would prove invaluable during the war and during Washington's presidency. Despite the difference in their ages—Knox was only twenty-five when he joined Washington—the two men would become close. Knox was smart and brave as well as physically imposing, both tall and portly. His wife, Lucy, was born into a wealthy loyalist family, who disowned her when she married Knox. They were devoted to each other, however, and together were devoted to the patriotic cause. Like Abigail Adams and Martha Washington, Lucy was a strong, independent woman. She once cautioned her husband, expressing her "hope that you won't consider yourself commander in chief of the house you own, but be sure there is such a thing as equal command."

This civilian and student of history and the military would distinguish himself repeatedly during the war. Washington held him in extremely high regard, and his approval was reciprocated. Knox formed an immediately favorable view of Washington, writing to Lucy, "General Washington is a great addition to his position and brings happiness and ease to all who surround him."

With Major General Charles Lee, his second in command, Washington had a more complicated relationship. A former British army officer who had joined the Americans, he gave the impression that he should be in charge, not Washington. Lee made a great show of showering praise on the commander and pledging his devotion. But it didn't take long for him to become a troublesome thorn. Lee was eccentric in looks and behavior, not exactly a model of the disciplined demeanor Washington was asking of his soldiers. His appearance, and the dogs that always accompanied him, made Lee stand out for all the wrong reasons. These would turn out to be the least of his sins.

As Washington began the process of surveying his troops, he was disappointed again and again. General Lee shared his frustration, writing to Robert Morris in Philadelphia, "We found everything exactly the reverse of what had been represented. We were assured at Philadelphia that the army was stocked with engineers. We found not one. We were assured that we should find an expert train of artillery. They have not a single gunner." It was a harsh reality check.

More serious was the overall lack of organization and discipline. No one could provide Washington an accurate head count. The number of troops was said to be around sixteen thousand, but fewer than fourteen thousand were actually present—far short of Washington's calculation of the need for at least twenty-two thousand.

Washington noted the lack of hierarchy in the ranks, which he judged was a function of New England's egalitarian culture. Obedience to authority was reputedly more natural to Southerners, and these independent New Englanders had to be taught what it meant to be soldiers—simultaneously bold and disciplined.

Washington referred to his men as his "military family," and he really saw them that way. But it wasn't a particularly united family. It drew from different regions and classes and exposed long-held prejudices between North and South, merchant and farmer; other divisions also created serious issues of trust within the ranks. Washington knew that an effective fighting force had to be of one mind on the field, and he had his work cut out for him with these men.

Washington had battlefield experience, but he had never received formal military training. As with much in his life, he was forced to teach himself. For this learning he often turned to European wisdom, in books such as *A Treatise of Military Discipline* by Humphrey Bland, a renowned Irish soldier who fought with the British in the War of the Spanish Succession (1701–15). This guidebook helped inform Washington's ideas about military discipline. However, he soon learned that his American army would require a special kind of leadership. With these independent-minded volunteers, many of them trained in the rough code of the militia, standard military forms of discipline wouldn't work. Rather than impose frequent severe whippings for transgressions, or death for more serious offenses such as abandoning their posts, Washington tried to inspire them with the greatness of their purpose, and to demonstrate the necessity of military discipline to their success.

Later that year, he would write to Colonel William Woodford, the commander of the Virginia Regiment, about the essentials of military command. It stands as one of the most succinct and well-considered philosophies on that subject in existence.

The best general advice I can give, and which I am sure you stand in no need of, is to be strict in your discipline—that is, to

require nothing unreasonable of your officers and men, but see that whatever is required be punctually complied with. Reward and punish every man according to his merit, without partiality or prejudice. Hear his complaints: if well founded, redress them; if otherwise, discourage them, in order to prevent frivolous ones. Discourage vice in every shape, and impress upon the mind of every man, from the first to the lowest, the importance of the cause and what it is they are contending for. Forever keep in view the necessity of guarding against surprises. In all your marches, at times, at least, even when there is no possible danger, move with front, rear, and flank guards, that they may be familiarized to the use; and be regular in your encampments, appointing necessary guards for the security of your camp. In short, whether you expect an enemy or not, this should be practiced; otherwise your attempts will be confused and awkward, when necessary. Be plain and precise in your orders, and keep copies of them to refer to, that no mistakes may happen. Be easy and condescending in your deportment to your officers, but not too familiar, lest you subject yourself to a want of that respect which is necessary to support a proper command. These, Sir, not because I think you need the advice, but because you have been condescending enough to ask it, I have presumed to give as the great outlines of your conduct.

One thing Washington had to make clear: the worst crime of a soldier was desertion. It had been a problem at Bunker Hill, with soldiers and even officers fleeing their posts. Others simply went home to sleep in their own beds. Creating discipline to keep the army at full strength was a high priority.

As commander of a sometimes unruly army, Washington also had to concern himself with their deep and long-held biases, which cut against unity and the spirit of the cause. One manifestation of these was the traditional Boston celebration of Pope's Day (a local version of England's Guy Fawkes Day), an anti-Catholic celebration during which the pope's effigy was set afire. This event personally offended Washington, and he also saw it as destructive to the cause, particularly in its insult to their French Canadian allies. He issued a general order decrying the custom and lamenting "that there should be officers and soldiers in this army so void of common sense, as not to see the impropriety of such a step at this juncture at a time when we are soliciting, and have really obtained, the friendship and alliance of the people of Canada, whom we ought to consider as brethren embarked in the same cause."

As Washington was busy with the task of organizing his troops, the Second Continental Congress that gave him his commission was engaged in a contrary endeavor: crafting an olive branch to the king. (After Washington left Philadelphia, the other delegates remained in session, and this congress would continue to conduct the nation's business until early 1781.)

Pennsylvania's John Dickinson, the primary author of the 1774 petition that had been rejected by King George, was trying again for reconciliation even in the midst of what was now an open war. He convinced the Congress to make one last effort to appease the king with the so-called Olive Branch Petition. The heated debate about whether to send this devolved into a loud confrontation between Dickinson and John Adams outside the hall. Dickinson threatened to walk away if the petition was not sent, while Adams shouted that he would not be threatened by the likes of him, and so on. They eventually calmed down, Hancock kept order on the floor, and the Olive Branch Petition was dispatched. Adams chose to be philosophical about the matter, writing to a friend about the "whimsical" nature of the Congress. "You will see a strange oscillation between love and hatred, between war and peace," he wrote. "Preparations for war and negotiations for peace. We must have a petition to the King and a delicate proposal of negotiations, etc. This negotiation I dread like death: But it must be proposed. We can't avoid it. Discord and disunion would be the certain effect of a resolute refusal to petition and negotiate."

In the end it didn't matter. The king, who had already issued a Proclamation of Rebellion against the colonies, refused to read the petition. It was too late. Fortunately, Washington's efforts had not been slowed by this sidebar.

General William Howe was the second British general to direct his side in a war that had barely started. He'd arrived in America in May 1775 to take his position as second in command to General Thomas Gage, but when the king yanked General Gage home after the Bunker Hill slaughter, Howe was elevated to commander. He was the picture of a soldier, a mirror image of Washington—six feet tall, forty-five years old, handsome and elegant, with a distinguished résumé from the French and Indian War. He came from a prominent family that had favored negotiation with America before the king put an end to that.

Howe was not an unreasonable man. Even as he sailed for America, he could not rid himself of the idea that the rebels were a troublesome minority, and the majority of Americans would soon see reason: "With respect to the few, who, I am told, desire to separate themselves from the Mother Country, I trust, when they find they are not supported in their frantic ideas by the more moderate, which I have described, they will, from fear of punishment, subside to the laws."

The reality on the ground was a terrible jolt to Howe's belief system. As he watched a thousand of his countrymen fall to an unrelenting American attack at Bunker Hill, he perceived the truth, and his heart was hardened.

Now that he was in charge of this mess, Howe had to shore up his resources and develop a strategy. He felt outmanned by the Americans, unable to either fight or move. He called on the British Navy to support him, but this was no easy matter, as the navy was essentially in mothballs after a lengthy period of peace.

Howe hunkered down in Boston, where he was rumored to be comforted by his beautiful mistress, Elizabeth Loring. Her husband, the local loyalist Joshua Loring Jr., had been conveniently dispatched to Halifax. Word of Howe's self-indulgence and lack of action reached London, where he was mocked:

Awake, arouse, Sir Billy
There's forage in the plain,
Ah, leave your little Filly,
And open the campaign.

Presumably, Howe believed that he could wait out the rebels. He didn't take them seriously, and this attitude filtered down to his men. A letter from a surgeon on a British ship, lying in the harbor, dripped with contempt: "This army . . . is truly nothing but a drunken, canting, lying, praying, hypocritical rabble, without order, subjection, discipline, or cleanliness, and must fall to pieces of itself in the course of three months. . . ."

Washington wasn't standing by and doing nothing. For him this pause was a valuable opportunity to prepare himself and his troops and to strategize about how the standoff would end. He was also burdened by Congress's demand that he press forward on a Canadian campaign, with the goal of bringing Canadian colonies into the fight on the American side.

Back in May, forces led by Ethan Allen, who served in the Connecticut militia called the Green Mountain Boys, and Colonel Benedict Arnold had seized Fort Ticonderoga from the British in a surprise attack. The fort, on Lake Champlain near the Canadian border, was an important northern beachhead, a strategic position now in American hands.

As summer dragged into fall, Washington grew concerned over the dwindling supply of gunpowder and arms. He was constantly aware that the British, controlling the seas, had ready access to reinforcements and supplies. He expected a barrage of heavy fire any day, and though it had yet to come, he had no illusions about its inevitability.

Volunteer enlistments plummeted, and the spirits of those who remained were low. Washington's men were getting itchy—bored and agitated. One Virginia regiment effectively mutinied against its leaders, bringing shame to Washington's home colony. When the army was asked to fight, no one could ask for a braver or more dedicated force. But when they were idle at camp, the determination and bravery drained out of them. They were there to fight, not to parade around aimlessly, waiting for action.

Washington was looking ahead at the long game, building his manpower and supplies in ways best calculated to make a future fight victorious. In a desperate search for more arms—especially heavy weaponry—he appealed to the colonies. He would need these reinforcements if he had any hope of driving the British out of Boston. But another source was soon identified.

In late fall, Henry Knox volunteered to lead a party some three hundred miles to Fort Ticonderoga and bring back cannons and gunpowder that had been seized in its capture. Washington agreed, and Knox's team set off, reaching their destination later than planned. By the time they began their return trip, it was January, and the route was treacherous, with ice-covered waterways and snow-slicked roads. On more than one occasion, as they attempted to cross a river, a cannon fell through the ice and sank, and they had to struggle in freezing temperatures to haul it out. Knox's "noble train of artillery" finally arrived in Cambridge on January 24, to great acclaim.

The long siege on unfamiliar ground was taking a toll on Washington. He longed to have his wife nearby, and he wrote to Martha—"Come to me." Martha complied, though the journey was long and potentially dangerous. She needed him, too, as well as a new way to be useful. Jacky and Nelly had recently had a baby, who died soon after the birth, and she invited them to come with her.

On the way they stopped in Philadelphia, where Joseph Reed met them with such fanfare that it bowled Martha over. She hadn't realized what a celebrity her husband was, and she herself by extension.

Washington eagerly awaited Martha's arrival, asking his secretary, Stephen Moylan, to secure some luxuries from a captured British ship: lemons and limes, sweets and pickles, along with ten baskets of oysters—Martha's favorite—and a variety of meats.

When Martha arrived in Cambridge, she found her husband staying in inadequate quarters as a guest of the president of Harvard. She soon had him moved to a larger and more comfortable residence. Her presence was a joy to him in a time that yielded few joys. Nathanael Greene wrote to his wife, Caty, "Mrs. Washington is excessive fond of the general and he of her. . . . They are happy in each other."

Five days after Knox returned from Ticonderoga, he and Lucy were invited to dine with the Washingtons. The younger couple—Henry twenty-five, Lucy twenty—became close friends with George and Martha.

When Martha toured the area, she was amazed at how physically close the standoff was. She could see across the harbor the

American sentries standing guard and troops busily tearing apart wharves for firewood. She felt alarm but made a supreme effort to keep her features still, wanting to be a credit to her husband.

Finally, after nearly a year, there was movement on the British side, as ships began to arrive in Boston Harbor, under the command of none other than Howe's brother, Vice Admiral Richard Howe, who had just been promoted to his position. Like his brother, the elder Howe had been open to making peace overtures, had even preferred that course, but that hope was dashed by the king. Now he was responsible for the British fleet sent to subdue the colonies.

Washington set his sights on Dorchester Heights, low hills overlooking Boston proper and the harbor, where Howe's ships lay. This commanding vantage point could give the Americans an advantage if they moved strategically.

The troop movement took place under cover of darkness on March 4, 1776. Major General John Thomas led eight hundred soldiers and more than a thousand workers up the heights to fortify the area. As they hammered away, the sound of construction was masked by cannon fire from another area. Finally, the cannons were moved up, the wagon wheels wrapped in straw to muffle the sound.

"Everyone knew his place," the Reverend William Gordon wrote approvingly of the effort. "All possible silence was observed." Work went on steadily throughout the night, and when morning dawned, the fortifications were in place. "General Howe was seen to scratch his head and heard to say by those that were about him that he did not know what he should do, that the provincials [he likely called them by some other name] had done more work in one night than his whole army would have done in six months."

Major John Trumbull wrote with excitement about the action that finally seemed imminent. From his perch on the heights, he could see the whole of the waterfront and watch the British board ships and approach the wharves. "We were in high spirits, well prepared to receive a threatened attack. Our positions on the summits of two smooth, steep hills, were strong by nature and well-fortified. . . . We waited with impatience for the attack, when we meant to emulate, and hoped to eclipse, the glories of Bunker's Hill."

Washington rode through the fortified positions as evening approached and was satisfied with the preparations. "Remember it is the fifth of March, and avenge the death of your brethren," he cried at one point, and his words were repeated down the line. No sooner had he completed his review than a heavy snowstorm blew in. Trumbull watched with glee as the high winds "deranged all the enemy's plan of debarkation, driving the ships foul of each other, and from their anchors in utter confusion, and thus put a stop to the intended operation."

As General Howe's men approached the heights, aiming to disable the cannons, they were hit by the snowstorm and forced to back off. Rather than planning a fresh assault when the weather cleared, Howe made a different choice. To the bafflement of many of his soldiers, he decided to leave altogether, abandoning Boston and the tactical disadvantage he perceived there. On March 17, 1776, more than eleven thousand British troops and hundreds of loyalists sailed out of Boston.

There was no time for celebration. Although the ships were headed north to Halifax, Washington was under no illusion as to Howe's ultimate goal: New York.

The colony of New York was a grand prize thanks to its centrality, its sophistication and relative wealth, and its waterways. Weighing in on the importance of a New York campaign, John Adams had written to Washington in January that "it is the nexus of the Northern and Southern colonies, as a kind of key to the whole continent, as it is a passage to Canada, to the Great Lakes and to all the Indian nations. No effort to secure it ought to be omitted."

Adams also noted a factor that was becoming increasingly clear: New York was a haven for "Tories" (loyalists), and their eradication was a critical component of the mission:

> Now if upon Long Island, there is a body of people, who have arms in their hands, and are entrenching themselves, professedly to oppose the American system of defense; who are supplying our enemies both of the Army and Navy, in Boston and elsewhere, as I suppose is undoubtedly the fact, no man can hesitate to say that this is an hostile invasion of American liberty, as much as that now made in Boston, nay those people are guilty of the very invasion in Boston, as they are constantly aiding, abetting, comforting and assisting the Army there; and that in the most essential manner by supplies of provisions. If in the city a body of Tories are waiting only for a force to protect them, to declare themselves on the side of our enemies, it is high time that city was secured. The Jersey troops have already been ordered into that city by the Congress, and are there undoubtedly under your command ready to assist in this service.

Knox, who had passed through New York City on his way to Ticonderoga, wrote to Lucy, "The people—why, the people are magnificent . . . in their pride and conceit which are inimitable, in their profaneness which is intolerable, in the want of principle which is prevalent, in their Toryism which is insufferable, and for which they must repent in dust and ashes."

Washington arrived in Manhattan on April 13 and established headquarters at Number 1 Broadway, at the southern tip of the island. The building was a mansion overlooking Bowling Green, vacated by a British naval captain, Archibald Kennedy. The advantage of its waterfront location was somewhat offset by the view of a large statue of King George III on the green.

In New York, Washington felt beset by enemies, both known and unknown. Aware of the strength of Tory sentiment in the colony, he was suspicious of the openly loyalist former governor, William Tryon, and his hand-selected mayor of New York City, David Mathews. Tryon had just returned from a triumphant trip to London the day Washington arrived.

In June, the New York Provincial Congress (the revolutionary provisional government) received evidence of a plot to arm citizens who backed Britain. Among others, Mayor Mathews was implicated in the plot and was placed under house arrest. Mathews named Thomas Hickey, a soldier on Washington's protective guard, as being involved in the plot and suggested that Washington's life might have been in danger.

Washington knew that he needed to make an example of Hickey and ordered his court-martial. During the trial, Hickey was brazen, seeming to taunt Washington by claiming that he was not the only one of the general's guard to have joined the plot. Hickey was found guilty and sentenced to death by hanging. On June 20, Washington ordered all available soldiers to attend his execution, hoping that his fate would serve as a warning. The next day, British ships began to arrive in New York Harbor.

On the day of Hickey's hanging, Washington wrote a note in his orderly book: "The unhappy fate of Thomas Hickey, executed this day for mutiny, sedition, and treachery, the general hopes will be a warning to every soldier, in the Army, to avoid those crimes and all others, so disgraceful to the character of a soldier and pernicious to his country, whose pay he receives and bread he eats."

While Washington was addressing disloyalties and planning his next campaign, in which he expected to face the full might of the

British forces, on land and water, Congress was in Philadelphia addressing the ultimate goal of the conflict.

Richard Henry Lee came from an influential Virginia family; his father had been a politician and governor of Virginia before his death in 1750. Lee the younger was considered pompous even in aristocratic Virginia circles, but John Adams thought his mind "masterly."

The Second Continental Congress had continued to meet in Philadelphia as a general governmental body, and various state bodies put forth initiatives. On June 7, 1776, Lee rose to make what would come to be known as the Lee Resolution:

> *Resolved*, That these United Colonies are, and of right ought to be, free and independent states, that they are absolved from all allegiance to the British Crown, and that all political connection between them and the State of Great Britain is, and ought to be, totally dissolved.
>
> That it is expedient forthwith to take the most effectual measures for forming foreign alliances.
>
> That a plan of confederation be prepared and transmitted to the respective colonies for their consideration and approbation.

On Saturday, June 8, Congress took up the issue, debating it that day and again on Monday. A group of delegates led by the voice of caution, John Dickinson, whom John Adams referred to sarcastically as a "piddling genius," was still imagining further petitions to the king. He was joined by James Wilson, Robert Livingston, and Edward Rutledge in arguing that, though they agreed in principle, the resolution was premature. The people— especially those of the middle colonies, Maryland, Delaware,

Pennsylvania, New Jersey, and New York—were not yet clamoring for independence. As Thomas Jefferson recalled decades later in his autobiography, the resistance was largely a matter of readiness—they "were not yet ripe for bidding adieu to British connection, but that they were fast ripening & in a short time would join the general voice of America."

It was also noted that some colonies had forbidden their delegates from declaring independence until their colonial governments had given the go-ahead. Those bodies were meeting independently to make that determination.

Some delegates were greatly concerned that America, once sliced off from the motherland, would receive no support from France or Spain, and that those foreign powers might even form an alliance with Great Britain in exchange for control of territories.

Adams, Lee, George Wythe, and others took the opposing position that the separation had already happened, in fact if not by declaration. They argued, Jefferson recalled, that "we had been bound to [the king] by allegiance, but . . . this bond was now dissolved by his assent to the late act of Parliament, by which he declares us out of his protection, and by his levying war on us, a fact which had long ago proved us out of his protection; it being a certain position in law that allegiance & protection are reciprocal, the one ceasing when the other is withdrawn."

These delegates forcefully declared that the matter was urgent, that they could not afford to lose time. Adams's celebrated biographer David McCullough described the agonies Adams experienced. "To Adams independence was the only guarantee of American liberty," McCullough wrote, "and he was determined that the great step be taken. The only question was when to make the move. If a decision were forced on Congress too soon, the result could be disastrous; independence would be voted down. But every day that independence was put off would mean added difficulties in the course of the larger struggle." Abigail stood with her husband in feeling this sense of urgency, quoting Shakespeare in a letter: "There is a tide in the affairs of men, Which taken at the flood leads on to fortune." And the only choice was to "take the current when it serves, or lose our ventures."

Early in 1776, Jefferson was a tormented man who was further upset by the sudden death of his mother. He'd dropped out of action in Philadelphia to stay in Monticello during her final illness, but by May was drawn back into the most significant debate the Congress had yet undertaken: If the colonies were indeed breaking from Great Britain, what would be the nature of this new state of independence?

Jefferson was well aware that many in the colonies were opposed to independence and viewed the fight with Great Britain as merely a defensive effort to achieve certain rights. In particular, the southern and middle colonies were reluctant to go so far as independence. According to Adams, the more eager New Englanders had been cautioned for some time not to "utter the word independence, nor give the least hint or insinuation of the idea."

However, those who favored independence from Great Britain were aided in their quest by the phenomenal popularity of Thomas Paine's widely distributed pamphlet, *Common Sense.* Paine's piety could be overwrought—for example, his claim that Americans' feelings about self-determination were implanted by the Almighty—but his point was clear: a call to action for Americans rightfully to claim an independent identity. His writing, with a poet's style and a revolutionary's passion, was instantly captivating. "We have every opportunity and every encouragement before us, to form the noblest, purest constitution on the face of the earth," Paine wrote. "We have it in our power to begin the world over again."

While some of the colonies were still wrestling with the decision, a committee was appointed to go ahead and draft a declaration of independence. That committee was composed of John Adams,

Ben Franklin, Thomas Jefferson, Roger Sherman, and Robert Livingston.

Which of them would be willing to tackle the first draft? Adams recalled that Jefferson suggested he be the one to draft the declaration.

Adams replied, "You shall do it."

Jefferson replied that Adams ought to do it.

But Adams said, "I will not."

Jefferson was puzzled. What was his reason?

With an impressive level of self-awareness, Adams explained it to him. "Reason first, you are a Virginian, and a Virginian ought to appear at the head of this business. Reason second, I am obnoxious, suspected, and unpopular. You are very much otherwise. Reason third, you can write ten times better than I can."

Jefferson caved and agreed to write the draft. He went to his lodging, the house of a Mr. Graff where he was renting the second floor. In the parlor of his rooms, bent over a portable writing box, he drafted the famous document, borrowing from his own writings and those of others, including great philosophers—patching together a document in the common language of human dignity, freedom, and self-determination.

He wasn't trying to be clever or even original. His purpose, he emphasized, was "not to find out new principles, or new arguments, never before thought of, not merely to say things which had never been said before; but to place before mankind the common sense of the subject . . . [in] terms so plain and firm as to command their assent; and to justify ourselves in the independent stand we [are] compelled to take."

It was intended, he said, to be "an expression of the American mind, and to give that expression the proper tone and spirit called for by the occasion."

When Jefferson had completed the draft, he shared it with Franklin and Adams, who made a few edits. For example, Adams's steel-trap mind bit into the phrase, "We hold these truths to be sacred and undeniable."

No, he said, the truths are not sacred, they are common and obvious—and thus "self-evident." And so the most famous line in the declaration became "We hold these truths to be self-evident, that all men are created equal . . ."

Other changes were small, and the committee decided the draft was in good enough shape to present to the Congress for review on Friday, June 28.

After a day of debate, often heated, a preliminary vote was taken on the substance of the declaration. Four colonies still held back from declaring independence—New York abstained for the moment, lacking directions from home. Pennsylvania and South Carolina flat-out voted no. Delaware's two delegates in attendance canceled each other out; the third and pro-independence member, Caesar Rodney, had not yet arrived.

The general sentiment was that the vote for independence should be unanimous, or nearly so. It wasn't acceptable that these four colonies would not be represented, especially at a moment when General Washington was in New York, facing the arrival of a massive British fleet.

The next morning opened with the good news of Rodney's arrival and thus the promise that Delaware's stalemate would be broken in favor of independence. Furthermore, the two strongest anti-independence voices in the Pennsylvania delegation, Dickinson and Robert Morris, were not in their seats. Although neither man could stomach voting in favor of independence, they chose to allow it by default. South Carolina gave in next, and though New York still abstained, there were no votes against the declaration.

Now the serious editing could begin. Adams may have smiled to himself, knowing what lay ahead for the young Jefferson, inexperienced in Congress. They would surely beat his beautiful prose into submission to the common will—not a particularly pleasant experience for an author. Jefferson endured the process with his mouth clamped shut and his face pale.

The finished document had three movements: (1) a stirring preamble—a defining statement of purpose; (2) a litany of grievances against the king; and (3) the strong declaration of independence. The preamble opened:

> When in the course of human events, it becomes necessary for one people to dissolve the political bands which have connected them with another, and to assume among the powers of the earth, the separate and equal station to which the laws of nature and of nature's God entitle them, a decent respect to the opinions of mankind requires that they should declare the causes which impel them to the separation.

And then to the heart of the matter:

> We hold these truths to be self-evident, that all men are created equal, that they are endowed by their Creator with certain unalienable Rights, that among these are Life, Liberty and the pursuit of Happiness.—That to secure these rights, governments are instituted among men, deriving their just powers from the consent of the governed,—That whenever any form of government becomes destructive of these ends, it is the Right of the People to alter or to abolish it, and to institute new government, laying its foundation on such principles and organizing its powers in such form, as to them shall seem most likely to effect their Safety and Happiness.

From there the declaration embarked on a staccato list of the grievances. This section was most difficult for those who had argued against independence, since it constituted an all-out indictment of the king.

Not wanting to burn every last bridge, Congress toned down several passages that some members thought were too abrasive. An example was this slap against the king, removed in the interest of maintaining a slight opening for reconciliation: "Future ages will scarcely believe that the hardiness of one man adventured, within the short compass of twelve years only, to lay a foundation so broad & so undisguised for tyranny over a people fostered & fixed in principles of freedom."

The most notable deletion was of a passage expressing an abhorrence of slavery. (Its inclusion in the first place seems to suggest Jefferson's conflicted view of the institution; in a distinct irony, an enslaved person tended to him even as he labored over the draft.) Most members were not yet prepared to renounce slavery, so they deleted the indictment of the king for having "waged cruel war against human nature itself, violating its most sacred rights of life and liberty in the persons of a distant people who never offended him, captivating & carrying them into slavery in another hemisphere. . . ."

Jefferson's soaring conclusion set forth, without hesitation, a pledge not to a king but "to each other" and a reliance not on any earthly power but on divine providence:

We, therefore, the Representatives of the united States of America, in General Congress, Assembled, appealing to the Supreme Judge of the world for the rectitude of our intentions, do, in the name, and by authority of the good People of these Colonies, solemnly publish and declare, that these United Colonies are, and of right ought to be Free and Independent States; that they are Absolved from all Allegiance to the British Crown, and that all political connection between them and the State of

Great Britain, is and ought to be totally dissolved; and that as Free and Independent States, they have full Power to levy War, conclude peace, contract Alliances, establish Commerce, and to do all other Acts and Things which Independent States may of right do. And for the support of this Declaration, with a firm reliance on the protection of divine Providence, we mutually pledge to each other our Lives, our Fortunes and our sacred Honor.

The Declaration of Independence is rightly known for its powerful prose, which often reads like poetry. But the most remarkable aspect of Jefferson's document may be its audacity. Until this moment, many Americans still held to the belief—or, perhaps more accurately, the illusion—that the rift between Great Britain and the American colonies could be mended to everyone's benefit. The declaration—the ultimate act of independence and also treason—dissolved that illusion. On September 9, Congress would officially declare that the new nation would be called the United States of America.

Many in Congress felt doomed, though resolute. Yet, as the delegates signed the document on July 4, some humor broke through the otherwise solemn mood. Jefferson would often recount a story from the corpulent Benjamin Harrison of Virginia, who told his thin colleague Elbridge Gerry of Massachusetts, "I shall have a great advantage over you, Mr: Gerry, when we are all hung for what we are now doing. From the size and weight of my body I shall die in a few minutes, but from the lightness of your body you will dance in the air an hour or two before you are dead."

In the wider world, the news of the Declaration of Independence was greeted with great celebration. When the announcement was made in Philadelphia, citizens reacted with pure joy.

Information disseminated slowly in 1776, so most Americans did not know about the Declaration of Independence right away. It wasn't as if they could wake up the next morning and read the headline, "America Declares Independence!" Philadelphians had the home advantage and learned of the signing quickly. Others found out more gradually, and even newspapers that printed the entire text lacked details about its meaning or how it came about. Many people learned of the Declaration of Independence by attending raucous public readings. One reading in Boston was reported by the *Massachusetts Spy*: "The Declaration of Independence of the United States was read to a large and respectable body . . . who testified their approbation by repeated huzzas, firing of musketry and cannon, bonfires and other demonstrations of joy." At some point the crowd went to the King's Arms tavern, tore down its sign recognizing the despot (with the approval of the innkeeper), and drank long into the night.

The document reached Washington in New York on July 9. At 6:00 that evening, he gathered thousands of men at the parade grounds in lower Manhattan for a reading of the declaration. It was greeted with roars of approval by the soldiers, who welcomed its confirmation that they were risking their lives not for vague concessions but for a noble and patriotic purpose.

Late that night a group of overly exuberant revelers headed for Bowling Green, at the foot of Broadway, where the British in 1770 had erected a four-thousand-pound gilded lead statue of George III, sitting astride a horse and clothed like a Roman hero. Already the statue was often desecrated with graffiti. Now the New Yorkers pulled it down and dragged it up Broadway, removing the monarch's head along the way. Most of the statue was shipped to Connecticut, where it was melted down for ammunition, but random pieces surfaced over the years; eight of them are preserved at the New-York Historical Society.

Things had sobered up by July 12, when Admiral Howe's flagship appeared on the horizon, with 150 more ships on the way. They made a grand show of superiority sailing into New York Bay near Staten Island. To Washington's consternation, he heard many reports of his men leaving their posts to gape at the ships.

On July 13, Admiral Howe sent a letter to Washington proposing a truce. Henry Knox and Washington's aide, Colonel Reed, went to greet the messenger, who said, "I have a letter, sir, from Lord Howe to Mr. Washington."

The letter was addressed to "George Washington, Esq., New York."

"Sir," replied Reed, "we have no person in our army with that address."

The officer wondered what the proper address was. "You are sensible, sir," said Reed, "of the rank of General Washington in our army?"

He and Knox refused to accept a letter so disrespectfully addressed to their commander. In any case, Washington did not trust that Howe was making a good-faith offer.

Howe did not give up. Soon after this, the adjutant general of General Howe's army appeared with a flag of truce. Washington agreed to meet with him, and he presented a letter, once again addressed to George Washington, Esq. It was an exceedingly polite encounter, but Washington ultimately sent him packing with no response.

This display of confidence on Washington's part belied the tremendous disadvantage faced by the Americans. General Charles Lee, who had been sent in advance to set up fortifications, had done little by the time Washington and his forces reached New York; they were still not ready when Howe's ships arrived.

The New York campaign began on Long Island on August 27. On the western end of the island—what is now Brooklyn—the

British army flexed its might. The ratio was two to one—twenty thousand redcoats against ten thousand shabbily clad Americans. General Howe finally had an opportunity to show his skill to his critics back home. He struck a blow that led to nearly one thousand dead and wounded in the American army.

The situation was so dire that Howe might have expected surrender. Even so, the Americans fought on against all odds, leading Washington to exclaim, "Good God! What brave fellows I must this day lose." But those brave fellows were in a state of near collapse. This was real war, not the start-and-stop action they'd experienced in Boston. It was a fight that tested their stamina.

Two days after the battle began, the British forced Washington's troops back to Brooklyn. Washington evaluated the situation and realized that his Brooklyn defenses were thin. He doubted that his men could withstand a serious onslaught from Howe's troops and decided to evacuate to Manhattan, forfeiting Long Island.

In Manhattan he divided the forces between Kip's Bay on the eastern side, Fort Washington in upper Manhattan, and Kingsbridge in the Bronx. The British struck first at Kip's Bay from the East River on September 15. The assault was so overwhelming that many American soldiers ran for their lives as their commander tried desperately to keep them in line. The following day, Washington reorganized his forces farther north, at Harlem Heights, a wooded area between the Hudson and Harlem Rivers.

The British rushed after them, a miscalculation. The Americans dealt with them harshly, a result that briefly lifted the spirits of the Continental Army. There would be no further attacks until October 12. Washington, hoping to keep the British off guard, moved his forces north of the city, but they were attacked by the British at Throgs Neck. Once again the Americans held them off and then continued north to White Plains, with the British in pursuit.

When Howe's forces arrived on October 22, they overwhelmed the Americans until Washington ordered a retreat.

By this point, Washington had serious doubts that they could defend Fort Washington. The British were exhibiting too much muscle on the Hudson River. But Nathanael Greene argued otherwise. He wrote to Washington, "Upon the whole, I cannot help thinking the garrison is of advantage, and I cannot conceive the garrison to be in any great danger." It is unknown why he felt so confident. Perhaps he was emboldened by the sheer necessity of holding this critical position, the last defense of the Hudson River. Greene was stationed across the river at Fort Lee, New Jersey, while Colonel Robert Magaw, formerly a Pennsylvania lawyer, commanded Fort Washington on the New York side.

There were only three thousand Americans to Howe's eight-thousand-man force of British and Hessian soldiers, but at first the Americans waged the stronger attack, inflicting severe casualties. On November 16, as British cannons fired on Fort Washington, thousands of British and Hessian soldiers began an assault, climbing up the side of the hill below the fort and forcing the Americans to retreat inside or be slaughtered.

Washington, who had gone ahead to establish headquarters in Hackensack, New Jersey, quickly rode nearly seven miles to Fort Lee, where he joined Greene and others. They could clearly see what was going on across the river. To Greene's horror, Washington suggested that they row over and observe the situation up close. Greene was fearful that in addition to losing the fort, this expedition might result in losing their commander as well. But he accompanied Washington, and they arrived just in time to see the Hessian climbers summit the hill. After Washington and Greene returned to the New Jersey side, Magaw surrendered the fort. One hundred and fifty-five of his men were killed and the rest taken prisoner. It was a tremendous loss—nearly three thousand men in a single battle. Washington ordered the evacuation of Fort Lee, as American troops fled through New Jersey, pursued by the British.

It was during this desperate time that a certain young man came to Washington's attention.

Alexander Hamilton, twenty-one, was born in the West Indies on the British island of Nevis and spent his formative years in St. Croix, a Danish colony. He came to the American colonies as a teenager in 1772 and proceeded to earn a good education. He was attending King's College (today's Columbia University) when the fighting started, and he immediately dropped out and volunteered with a local militia, which later merged with Washington's army. In March 1776, he became the captain of an artillery company. Others took note of his fearless determination and his boundless energy, and he really shined during Washington's flight through New Jersey.

As they approached the Raritan River near New Brunswick, Washington's army, depleted in both numbers and stamina, faced a fierce enemy in pursuit. Hamilton took a position with artillery on the riverbank and held off the British with a cannonade of fire that allowed Washington's troops to get away. Washington noted his performance with admiration.

Historian Willard Sterne Randall painted this picture of Hamilton's courage and leadership:

For several hours, the slight, boyish-looking captain could be seen yelling, "Fire! Fire!" to his gun crews, racing home bags of grapeshot, then quickly repositioning the recoiling guns. Hamilton kept at it until Washington and his men were safely away toward Princeton. Halfway there, the general dispatched a brief message by express rider to Congress in Philadelphia: "The enemy appeared in several parties on the heights opposite

Brunswick and were advancing in a large body toward the [Raritan] crossing place. We had a smart cannonade whilst we were parading our men."

Although Hamilton's actions guaranteed that Washington and his struggling men would live to fight another day, the men who had slipped out of Howe's grasp still seemed to face insurmountable odds.

Less courage and skill were displayed by Washington's second in command, General Lee. It was no secret that Washington and Lee didn't get along. Lee had always believed that he was better suited to lead the Continental Army than Washington, and his fundamental disloyalty was troubling. Worse was his behavior in battle. After the loss of Manhattan, as Washington worked to regroup in New Jersey, he sent urgent word to Lee to join him there as soon as possible.

Rather than rushing to his commander's side, Lee delayed, and his forces didn't arrive in Morristown until December 12. Instead of seeking out Washington, Lee headed for Widow White's Tavern at Basking Ridge, about nine miles away.

British officers nearby got wind of Lee's presence, and the next morning they began to fire on the tavern. The Americans returned fire but soon realized they were outnumbered. Lee was offered a deal: if he surrendered, his life would be spared. Still in his nightgown, he presented himself to the British and was taken to New York. He would be released in a prisoner exchange in 1778, just in time to do more damage.

By now, Washington's army was outmanned and outgunned, exhausted and bereft—nearing its breaking point. And yet, as grim as things seemed, it was not the end of the road, as many feared. This was due chiefly to the character of two men, General Washington and General Howe. Historian Edward G. Lengel provided an interesting perspective on the character of these commanding generals. Of Washington he wrote, "If Abraham Lincoln had been president of Congress in 1776, he might have said of Washington instead of Ulysses S. Grant that, 'I can't spare this man, he fights!' Both men hated idleness and were temperamentally inclined for battle." By contrast, Lengel noted, "If William Howe had been even half as daring as Robert E. Lee, Washington might have ended his career in 1776 as a British prisoner in lower Manhattan."

Thomas Paine, who accompanied the American forces in their retreat, reflected thoughtfully on Washington's character from a contemporary viewpoint: "Voltaire has remarked that King William never appeared to full advantage but in difficulties and in action; the same remark may be made on General Washington, for the character fits him. There is a natural firmness in some minds which cannot be unlocked by trifles, but which, when unlocked, discovers a cabinet of fortitude; and I reckon it among those kind of public blessings, which we do not immediately see, that God hath blessed him with uninterrupted health, and given him a mind that can even flourish upon care."

CHAPTER SIX

"VICTORY OR DEATH"

On December 23, 1776, Benjamin Rush, a doctor and a Pennsylvania delegate to the Continental Congress, visited Washington at his headquarters four miles from the Delaware River. On this visit, he formed the impression that the commander was depressed about his dissolving army.

It was true that conditions were dire, and that Washington's forces were depleted, his remaining troops eyeing the calendar, as their enlistment period would expire on December 31. Days earlier, Washington had written to Hancock, analyzing the enemy's strength: "This strength, like a snowball by rolling, will increase, unless some means can be devised to check effectually, the progress of the enemy's arms." And what might that means be?

What Rush characterized as depression was more likely a state of intense concentration, because Washington was about to set in motion an audacious plan. While they talked, Washington doodled with pen and ink on small pieces of paper. "One of them by accident fell upon the floor near my feet," Rush recalled. "I was struck by the inscription upon it. It was 'Victory or Death.'"

Unknown to Rush, "Victory or Death" would become the countersign (password) for a dramatic surprise. "Christmas day at night, one hour before day is the time fixed upon for our attempt upon Trenton," Washington instructed Colonel Joseph Reed on the 23rd. "For heaven's sake keep this to yourself, as the discovery of it may prove fatal to us."

Across the Delaware, the British were well fortified along the Jersey shoreline, from Trenton to Princeton and in between, including a contingent of fifteen hundred Hessian mercenaries, who had joined the fight and were encamped at Trenton. The strength of his forces combined with the severity of the weather gave Howe confidence that his army was safe from attack that Christmas. "I can hardly believe that Washington would venture at this season of the year to pass the Delaware at Vessels Ferry as the repassing it may on account of the ice become difficult."

Colonel Johann Rall, a fifty-year-old officer of long military experience, who was commanding the Hessian troops, wasn't so sure. He warned his immediate superior, Colonel Carl von Donop, of the potential for an attack, and von Donop passed on the concerns to Major General James Grant.

Grant was contemptuous of the American army and annoyed by Rall. "I am sorry to hear your brigade has been fatigued or alarmed," he replied testily. "You may be assured that the rebel army . . . does not exceed eight thousand men, who have neither shoes nor stockings, are in fact almost naked, starving for cold without blankets, and very ill-supplied with provisions."

So convinced were the British of the absence of any threat that Colonel von Donop left his post at Bordentown to bunk down for several days at the home of a beautiful Mount Holly widow. As Captain Johann Ewald, a Hessian soldier who kept a diary of the war, observed, "The fate of entire Kingdoms often depends upon a few blockheads and irresolute men."

On the frigid morning of December 25, the skies were clear, but Washington's men, their clothing ragged and their hunger barely sated, shivered as they stood to receive their commander's Christmas message before leaving their encampment. According to many historical accounts, which have combined to become legend, Washington asked for a reading from the new pamphlet published by Paine. The passage would become one of the most often quoted in the nation's history.

These are the times that try men's souls. The summer soldier and the sunshine patriot will, in this crisis, shrink from the service to his country, but he that stands it now deserves the love and thanks of man and woman. Tyranny, like hell, is not easily conquered; yet we have this consolation with us, that the harder the conflict, the more glorious the triumph.

They began to march, twenty-four hundred men. Their destination, long hours away, was McKonkey's Ferry on the Delaware. There, in the dark, they would board large boats borrowed from an ironworks operation and from local residents to cross the river. Although the ground was covered with hardened snow, the river looked passable.

Knox was in charge of artillery, his "deep bass voice" roaring above the sound of the wind. Alexander Hamilton had been desperately ill, bedridden in a local farmhouse when the Christmas attack began. He dragged himself out of bed to join the fight.

The plan relied on flawless timing and perfect execution. The men would cross to the other side of the river, along with four hundred tons of artillery and horses, and then march nine miles to an encampment of some fifteen hundred Hessians, where they would launch a predawn attack. Washington assumed the enemy would be sleeping off its holiday celebration.

Washington crossed first and then sat on a wooden box (formerly a beehive) to watch the rest of the movement. He was deeply worried, as they were hours behind schedule.

Freezing rain slashed at them, chilling them thoroughly. The wind howled, battering them from every side. The flat-bottomed boats were difficult to maneuver through the icy waters. The weather served as both an impediment to their swift progress and a strange gift, in that the Hessians never imagined them making the trip.

Imagine twenty-four hundred men marching for nine miles in complete silence. When boots crunched on the frozen snow, those who still wore boots were ordered to wrap them in rags to muffle the sound. Those without shoes wrapped their bare, cold feet, but their raw skin still left spatters of blood on the snow-packed ground.

Knox described the scene in a letter to Lucy, writing that "a part of the army consisting of about 2500 or three thousand passed the river on Christmas night with almost infinite difficulty, with eighteen field pieces. Floating ice in the river made the labor almost incredible however perseverance accomplished what at first seemed impossible—about two o'clock the troops were all on the Jersey side—we then were about nine miles from the object, the night was cold and stormy. It hailed with great violence. The troops marched with the most profound silence and good order."

Elisha Bostwick, a soldier, wrote about the long march.

. . . About day light a halt was made at which time his Excellency [Washington] and aides came near to the front on the side of the path where soldiers stood. I heard his Excellency as he was coming on speaking to and encouraging the soldiers. The words he spoke as he passed by where I stood and in my hearing were these: "Soldiers, keep by your officers. For God's sake, keep by your officers!" Spoke in a deep and solemn voice.

While passing a slanting, slippery bank his Excellency's horse's hind feet both slipped from under him, and he seized his horse's mane and the horse recovered.

Our horses were then unharnessed and the artillery men prepared. We marched on and it was not long before we heard the out sentries of the enemy both on the road we were in and the eastern road, and their out guards retreated firing, and our army, then with a quick step pushing on upon both roads, at the same time entered the town. Their artillery taken, they resigned with little opposition, about nine hundred, all Hessians, with 4 brass field pieces; the remainder crossing the bridge at the lower end of the town escaped. . . .

Johann Rall was a casualty of the fighting, shot twice in the side. He was removed from battle to the home of a Tory friend, and as he lay on his deathbed, he called for Washington to visit him so he could surrender to him personally. Though flawed as a strategist, Rall was beloved by his men, whom he always treated with kindness and respect. Mindful of their fate, he made a last request to Washington: that his men be treated with humanity. Washington promised that they would be, and he kept his promise.

On December 31, as the last light of a fateful year began to fade, Washington surveyed a bedraggled regiment of New Englanders, who had been with him the whole way from Boston. Sitting astride his horse, he assured them of his deep regard and admiration for their patriotism, and he asked them to consider one more offer: if they extended their enlistment period by six weeks, he would pay them a bounty of $10.

A call went out for volunteers, but not a single man responded in the affirmative. Washington began to ride along the line, speaking as persuasively as he knew how: "My brave fellows, you have done all I asked you to do, and more than could be reasonably expected.

But your country is at stake, your wives, your houses, all you hold dear. You have worn yourselves out with fatigue and hardships, but we know not how to spare you. . . ."

Slowly, the men began to respond, stumbling forward to pledge their last measure of strength to the cause. In the end, half of the twenty-four hundred signed up to stay another six weeks.

While Washington's men were buoyed by the victory at Trenton, their physical condition remained poor. Fewer in number and still barely clothed against the cold, they would soon face their next confrontation with the enemy, in Princeton, just thirteen miles to the north.

Approaching Princeton, Washington felt the full gravity of their situation. As his step-grandson George Parke Custis wrote dramatically, "He was aware that his hour was come to redeem the pledge he had laid on the altar of his country when he first took up arms in her cause to win her liberties or perish in the attempt. Defeat at Princeton would have amounted to the annihilation of America's last hope. . . ."

Yet, as had happened before, Washington believed that providence was with them in the coming battle. As they rested on the night before their approach to Princeton, a sudden cold front blew in, freezing the roads, which had been muddy and difficult to negotiate. Now they were as smooth and hard as a city pavement. Washington roused his men and ordered them to march under cover of darkness. What might have been a slog was now an easier march. As dawn broke on January 3, they reached a hill near Princeton, where they paused briefly to reconnoiter, then attacked.

The fighting was brief but intense. One friend observed Hamilton, so recently in his sickbed, offering "a model of discipline" as he led his company into Princeton. Washington urged his men on, calling to them to have no fear, that the enemy wasn't that strong.

His aide John Fitzgerald, watching the commander sitting tall on his white horse, covered his eyes, unable to bear the expected sight of seeing him fall. But he didn't fall, instead driving the enemy back, and as a bonus capturing a wagon train of much-needed supplies. (Washington neglected to mention this haul in his report to Congress, lest they get any ideas about reducing his request for equipment.)

Washington was proud of his men, and they in turn gave him all they had. One young man, a sergeant, made a frank (and charming) confession in his diary: "In this battle and that of Trenton, there was no ardent spirits in the army, and the excitement of rum had nothing to do in obtaining the victories. As I had tried powder and rum on Long Island to promote courage, and engaged here without it, I can say that I was none the less courageous here than there."

When these critical battles were over, Knox wrote to Lucy: "Every American friend will be enthralled to see the intrepidity of our people in fighting the enemy and preventing them from forming in their town."

Washington led his army to Morristown, where they established winter quarters. It was strategically located between New York and Philadelphia, and the terrain made it easy to defend. Washington established his headquarters at Arnold's Tavern, the centerpiece of the town. During the winter he made public health his priority, ordering inoculations against smallpox and taking other health and hygiene measures. Smallpox was rampant throughout the army, and it was usually fatal, but even so, the men greatly feared inoculation. It meant being injected with a small amount of live smallpox, and it did make people sick. There was substantial resistance among troops who already felt weak and exhausted, but Washington ultimately got his way, calling smallpox "more destructive to an army in the natural way than the enemy's sword." His order that every soldier and new recruit be inoculated ultimately saved the army from being defeated by disease.

The army stayed in Morristown until spring, but for many of them this rest wasn't enough. Conditions were poor, and it was difficult to get necessary resources from Congress. Desertion was an ongoing problem. Congress had finally agreed to longer-term enlistments, which helped somewhat, but civilians weren't rushing to sign up.

Alexander Hamilton's fortunes changed during this time. No sooner had the army camped in Morristown than Washington sent Hamilton a message, requesting his service as aide-de-camp—a promotion that carried the rank of lieutenant colonel. A man of many talents, Hamilton quickly took charge of daily official matters, freeing his boss to attend to larger concerns. Their relationship became close, nearly symbiotic. Hamilton biographer Ron Chernow pinpointed the way each man served the other, noting that with his "sterling character and clear sense of purpose," Washington provided guidance to the younger man. "Hamilton, in turn contributed philosophical depth, administrative expertise, and comprehensive policy knowledge that nobody in Washington's ambit ever matched. . . . As a team, they were unbeatable and far more than the sum of their parts."

Congress was trying to lend aid from afar, but its idea of helping wasn't always welcome—as was the case when it introduced Washington to a French officer who wanted to join the fight. Only nineteen years old, Gilbert du Motier, the Marquis de Lafayette, was extremely bright and *very* wealthy, and he came highly recommended. Still, in Washington's experience, these foreign volunteers were sometimes more trouble than they were worth. There were too many of them floating around, and many of them bore Ben

Franklin's questionable imprimatur—he wasn't always so careful with his vetting. Washington complained about this, calling their presence an embarrassment.

However, Congress was convinced that Lafayette was an exception, and Washington was persuaded to meet with the young man on August 5 at the City Tavern in Philadelphia. The favored gathering place of Congress, the City Tavern also offered lodging, and Washington and his aides stayed there for three days while the commander held meetings.

Washington had many concerns when he met Lafayette. The British were marching toward Philadelphia, determined to seize this symbolic jewel. Washington knew he did not have the resources to fully defend the city—it was just too big and spread out. His strategy was to fight the enemy before it reached Philadelphia.

Lafayette cut an impressive figure at their meeting—tall and elegantly dressed in an officer's attire, his receding hairline belying his youth. Although he struggled with English, he got by, and his sincerity shone through. He was enormously charming. Normally an emotionally cautious man, Washington was immediately taken with Lafayette, and he would never have reason to question this first impression. He saw a young man mature beyond his years, who was sincerely devoted to the cause—who in fact had bucked his family's wishes to be there and who offered his services without pay.

Perhaps Lafayette prodded an old memory in Washington, of a time when he himself was young and green, and older men took him under their wings, even when he screwed up. He felt drawn to Lafayette and wanted to give him a chance. For his part, Lafayette was starstruck by the general, hailing his "majestic figure and deportment." He was ready and willing to learn from such a master. In the years to come, Lafayette would become one of Washington's most valuable advisors and a dear friend.

At their first meeting, Washington asked Lafayette if he would like to join him for a tour of the city's military defenses the next day. Soon Lafayette was on board, sharing Washington's house with his top military aides, and ready to go into battle.

The French officer soon had an opportunity to show what he was made of. With the British pressing north toward Philadelphia, Washington faced a critical series of battles, beginning with a strong defense of the city from an area to the south, at Brandywine Creek.

Before heading south, on August 24 Washington arranged to parade through the streets of Philadelphia. His purpose was to demonstrate a military strength that barely existed and to persuade the city's Tories—of whom there were many—to abandon their support for Britain and come over to the patriot side. It seemed like every Philadelphian came out to watch the parade and cheer the men, who marched as tall as they were able. Green sprigs were attached to their hats in lieu of full uniforms—Lafayette's idea.

Their appearance boosted the mood of the locals, though John Adams, watching from outside the State House, expressed a frustration undoubtedly felt by many: "Our soldiers have not yet quite the air of soldiers. They don't step exactly in time. They don't hold up their heads quite erect, nor turn out their toes exactly as they ought. . . ." Had Washington heard this judgment, he would probably have lost his temper. If his men were ill-equipped, it was in large part due to Congress's failure to expedite the delivery of funds and equipment. The delegates sat in their fine hall and lived in the best accommodations while his troops shivered and went hungry.

As they marched toward Brandywine Creek, Washington ordered his men not to loot the farms they passed. These were citizens like themselves, he told them, who needed their provisions. The army, in turn, needed their goodwill, and plundering farms would destroy that bond.

Howe's army did not exercise the same restraint. According to local historians, "For years after the battle, Chester County residents were recovering from the damages (depredations) that the British had wreaked from their commandeering of animals, food, crops, clothing, and other items. It is important to note that this was harvest time and as fruit and crops were being gathered, suddenly two armies descended on the county."

When those armies met near Chadds Ford, Washington's troops fought valiantly but to no avail. On September 11, over twelve hundred were killed, wounded, or captured at Brandywine Creek, outside of Philadelphia. As the British turned toward the city, Washington sent Hamilton and officer Henry Lee (later the father of Robert E. Lee) ahead to burn the flour mills on the Schuylkill River.

Lafayette, fighting hard, did not at first notice when a ball struck his left leg below the calf. Only when blood began to fill his boot did he see that he was wounded. He was carried off the field but recovered within a few weeks.

Philadelphia, however, did not escape. On September 18, with the enemy upon them, Hamilton managed to send an urgent message to Hancock at the Continental Congress:

Sir,

If Congress have not yet left Philadelphia, they ought to do it immediately without fail, for the enemy have the means of throwing a party this night into the city. I just now crossed the valleyford, in doing which a party of the enemy came down & fired upon us in the boat by which means I lost my horse. One man was killed and another wounded. The boats were abandoned & will fall into their hands. I did all I could to prevent this but to no purpose.

"Congress was chased like a covey of partridges from Phila-delphia. . . ." lamented Adams, who had been roused from his bed in the middle of the night to receive Hamilton's message. He described the event in his diary:

At 3 this morning was waked by Mr. Lovell, and told that the members of Congress were gone, some of them, a little after midnight. That there was a letter from Mr. Hamilton aide de camp to the General, informing that the enemy were in posses-sion of the ford and the boats, and had it in their power to be in Philadelphia, before morning, and that if Congress was not removed they had not a moment to lose.

Congress departed the city, vowing to remain an official body. Traveling west, they stopped in Lancaster, remaining for a day before establishing themselves at the county courthouse in York, about one hundred miles from Philadelphia.

When Franklin heard in Paris that Howe had captured Philadel-phia, he responded, "No, Philadelphia has captured Howe."

Technically, Howe had won at Brandywine, yet questions lingered about his willingness to fight the war. He did not pursue Washing-ton's forces to try to deliver a fatal blow. Instead, he let them go and turned toward the city, a questionable prize. "The feeling that Howe lacked something essential as a commander in chief grew in late 1777 and continued to dog him," wrote historian Robert Middle-kauff. "It is difficult not to conclude that he lacked the intellectual power to understand the war he was fighting. Coupled with a dis-position to take his ease, to wait rather than act, there was a feeling that for all his courage and his long years of experience in the army, he was out of place—in over his head—as commander."

The Continental Congress in exile refused to be defeated. Re-convening at the courthouse in York, they completed the Articles of

Confederation. After the Declaration of Independence was signed, the Confederation Committee, headed by Dickinson (who, ironically, had voted against the declaration), had begun the work of drafting what amounted to a constitution.

It wasn't the first effort of its kind. Franklin had drafted a plan for a government as early as the 1750s, long before the quest for independence had gained popularity. It didn't go anywhere. Now Dickinson presented his draft, titled "Articles of Confederation and Perpetual Union."

Jane E. Calvert, who has written extensively about Dickinson and Quaker thought in early America, notes, "He put forth several key provisions that deserve mention, provisions that, had they been adopted, would have launched America on a very different course: a strong central government; protections for Indians; the abolition of slavery; religious liberty; and the rights of women." She credits Dickinson's close association with the Quakers for many of his advocacies, calling it "Quaker constitutionalism." But Dickinson's more progressive ideas were rejected by the Congress.

Debates were held during the summer of 1776. Then the effort was paused as the war took precedence; discussion did not resume until Congress was settled at the county courthouse at York in September. Franklin wasn't present this time, having been sent to Paris to convince the French government to back America in the war. Jefferson was also absent, essentially working from home in Virginia.

The Articles of Confederation, adopted on November 15, were not exactly a constitution. Article III described the arrangement as a "firm league of friendship" among states, with each state retaining "its sovereignty, freedom, and independence, and every power, jurisdiction, and right, which is not by this confederation expressly delegated to the United States, in Congress assembled." The national body had sharply limited powers, a fact that would create difficulties as time went on.

Meanwhile, taking their ease in Philadelphia, Howe and his officers occupied the finest homes and looked forward to a much more pleasant winter than their opponents. Howe sent for his mistress, Mrs. Loring, and made sure that she was set up comfortably. He was once again mocked in poetry for his exploits:

Sir William, he, as snug as flea
Lay all this time a-snoring;
Nor dreamed of harm, as he lay warm
In bed with Mrs. Loring.

Washington's troops suffered a very different fate. The contrast between the two sides during the coming winter was stark—one comfortable and confident of an easy victory, the other tested by trials worthy of Job.

In a 2005 speech at Brigham Young University, the great historian David McCullough, who died in 2022, spoke of an aspect of Washington's character that enabled him to keep coming back from his failures. McCullough noted that Washington "made dreadful mistakes, particularly in the year 1776. They were almost inexcusable, inexplicable mistakes, but he always learned from them. And he never forgot what the fight was about—'the glorious cause of America,' as they called it. Washington would not give up; he would not quit."

CHAPTER SEVEN

WASHINGTON'S CRUCIBLE

"There comes a soldier, his bare feet are seen through his worn out shoes, his legs nearly naked from the tattered remains of an only pair of stockings, his breeches not sufficient to cover his nakedness, his shirt hanging in strings, his hair disheveled, his face meagre; his whole appearance pictures a person forsaken and discouraged. He comes, and cries with an air of wretchedness and despair." This vivid account comes from the diary of Albigence Woldo, a surgeon with the Continental Army, who witnessed the suffering experienced by Washington's men in December 1777, when they settled at Valley Forge for the winter.

Twenty miles north of Philadelphia, Valley Forge seemed to be the end of the line for the army. It felt like a wasteland. A few scattered farmhouses stood in the forest overgrowth near the ruins of an iron forge and abandoned gristmill, bordered by the Schuylkill River and Valley Creek. To look at it was to despair of comfort or warmth as the mid-Atlantic winter approached.

The site had been chosen for its distance from the occupying British; it was near Philadelphia but not so near as to draw the enemy into a battle. Washington had decided not to fight for Philadelphia—at least not yet.

As Lafayette, recently recovered from his Brandywine injury, put it, "There we shall be quiet, there we can discipline and instruct our troops, we can be able to begin an early campaign, and we shall not fear to be carried into a winter campaign if it pleased General Howe."

Washington immediately ordered the men to build huts for their shelter, in what historian Douglas Freeman called a "strange" race against time—"between the axes of the men building huts and the harsh wear-and-tear on the remaining garments of those who still had sufficient clothing to permit outdoor duty."

Washington's men were in pathetic shape. Aside from their other woes, they were hungry, subsisting on firecakes, a tasteless, fire-roasted brick made of flour and water. They'd had no meat in many days, and on December 21 an anguished cry went up in the camp: "No meat! No meat!"

Such misery led, Washington saw, to a "longing, and hankering after their respective homes"—how could it not? He worried that many officers and soldiers were once again prepared to leave when their enlistment period ended on December 31.

For the first time, a chorus of criticism rose against Washington. Not only did the Americans appear to be losing the war, but also they were starving and afflicted with disease. Perhaps, some said, it was time to consider replacing Washington with a more competent commander. Ironically, such voices found ammunition in the cheering news, back in September, of a victory at Saratoga, New York, by American forces led by Horatio Gates.

The army's misfortune also raised the pressure for Franklin to succeed in bringing the French into the war. It no longer seemed possible, many acknowledged, that Washington's struggling army could defeat Great Britain on its own. It was time for the larger world to get involved.

It would be a tough sell. France had to be convinced that it was worth its while to reengage with Great Britain during a time of relative peace in Europe. The eleven-year war in America was hardly a distant memory; nor was the fact that Americans fought on the side of Britain against the French. Perhaps no other man than Franklin could have had a chance of winning them over.

The French loved Franklin personally, and he knew how to manipulate their worship. When he received word of the American victory at Saratoga, he played it up dramatically, virtually signaling that the war was all but lost by the British. His claim caught the attention of Louis XVI, as it was meant to do, and the king began to reconsider the prospect of support for the Americans. Things were looking up.

But the undermining of Washington by those comparing his leadership unfavorably to Gates continued through the early part of 1778.

Writing to Patrick Henry in January, Benjamin Rush, who had earlier doubted Washington before his brilliant crossing of the Delaware, expressed new worries: "Sir we have only passed the Red Sea. A dreary wilderness is still before us, and unless a Moses or a Joshua are raised up in our behalf, we must perish before we reach the promised land." Rush noted that the Saratoga victory, which did not involve Washington directly, "has shown us what Americans are capable of doing with a *General* at their head." He went on to claim, "A Gates, a [Charles] Lee, or a [Thomas] Conway would, in a few weeks, render them an irresistible body of men."

Of course, no one would have been happier to dismiss any talk of heroism than Washington himself. He knew better than anyone his own very human flaws. But he was hurt to learn that some of his most outspoken critics were his own officers. One of these was the man Rush cited, the Irish-born, French-raised general Thomas Conway, who wrote an incendiary letter to General Gates: "Heaven has been determined to save your country, or a weak general and bad councilors would have ruined it."

News of the letter was leaked to Washington by a supporter. When Washington challenged him, Conway denied that he'd ever used the phrase "weak general." Congress, seeming to give some credence to Conway, promoted him to inspector general and gave him the rank of major general. Many of Washington's old allies in Congress were beginning to doubt him. The Board of War, established to oversee Washington, appointed Gates as its president.

Expressing his frustration to Henry Laurens, the South Carolinian who had replaced Hancock as president of the Continental Congress, Washington said, "My enemies take an ungenerous advantage of me. They know the delicacy of my situation and that motives of policy deprive me of the defense I might otherwise make against their insidious attacks. They know I cannot combat their insinuations, however injurious, without disclosing secrets it is of the utmost moment to conceal."

Laurens's son John was in Washington's command, and his father wrote to him anxiously. "I know the cruelty of tongues speaking the fullness of designing hearts. Nevertheless I am afraid there may be some ground for some of these remarks." John defended his commander, and the elder Laurens ultimately came around.

Even Lafayette briefly flirted with the campaign against Washington. Lafayette had great admiration for Gates and was initially swayed in his favor. Later, he would be chagrined by his naivete. "I thought that here almost every man was a lover of liberty," he confessed to Washington. Instead, he was shocked to find in Congress "stupid men who without knowing a single word about war undertake to judge you . . ."

Washington forgave his young acolyte, writing to him with unusual sentimentality that, after the war, "if you will give me your company in Virginia, we will laugh at our past difficulties and the folly of others."

Washington didn't say so, but what came to be known as the Conway Cabal was effectively a coup attempt. Conway began a back-channel correspondence with Gates, full of plans to replace Washington, while Rush sowed doubt behind the scenes. When Washington learned of the correspondence and the plot, it collapsed. Congress was instantly back in Washington's camp, as letters of support from his generals poured in.

Conway resigned from the army in March 1778. In the summer, he accepted the challenge to a duel by one of Washington's Pennsylvania friends, General John Cadwalader. Conway was wounded and, thinking himself dying (he wasn't), wrote an apology to Washington.

Gates did not suffer measurably from his association with Conway, though many, possibly including Washington, thought that he was implicated in the cabal. He fought on, stumbling only late in the war.

Washington could be oversensitive, so it's likely that he was wounded by the betrayal and lack of confidence on the part of men he trusted. He admitted as much to Henry Laurens. But his greater concern was always with the welfare of the army and the need to cut out the "malignancies" that could weaken it.

Washington's chief occupation as the winter of 1777 advanced was to shore up the supply chain of food, including hay and oats for the horses. By February, the food situation was critical. Men were languishing and horses were dying. Opportunistic diseases spread through the camp. Even so, Washington still hesitated to commandeer supplies from the surrounding country folk, though he had permission from the Congress to do so. The army relied on the confidence and support of its civilian friends, he argued. Plundering their food and clothing would turn them into enemies. Instead, he sent a group led by Nathanael Greene to purchase grain, cattle, and other goods from farmers within a twenty-mile radius of their encampment, and this solved the immediate problem.

On February 22, Washington's forty-fifth birthday, his mood was lifted by a serenade performed outside his headquarters by a group of soldier musicians. He was so delighted that he gave each of the fifers and drummers one pound ten shillings as a gift. Then he returned to his deeper worries: how to strengthen the fighting force.

On February 23, Washington mounted his horse and headed west from Valley Forge for an important rendezvous. Traveling toward him on the eighty-mile journey from York, Pennsylvania, was Baron Friedrich Wilhelm von Steuben, a former Prussian lieutenant general and protégé of Prussia's Frederick the Great. At the behest of Ben Franklin, von Steuben had met with members of Congress in York; the next step was to meet Washington.

Franklin, who had met von Steuben in Paris, had sung his praises to Washington, in the process embellishing his record. His rank had never been as high as reported, and his current status was unemployed and down on his luck. Even so, there was little doubt about von Steuben's sincerity or his ability when it came to training soldiers. In December, von Steuben wrote to Washington with a convincing entreaty, stating that "the object of my greatest ambition is to render your country all the services in my power, and to deserve the title of a Citizen of America by fighting for the cause of your liberty." Washington left the final decision to Congress, which gained a positive impression of von Steuben—especially when he declined rank or pay for his services, only requesting reimbursement for his expenses if America won the war.

Now Washington saw von Steuben approaching on the road from York, elegant in the crisp uniform of a Prussian general, accompanied only by two aides and his sleek Italian greyhound, Azor. Washington was immediately struck by the dignity and charm of the man, and his animal lover's heart was lifted by the sight of the beautiful greyhound striding alongside his master's horse.

He soon discovered that von Steuben couldn't speak a word of English, but no worry: Hamilton and Lafayette were happy to translate for him.

Von Steuben's methods were specific and highly effective. He took a disorganized army and trained them in a proven set of drills and maneuvers, along with emphasizing improved personal discipline. His personal and supportive approach transformed the army's overall character in just a few months. Von Steuben worked directly with the men, communicating through translators. He wrote out a drill manual in French, and Hamilton translated it. His leadership began to lift the soldiers' mood.

Further aiding morale—including his own—Washington welcomed some of the officers' wives to camp. Martha arrived in February and stayed though the winter. Von Steuben's secretary, Peter S. Duponceau, looked on with admiration: "In the midst of all our distress there were some bright sides of the picture which Valley Forge exhibited. . . . Mrs. Washington had the courage to follow her husband to that dismal abode. Other ladies also graced the scene. Among them was the lady of General Greene, a handsome, elegant, and accomplished woman." Others included Lucy Knox; Sara Stirling, the wife of Lord Stirling, a Scottish American major general; and Rebekah Biddle, the wife of Colonel Clement Biddle, who organized one of the first Quaker units under Washington. Duponceau recalled cheerful evenings when the ladies would gather for tea and conversation and song, lifting the spirits of those who heard them.

Besides these distinguished guests, several hundred women lived at the camp: wives of enlisted men, who had become a critical support system for the army. There were also at least a few unmarried women and prostitutes.

With Martha on hand, the Washingtons' lodgings became a focal point of aid to the well-being of soldiers and their families. Women felt comfortable coming to her with their concerns. In addition to this social support, the ladies knit and mended socks, thus saving many soldiers from the torment of blistered, frozen feet.

Martha was also helpful in local diplomacy. After a group of Quaker men in Pennsylvania were arrested for refusing to pledge allegiance to the new nation or take up arms, their wives came to Valley Forge to plead their cause. Martha received them with her husband. They were invited to dinner and then joined Martha in her bedroom. What transpired is not exactly clear, but their husbands were soon released, and the women saw Martha's hand in the effort.

Even with these positive developments, by late April Washington still did not know how they would rise to the challenges of any fresh assault. Then came a gift of hope from overseas. Franklin had succeeded in his mission, and France recognized the United States as an independent nation. On February 6, 1778, months before the news made its way to Washington, Franklin arrived at Versailles to great fanfare to sign two treaties. One was the Treaty of Amity and Commerce, which, in recognizing America as a sovereign nation, also promoted trade between the two countries. The second treaty, the Treaty of Alliance, made America and France allies in the war with Great Britain.

"Vive Franklin!" cheered the French crowds when the diplomat appeared at Versailles. The crowds were thrilled to see him. Perhaps the only person in France not enamored of Franklin's pioneer spirit and wide-ranging genius was Marie Antoinette. She sniffed that a mere printer's foreman would never have achieved such status in Europe. Had Franklin been asked about the remark, he might have responded, "Exactly!" For the beauty of the new republic being conceived in America was that a printer's foreman could lead the way.

When Washington finally received word of the treaty, on May 5, he gathered his troops and directed that "upon a signal given, the whole army will huzza, 'Long live the King of France.'"

The advantages of France's support were innumerable. It immediately dampened England's fervor, as few could stomach the prospect of another long war with France. And as a practical matter, France provided indispensable aid to Washington's flagging army in the form of funds, arms, ships, soldiers, and other personnel.

Simultaneously with the news that France was coming to the Americans' aid, General Howe requested to be relieved of his command. His appointed replacement was Henry Clinton. Short and stocky, with an unpleasant personality and an imperious attitude, Clinton had been raised in America, where his father was the royal governor of New York from 1743 to 1753. He'd joined the British army and served in Germany before returning to America to fight the colonists at Bunker Hill. He had taken part in every major campaign since then.

Howe's farewell celebration was a lavish and expensive extravaganza in the style of a Mischianza (Italian for a medley of events). There was jousting, a river parade, and a costume ball with fireworks, dancing, and an enormous midnight supper. This over-the-top display celebrated a man who had wasted every opportunity for victory during his command.

Fearing that they'd be unable to hold the city once French ships arrived, the British abandoned Philadelphia on June 18. The British loyalists were horrified, feeling exposed and betrayed. Some managed to board British ships bound for the motherland, but others were not so lucky. Howe's secretary, Ambrose Serle, wrote in his journal about one civilian friend "left to wander like Cain upon the earth without home and without property. Many others are involved in the like dismal case for the same reason—attachment to the King and country, and opposition to a set of daring Rebels."

Washington had endured his crucible at Valley Forge, a time that posed the ultimate test of his resolve, his stamina, and his leadership. He would take the opportunity offered by his newly strengthened army, the promise of French support, and the British flight from Philadelphia, and make the most of it.

General Charles Lee, who had been captured by the British in New Jersey in 1776, was back, having been released in a prisoner exchange. The British had hoped to trade him for a high-value general of theirs, but the negotiations slogged along; it was obvious that the Continental Army didn't consider Lee a valuable trade. They finally accepted a deal and handed over a lesser British general. Washington might have felt reluctant to give Lee much authority, but he was respectful of Lee's seniority, so once again Lee would be in a position of command. Washington had no idea that, during his time in prison, the British-born Lee had served as an informal advisor to his captors, suggesting ways of overwhelming Washington's army. Much later it was learned that he'd written several letters to Howe containing such recommendations. When Lee returned to Washington's army, however, there was no hint of his betrayal.

Washington was intent on pursuing General Clinton's army north through New Jersey. He assigned Lee to take an advance force to launch a forward attack, while Washington brought the remainder of the army from Valley Forge.

Clinton's army, on the move since departing from Philadelphia in mid-June, had stopped to rest at Monmouth Court House (in modern-day Freehold Township) in central New Jersey, and that's where Lee found them. While Washington's instructions were not particularly explicit, Lee stumbled in his attack. His advance was disorganized and burdened with uncertainty, and he quickly decided that he was no match for Clinton. By the time Washington and his forces arrived, Lee and his men were in retreat.

Washington confronted Lee, in a rage over the latter's insubordinate choice to retreat rather than fight. According to one report, the commander "swore that day till the leaves shook on the trees." He pulled Lee from authority and assembled a powerful team of Greene, Hamilton, Lafayette, and the Pennsylvania-born Anthony Wayne, who had comported himself bravely at Brandywine, for a surprise attack against the British. Throughout the Battle of Monmouth, fought on June 28 in blistering, hundred-degree heat, Washington rode among his troops, urging them on. They finally drove the British into retreat. Seeing that his men were exhausted, Washington decided not to pursue Clinton, settling for the victory and heaping praise on his soldiers for their courage. The men sensed that they had at last come back from their low point at Valley Forge. Putting von Steuben's training to the test, they had prevailed.

Lee's fate was harsh. He was arrested for disobeying orders and later court-martialed. In January 1780, he was dismissed by Congress and returned to Philadelphia, where he died a civilian before the end of the war.

A great marvel and mystery for us, looking back on the war for independence from the twenty-first century, is how on earth the Americans prevailed. The struggle lasted for eight years, and the combatants were grossly unequal. The Americans piled up defeats, some devastating enough to put an end to their fight. Yet somehow they always climbed out of what seemed like certain doom. The entry of the French in 1778 was met with exhilaration and brought a sense that victory was within America's grasp. Even though it took five more years, there was never again the undercurrent of despair that had marked the war's early years.

Most historians credit Washington's leadership, but what exactly was it about his command that was so effective? As Thomas Fleming sagely put it in *The Strategy of Victory*, a winning military strategy is essentially "a cluster of ideas and insights, all linked to a way of winning a specific war." In that respect, Washington had a gift for the big picture. He could visualize the scope of the war and avoid being distracted by individual defeats. He understood that losing a battle did not preclude a victory in the war, and thus was able to inspire his men to keep on and prevail the next time.

Through it all, Washington displayed, in the words of the late James C. Rees, former executive director of Mount Vernon, "courage in the raw—an intuitive, visceral bravery" that was integral to his character. He rode beside his soldiers. He fought with them. He shared their agonies and their victories. He saw them through.

The site of Washington's Virginia birthplace, signifying the beauty and promise of the new world. *By J.G. Chapman. The Miriam and Ira Wallach Division of Art, Prints and Photographs: Print Collection, The New York Public Library*

Washington had a difficult but ultimately loving relationship with his mother, Mary Ball Washington. She lived to see him become president but died soon after in August 1789. This illustration depicts Washington's last visit before her death. *Courtesy of Mount Vernon Ladies' Association.*

Beautiful, vivacious, and intelligent, Martha Dandridge first caught the eye of the wealthy Daniel Parke Custis, who would suffer an early death. A widow with two children, she was courted by many before she and Washington found each other. *The Miriam and Ira Wallach Division of Art, Prints and Photographs: Print Collection, The New York Public Library*

The wedding of George Washington and Martha Dandridge Custis. Martha's children are also pictured. *After Junius Brutus Stearns. Courtesy of Mount Vernon Ladies' Association.*

Washington, Martha, and the children at Mount Vernon.
Although Washington never had children of his own, he became
a loving stepfather to Jacky and Patsy. *The Miriam and Ira
Wallach Division of Art, Prints and Photographs: Print Collection,
The New York Public Library*

This illustration
depicts General George
Washington standing on
a bluff above the Hudson
River, with his enslaved
valet William Lee on
horseback to his right. Lee
remained with Washington
for life, and Washington
freed him with an annuity
in his will. *By John
Trumbull. The Metropolitan
Museum of Art, Bequest of
Charles Allen Munn, 1924*

Whenever she could, Martha visited Washington at his headquarters, spreading welcome warmth and support to his men. Other officers' wives sometimes joined her. This illustration depicts her arriving at Washington's headquarters at Valley Forge. *Breuker & Kessler. National Museum of American History*

George Washington's autograph. *Manuscripts and Archives Division, The New York Public Library*

On June 28, 1776, Thomas Jefferson presented a draft of the Declaration of Independence to John Hancock at the Pennsylvania State House in Philadelphia. *By John Trumbull. Smithsonian American Art Museum, Gift of International Business Machines Corporation*

On Christmas Eve 1776, Washington prepared to lead his men across the Delaware River. The campaign was a desperate effort by a beleaguered army to gain an advantage. Washington's call sign for the campaign was "Victory or Death." *After John Cameron. The Metropolitan Museum of Art, Bequest of Adele S. Colgate*

The Quaker patriot Nathanael Greene became one of Washington's
most skilled officers, and a strong bond formed between the two men.
By Valentine Green. National Portrait Gallery, Smithsonian Institution

"Hour of Victory": The march to Trenton. *By Edward Percy Moran. Courtesy of Mount Vernon Ladies' Association*

During a brutal winter at Valley Forge, as Washington struggled to restore the strength of his exhausted force, he welcomed the arrival of a young French officer, the Marquis de Lafayette, who would become a valuable officer and a devoted friend. *John Ward Dunsmore. Library of Congress*

Washington and his staff at Valley Forge. The officers on horseback are the Marquis de Lafayette, Nathaniel Greene, Anthony Wayne, and Henry Knox. Standing in the background on the right is Col. John Brooks. *By Vernon Fletcher. Mabel Brady Garvan Collection, Yale University Art Gallery*

On December 4, 1783, Washington resigned his commission and bid farewell to his men "with a heart full of love and gratitude." *The Miriam and Ira Wallach Division of Art, Prints and Photographs: Print Collection, The New York Public Library*

The British surrender their arms to Washington. Among those shown are Benjamin Lincoln, Lafayette, and British General Charles Cornwallis—although Cornwallis had refused to attend the ceremony and was not present.
Courtesy of Mount Vernon Ladies' Association

A replica of the Assembly Room of the Pennsylvania State House where the Constitution was debated in 1787. *National Park Service*

James Madison, known as the chief architect of the Constitution, was a dedicated federalist who would become the nation's fourth president. *Library of Congress*

The signing of the Constitution was a somber occasion. In this depiction Washington presides over the process. Benjamin Franklin, seated in front, had reservations about the Constitution, but he urged everyone to sign for the sake of unity. *By Howard Chandler Christy, 1940. House Wing, East Stairway, U.S. Capitol Building. Architect of the Capitol*

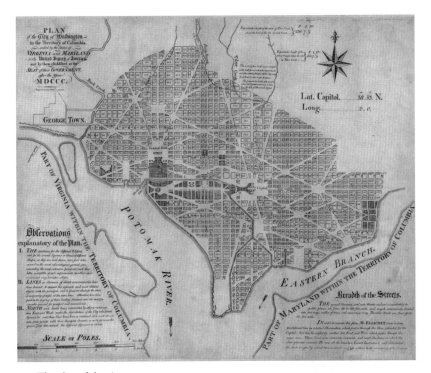

The plan of the city of Washington in the territory of Columbia, which was ceded by Virginia and Maryland to the United States to become the seat of its government.
Library of Congress

The Rising Sun chair. The mahogany armchair with a carved sun in the top crest rail was made by John Folwell for the Speaker of the Pennsylvania Assembly. During the Constitutional Convention it became Washington's seat as he served as the convention president. *National Park Service*

On April 30, 1789, George Washington took the presidential oath of office for the first time. The location was Federal Hall in New York City. *National Park Service*

Vice President John Adams. Adams's contribution to the birth of the nation is without parallel. After serving two terms as Washington's vice president, he would become the nation's second president.
Library of Congress

Alexander Hamilton.
Artist: John Trumbull.
Gift of Henry G.
Marquand,
The Metropolitan
Museum of Art

A view of Mount Vernon. *National Gallery of Art,
Gift of Edgar William and Bernice Chrysler Garbisch*

The first cabinet (l to r): President Washington; Henry Knox, Secretary of War;
Alexander Hamilton, Secretary of the Treasury; Thomas Jefferson, Secretary of
State; Edmund Randolph, Attorney General. *Currier & Ives. Library of Congress*

The busts of the Founding Fathers ring the beautiful windowed Reading Room of the George Washington Presidential Library. Washington holds a prominent position. *Photograph by Daniel Schwartz*

George Washington's personal copy of the Acts of Congress is housed in the Rare Book Suite of the George Washington Presidential Library at Mount Vernon. Glancing through it and seeing his annotations brings the early history of the nation to life. *Photograph by Daniel Schwartz*

Chapter Eight

The Final Fight

Benjamin Lincoln was short, wide, and hobbled by a leg injury—one leg was two inches shorter than the other, from a wound suffered at Saratoga, where he'd fought with Horatio Gates to achieve an important victory in the war. A product of the Massachusetts militia, he had become one of Washington's most reliable officers. On October 3, 1778, as soon as Lincoln's shattered ankle had sufficiently healed, Congress decided that he was the man to lead the Southern front of the war. Washington himself was focused on what he considered the grand prize—New York City and the surrounding area. He could scarcely spare men to fight in the South, but he trusted Lincoln.

For a New Englander like Lincoln, the new assignment was tantamount to fighting on foreign soil—in both terrain and culture. But Congress hoped that his presence would serve as a clear signal that the North and South were fighting the war as one army.

Once again, the Americans would be challenging the British in areas where loyalty to the cause of independence was in question. The British firmly believed—and many Americans feared—that the South was a loyalist stronghold, especially Georgia and South Carolina. This belief remained untested, but the British were developing a Southern strategy that relied in part on support from the locals.

Lincoln started his mission at a disadvantage, reaching the South too late to prevent the British capture of Savannah very late in 1778, by an expeditionary force led by Sir Archibald Campbell. Campbell was captured and taken prisoner by the Americans early in the war and had been released only recently in exchange for Ethan Allen, captured after the Battle of Fort Ticonderoga. (At one time there was talk of exchanging Campbell for General Lee, but Lee had already been released.) Savannah was an easy win for the British. Lincoln settled in Charleston, where he prepared a plan to retake Savannah with the support of the French. That effort failed in December 1779; after that, Lincoln's main goal became the protection of Charleston.

Charleston was the jewel of the South, then America's fourth largest city, its harbor bustling with commerce. Defending the city was crucial to the American cause, and Lincoln hoped that Savannah's fall would serve as a wakeup call to Congress. But he was disappointed in his poorly prepared garrison. He wrote to Washington, complaining that "we remain unsupported by troops, unsupplied with many essential articles, and uncovered with works."

He would soon learn that the British, too, were eyeing Charleston as key to control of the South. Clinton himself was heading south with a force of eight thousand, while Lincoln had barely managed to organize a paltry fourteen hundred. He desperately tried to raise a militia and proposed that enslaved Blacks should be allowed to join the fight—an idea that was rejected by South Carolina governor John Rutledge. Rutledge wrote dismissively to Lincoln that his plan was impractical. Furthermore, he insisted that Lincoln had all he needed to protect the city—and stressed that he *must* protect the city. Lincoln felt demoralized by this response. He knew that he didn't have what he needed to hold Charleston, though Rutledge and others seemed blind to this fact.

By the end of March 1780, Clinton had moved his forces by land and sea to surround Charleston. British warships appeared, one after the other, like a fateful mirage on the horizon. Lincoln had received some reinforcements by then. His fortifications, erected with aid from the French, were substantial and well crafted to thwart the enemy. Yet his garrison still lacked the tools and manpower to combat Clinton's massive forces, he realized. Moreover, his potential evacuation routes were rapidly closing. The Americans were essentially trapped.

On April 10, Clinton sent a message to Lincoln, calling on him to surrender. Lincoln refused: he hadn't abandoned the city in the sixty days since Clinton's offensive was revealed, he said, and he wasn't about to do so now. He was determined to defend Charleston to the last.

The bombardment that followed was so fierce and unceasing that many civilian structures were left nearly in ashes. Lincoln expedited the escape of Governor Rutledge and kept fighting. His officers and men were with him all the way, but by April 20 it was clear to everyone that they would not prevail. Solemnly, they agreed to make a surrender offer to Clinton.

On April 21, Lincoln raised a flag of truce and dispatched a list of surrender recommendations. His greatest concern was that his men be allowed to evacuate with the honors of war, which was traditional. However, Clinton rejected the terms and immediately resumed the assault.

Without a means of evacuation, the Americans had no choice but to fight on. By May 11, Lincoln's men were pleading for surrender, and Lincoln capitulated the next day. There were to be no honors of war and no favorable terms. While militia members would be allowed to return to their homes, Continental Army soldiers would be held prisoner.

When Lincoln's troops marched out of the garrison, a British officer observed, "Lincoln limped out at the head of the most ragged rabble I ever beheld." The general would become a prisoner of war, paroled to the north, while fifteen hundred of his soldiers remained prisoners in South Carolina.

General Charles Cornwallis, Clinton's second in command, had joined him for the siege of Charleston. Afterward, Clinton returned to New York and left Cornwallis to head up the Southern campaign. Cornwallis had been chasing Washington throughout the war, and ever since losing the advantage at Trenton, he'd had one ambition: "bagging the old fox"—meaning Washington. Now he had an opportunity in the South, with the British success at Charleston heralding an anticipated rout.

Once Congress received word that Lincoln was out of action, it appointed Horatio Gates to replace him in the South. Gates arrived in July 1780, as the British were heading inland under the command of Cornwallis. They met on August 16 at Camden, South Carolina, where Gates's army was nearly obliterated. Nearly nine hundred of Gates's men died, and about one thousand were captured, and Gates was left with a fragmented and poorly equipped force. Not long after that, Gates learned that his only son had become ill and died.

Washington pulled Gates from the field and sent Nathanael Greene in to command the Southern forces. In his instructions to Greene, Washington acknowledged his lack of information about the enemy's Southern operations but expressed full faith in him: "I can give you no particular instructions but must leave you to govern yourself entirely according to your own prudence and judgment and the circumstances in which you find yourself."

When Greene arrived in Charlotte, North Carolina, in early December, he found a demoralized Gates and a broken army—as he wrote to his wife, "nothing but a few half-starved soldiers who are remarkable for nothing but poverty and distress." Gates was a shell of his former self, his battlefield losses cruelly capped by the death of his son.

Now the fate of the South was in the hands of Greene; the thirty-eight-year-old Quaker would face off against Cornwallis, Britain's most fearsome military legend of the day. Cornwallis not only had more men, but they were much fitter. Greene could see that his army was depleted and on the verge of ruin. He wrote to von Steuben, "I arrived at this place . . . and found the army under General Gates in a most deplorable situation, entirely without tents and almost starved with hunger and cold. The Virginia troops are literally naked and undisciplined."

Hoping to improve his chances, Greene made a fateful decision—to divide his army in two, a strategy, he wrote, that "makes the most of my inferior force, for it compels my adversary to divide his, and holds him in doubt as to his own line of conduct."

He put six hundred of his best troops under the command of Brigadier General Daniel Morgan, a six-foot-tall, strapping New Jerseyan, who had fought—and been wounded—in the French and Indian War. Morgan also carried scars from his stint with Braddock's army, when he was flogged for bad behavior. Five hundred lashes had left permanent stripes on his back, but he joked that he owed the British one more stripe because they'd miscounted. This indomitable force of nature led a battalion that Greene bestowed the title "the Flying Army."

Greene's bet paid off in January 1781, when Morgan won a victory over the British in an open field in South Carolina called the Cowpens. About to face off with British Lieutenant Colonel Banastre Tarleton, Morgan is said to have remarked, "Here is

Morgan's grave or victory." As his troops made camp in the pasture, fortified by a rare and generous meal of fresh local beef, Tarleton approached just before dawn. Morgan woke his troops and lined them up in a brilliant formation: three lines, advancing in order, each required to fire three volleys before leaving the field to the next line.

"Just hold up your heads, boys, three fires and you are free," he ordered, "and then when you return to your homes, how the old folks will bless you, and the girls will kiss you for your gallant conduct."

The first line was composed of seasoned militia and sharpshooters at the bottom. The second was also militia, and in the third were veterans of the Continental Army and the South Carolina militia. They executed Morgan's plan like clockwork. When the British saw men running from the lines, they thought their foes were defeated, not recognizing that it was all part of the plan. The British were rapidly dispatched, with over a hundred dead, two hundred wounded, and five hundred captured.

Meanwhile, Greene was leading Cornwallis's main force on a chase across the South, toward Guilford Courthouse in North Carolina. After a nighttime ride through the country around present-day Greensboro, Greene stopped at a local tavern. The owners were patriots, but a portrait of George III still hung over the fireplace from before the war. Before he ate, Greene turned the portrait so it faced the wall and wrote on the back, "Hide thy face, George, and blush."

On February 9, Greene's troops arrived at Guilford Courthouse. By then, Cornwallis was only twenty miles away with twice as many men, and they were in much better physical condition. Greene decided to make a run for the Dan River, hoping to put it between him and the enemy. The ploy worked: Greene managed to assemble enough boats to get everyone across the river, and by the time Cornwallis and his troops arrived at the Dan, they could see Greene's campfires burning on the other side.

This gave Greene's men a two-day respite, during which they rested and ate better than they had in some time, thanks to supportive locals. Volunteers from militia groups continued to arrive, so when Greene's army finally recrossed the river, it was a stronger force.

Cornwallis continued to pursue Greene, and Greene continued to slip out of his grasp. When Cornwallis finally faced Greene at Guilford Courthouse with his divided army, he had fewer troops than the Americans. It was a hard fight, ending in Greene's strategic withdrawal from the arena, leaving Cornwallis with a de facto victory. But the British suffered many casualties. As Greene wrote to von Steuben, "The enemy got the ground the other day, but we the victory. They had the splendor, we the advantage."

For all the courage displayed by the American fighting forces, there were shameful stories as well. One man came to represent, to this day, the definition of a traitor to all the noble values the patriots fought and died for.

Benedict Arnold had been a reliable and often heroic performer earlier in the war, beginning with the remarkable victory at Ticonderoga. Wounded at Saratoga, he was appointed by Washington to serve as military commander of Philadelphia, but Arnold soon sank into a state of psychological misery. His service hadn't worked out for him as he'd once dreamed; he felt disposable and underappreciated by his commander. He was also in debt. His feelings of resentment only grew when he was later put in charge of the Hudson Valley and its strategically valuable fort at West Point, towering over the Hudson River sixty miles north of New York City. There, in his miserable state, he fell prey to temptation.

Major John André, who was Britain's chief spy in America and headed its secret service, easily sniffed out Arnold's inner conflict and resentment. The British had set their sights on capturing West Point, which would assure their control of the Hudson, and André believed that the weak and conflicted Arnold presented a rare opportunity. He arranged secret meetings with Arnold in 1780, leading to a tantalizing offer: in exchange for Arnold's agreement to turn over West Point to the British, Arnold would receive money, a command in the British army, and the status of hero in Great Britain.

The plot might have succeeded had not André been captured in September, while crossing between British and American lines. He was carrying papers that proved Arnold's treason. It so happened that Arnold at the time was awaiting a visit from Washington, who was riding through the area. Arnold was at dinner when a messenger arrived with the news of André's capture. He rose quickly, telling his companions he had been called to West Point and would be back in an hour to meet Washington. He never returned. Washington arrived and waited for him for some time before hearing about André. As it became clear that Arnold wasn't returning, his young wife, Peggy, appeared to be inconsolable. Before he could be caught, Arnold managed to reach the safety of British lines and then escape to Great Britain. Joining him there was Peggy, who, it turned out, was not so innocent after all.

Unable to punish Arnold, a furious Washington needed to make an example of André. He was brought to Tappan, south of West Point, where Washington had set up headquarters. The local watering hole, Mabie's Tavern, was turned into a prison. Washington quickly assembled a board for a military trial, and after a brief hearing, the verdict was death by hanging.

At noon on October 2, Washington ordered fifteen hundred soldiers to witness the execution, which took place on a hill behind the tavern. As André was led toward the hill, he recoiled at the sight of the noose and begged to be shot instead of hung, to no avail. He trembled visibly and gasped as he approached his fate. But as the noose was placed around his neck, he stood still. It was over in moments.

Today, a monument stands at the spot, and André's "prison" remains in business as the Old '76 House, the oldest tavern in America.

Although Arnold escaped punishment, he did not escape the permanent stain of his treason. Washington used the announcement of this betrayal as an opportunity to praise his army and express gratitude for divine providence. He noted, "The brightest ornament in the character of the American soldiers is their having been proof against all the arts and seductions of an insidious enemy."

Arnold capped his treason by becoming a brigadier general in the British army. Ironically, he became as unpopular among the British as he was with Americans; no one could stomach a traitor. After the war, he moved to Canada and was reviled there as well. He lived for twenty years after making his deal with André, but they were tormented years.

By the end of 1780, Washington was again struggling to keep his Northern army together. In January 1781, the Continental troops of the Pennsylvania line staged a mutiny at Morristown and began heading toward Philadelphia to collect their back pay. As Washington tried to reason with the mutineers, Clinton saw an opportunity, sending an offer of immunity and compensation if they would join the British. With Arnold's betrayal fresh in their minds, they refused but demanded a settlement from Washington. He finally agreed to dismantle this regiment, a loss he could ill afford. The men were either discharged or furloughed. When Washington heard that another division was flirting with mutiny, he shut it down as well.

Around this time, Washington was collaborating on the next major move with his French counterpart, Lieutenant General Jean-Baptiste-Donatien de Vimeur, comte de Rochambeau. Rochambeau had served with distinction in the Seven Years' War and arrived in Rhode Island in the summer of 1780. He and Washington met regularly to plan a major joint operation they hoped would end the war. Rochambeau was ordered to serve under Washington, and their collaboration became a model, even when they disagreed.

They mainly differed over where to go after the British next. Washington had long believed that the decisive battle of the war would be fought in New York City. Rochambeau doubted that they had sufficient troops to take on such a large and well-defended area, but he obediently brought his army to rendezvous with Washington's at Dobbs Ferry, north of the city. Surveying their combined forces, Washington began to face the uncomfortable reality that Rochambeau was right. They didn't have the strength to overcome the British in New York.

Then Cornwallis presented an opportunity elsewhere.

In September 1781, the British general was encamped with about nine thousand troops at Yorktown and Gloucester Point in Virginia, located on a peninsula where the York and James Rivers empty into the lower Chesapeake Bay. He was waiting for supplies and reinforcements from the Royal Navy, and he hoped to stay off the radar until that happened. Informed of his location, his entrenchment, and his vulnerability, Washington and Rochambeau decided that they could pick off this sitting duck.

With French support, Washington had received a critical infusion of soldiers and heavy weaponry, and unlike his own men, Rochambeau's forces were fit, fresh, and well fed. Furthermore, the arrival of the French navy would cut off Cornwallis's anticipated reinforcements from the sea. The scale of the proposed joint operation was unprecedented in this war.

Hamilton, still serving as Washington's aide-de-camp, was desperate to get back into the fight, but his repeated pleas had gone unacknowledged. Newly married to Eliza Schuyler, the daughter of one of Washington's generals, Hamilton grew more self-assured and demanding. As he prepared to leave for Yorktown, Washington finally agreed to put Hamilton in the field, assigning him to the Marquis de Lafayette's division. Hamilton happily complied. His old friend Henry Knox would serve as chief of artillery.

By early October, Washington and Rochambeau had organized nearly twenty thousand troops in Virginia—double the size of Cornwallis's army. On October 9, they fired the first volley. A moment of symbolism marked the beginning of the siege: "His excellency George Washington put the match to the first gun," James Thatcher, a Massachusetts doctor on the scene, wrote in his diary. From then on, Washington was a steady presence, directing every detail. He constantly addressed his troops, urging them on, bucking them up. By his side was Benjamin Lincoln, freed in a prisoner exchange and returned to the battlefield.

Cornwallis never received his anticipated reinforcements, and his men were subjected to a constant bombardment from all sides from the French and Americans.

Knox and Hamilton fought bravely side by side to take Redoubt 10, one of the most significant British fortifications. At one point they engaged in a minor dispute. Knox had ordered his men to yell, "Shell!" when an incoming shell was fired by the enemy. Hamilton thought that this practice was nonsense. As they argued about it, a Knox soldier yelled, "Shell!" and the two men dove into a trench for cover, Knox landing on top. "Now do you feel we should yell *shell*, Mr. Hamilton?" Knox asked. Soon after, they captured the redoubt.

Within two weeks of the first attack, the British were overwhelmed. Early on October 17, a drummer appeared atop a parapet on Cornwallis's line, beating a solemn parlay, as an officer walked out waving a white handkerchief. He brought a message from Cornwallis requesting a twenty-four-hour cease-fire to discuss terms of surrender.

Washington gave him the day and spent it working on the terms. The final document of capitulation stipulated that Cornwallis's men would be held as prisoners of war, and the officers would be paroled.

Stunned in defeat, Cornwallis did not attend the surrender ceremony, claiming to be ill. He sent General Charles O'Hara in his stead to deliver the symbolic sword. Washington, unwilling to accept the sword of a subordinate to Cornwallis, called on Lincoln, who had been denied an honorable surrender at Charleston, to do the honors.

The legend took hold that when the British army surrendered, their band played an old English ballad, "The World Turned Upside Down."

> Listen to me and you shall hear,
> news hath not been this thousand year:
> Since Herod, Caesar and many more,
> you never heard the like before.

This legend didn't appear until long after the war but has survived the centuries—including as a backdrop to a powerful scene of the Yorktown battle in the musical play *Hamilton*. It can even be found in some textbooks. Although the story is unlikely, it certainly captures the mood of the victorious Americans and the defeated British.

After the surrender, Washington called upon his aide Colonel Tench Tilghman to ride the three hundred miles to Philadelphia and deliver news of the victory to Congress. One of his most loyal soldiers, Tilghman had been by Washington's side since 1776. Washington may or may not have been aware that he was falling ill (possibly with malaria), yet despite fever and chills, Tilghman faithfully undertook the long journey, arriving in a state of deep exhaustion. He was so wobbly that observers thought he was drunk. Elation spread throughout the city. So thrilled were the members of Congress with Tilghman's news that they presented him with a horse and a sword.

The Siege of Yorktown effectively ended the war, but it would take two more years to fully settle matters between Great Britain and America, including national boundaries, and to resolve the disputes with countries that had supported the United States, including France and Spain.

The thrill of victory thrummed in the hearts of the Americans, and even in the face of defeat, some of their enemies admired the superhuman levels of resolve that led to this moment. In his diary, Captain Johann Ewald, a Hessian officer serving with Cornwallis, wrote, "With what soldiers in the world could one do what was done by these men, who go about nearly naked and in the greatest privation? Deny the best-disciplined soldiers of Europe what is due them and they will run away in droves, and the general will soon be alone. But from this one can perceive what an enthusiasm—which these poor fellows call 'Liberty'—can do!"

• • •

In Paris, Franklin cut quite a figure, especially with women. Despite his advancing age, ladies were in thrall to him, and he happily accepted their attentions—something the more puritanical Adams observed with dismay when he joined Franklin there in 1782 to hammer out a peace treaty with England. In almost every way, including this one, the two men were opposites, though they had one thing in common—their love of America. As it turned out, the team of Franklin, Adams, Henry Laurens, and John Jay would prove to be a formidable peace commission.

While the treaty was being crafted in Paris, Washington was facing a crisis at home with his own soldiers. The issue was pay. In 1780, Congress had resolved that retired soldiers should receive half pay, but as Congress had no authority to force the states to comply, the payments had not been made. By 1783, as the official end of the war neared, this increasingly became a point of contention, as the soldiers were egged on by the likes of Hamilton and Horatio Gates.

Matters came to a head on March 10, 1783, when an inflammatory address written by Major John Armstrong, a Gates aide-de-camp, was circulated among the men at Washington's Newburgh, New York, encampment.

Armstrong's address is one of the most stirring defenses of war veterans ever produced. It captured the essence of the struggle faced by the survivors of combat, in any era, when a nation turns to peace. Detailing the failures of the states to pay their due, he wrote:

> If this, then, be your treatment, while the swords you wear are necessary for the defense of America, what have you to expect from peace, when your voice shall sink, and your strength dissipate by division? When those very swords, the instruments and companions of your glory, shall be taken from your sides, and no

remaining mark of military distinction left but your wants, infirmities and scars? Can you then consent to be the only sufferers by this revolution, and retiring from the field, grow old in poverty, wretchedness and contempt? Can you consent to wade through the vile mire of dependency, and owe the miserable remnant of that life to charity; which has hitherto been spent in honor? If you can—GO—and carry with you the jest of Tories and scorn of Whigs—the ridicule and what is worse, the pity of the world. Go, starve, and be forgotten.

Armstrong offered the soldiers two alternatives to helplessly accepting their fate. He called upon them to issue an ultimatum to Congress: if payments were not forthcoming, the army should disband and go home—or failing that, to refuse to disband after a peace treaty was signed, effectively staging a military coup. Armstrong called for a general meeting of officers the next day to discuss their options.

Washington quickly learned of the plan and knew he must act decisively. He sympathized with the plight of his men, but he needed to head off an action that would be destructive to their interests during the uncertain period before a treaty was signed. He offered them another option.

In his March 11 General Orders, Washington noted that he was aware of the address (though he called it anonymous) and the plan to meet. Referring to himself in the third person, he wrote that the commander in chief considered that

. . . his duty as well as the reputation and true interest of the Army requires his disapprobation of such disorderly proceedings, at the same time he requests the General and Field officers with one officer from each company and a proper representative of the staff of the Army will assemble at 12 o'clock on

Saturday next at the Newbuilding to hear the report of the Committee of the Army to Congress.

After mature deliberation they will devise what further measures ought to be adopted as most rational and best calculated to attain the just and important object in view. The senior officer in rank present will be pleased to preside and report the result of the deliberations to the Commander in Chief.

Washington's action temporarily quelled the dissent, and on March 15, he appeared before the officers and appealed to their patriotism. It was a lengthy statement, but the most moving portion was his call for them to consider their role in posterity as the saviors of the world.

By thus determining—and thus acting, you will pursue the plain and direct road to the attainment of your wishes. You will defeat the insidious designs of our enemies, who are compelled to resort from open force to secret artifice. You will give one more distinguished proof of unexampled patriotism and patient virtue, rising superior to the pressure of the most complicated sufferings; and you will, by the dignity of your conduct, afford occasion for posterity to say, when speaking of the glorious example you have exhibited to mankind, "had this day been wanting, the world had never seen the last stage of perfection to which human nature is capable of attaining."

As he read his statement, Washington paused once to put on his glasses, joking, "I have not only grown gray, but almost blind in service to my country."

In Paris, months later, the peace treaty was signed on September 3. It took another two months for the last of the British troops to sail from Long Island. As their ships faded from view, Washington sent an invitation to his officers to celebrate with him at Fraunces Tavern in lower Manhattan. They gathered in high spirits, as the *New York Gazette* reported emotionally:

> **Last Thursday noon (December 4), the principal officers of the army in town assembled at Fraunces Tavern, to take a final leave of their illustrious, gracious, and much loved comrade, General Washington. The passions of human nature were never more tenderly agitated, than in this interesting and distressful scene. . . . [His] words produced extreme sensibility on both sides. . . .**

As Colonel Benjamin Tallmadge recounted in his memoir almost fifty years later, in 1830, "We had been assembled but a few moments when his excellency entered the room. After partaking of a slight refreshment in an almost breathless silence the General filled his glass with wine and turning to the officers said, 'With a heart full of love and gratitude I now take leave of you. I most devoutly wish that your latter days may be as prosperous and happy as your former ones have been glorious and honorable.'"

After each officer had a glass in hand, Washington said, "I cannot come to each of you but shall feel obliged if each of you will come and take me by the hand." Knox, the closest officer to Washington, walked up to the General, and the two embraced, tears running down their faces. Tallmadge watched as every officer repeated the process. "Such a scene of sorrow and weeping I had never before witnessed and fondly hope I may never be called to witness again."

At that moment, Washington was arguably the most powerful man in the country. He had chosen to retire from the army, but he could have remained in some titular position of power had he wanted to. He did not. He knew his power had been on loan. The very democratic principles that guided his mission demanded that he step away and return to civilian life. Looking on, his devoted colleagues could hardly fathom that this might be their last sight of him.

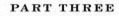

PART THREE

RESCUING THE CONSTITUTION

CHAPTER NINE

THE UNRAVELING UNION

A surge of anticipation carried Washington home. As he rode toward Virginia in December 1783, he felt an unfamiliar sense of lightness. The weight of the war fell away, and his mind filled with images of Mount Vernon, the place where he could finally live the home life he'd dreamed about so often on the field. It was a long journey, the air growing cold as he rode. One can imagine him turning contemplative, marveling at the events of the past years, savoring the victory.

The success of the Continental Army under Washington's leadership is a complicated story, pored over by historians for centuries. But perhaps it was simpler from Washington's perspective. For him, leadership entailed the need to constantly reinforce the grander vision—never allowing individual defeats (of which there were many) to take hold and shake his army's confidence. They were always on the move, not just physically but mentally, calculating strategies for the next confrontation. Even at the lowest point, that frozen winter at Valley Forge, Washington never tolerated wallowing in misery. He replaced despair with an elixir compounded of confidence and training, the latter thanks to von Steuben. He weeded out the naysayers and troublemakers.

At times, Washington's greatest conflict was with Congress, which was tight-fisted about distributing money and supplies, even when most urgently needed. In fairness, Congress lacked authority to force compliance among the citizenry, and there was no strong national civilian leader to inspire public support. Washington never allowed his disputes with Congress to devolve into open conflict, however. Instead, he calculated how to inspire strong allies in their midst.

Throughout the war, Washington recognized that his most important role as a leader was to raise up other leaders. A war on multiple fronts could not be a one-man show. He could not be everywhere all at once. He was grateful for the courage and stamina of some of the great men in his command—Greene, Knox, Hamilton, Lafayette, Lincoln, and von Steuben.

Never once in eight years did Washington have the luxury of a fully rested, fed, and equipped force. He always had to scramble for more bodies and more resources. Enlisting and retaining men was a constant struggle, and there wasn't always time to train them before the next battle.

With all the forces of man and nature arrayed before the Continental Army, the single consistent factor that kept them going was the constancy of their leader. Washington had learned the value of patience earlier in life, and he put that lesson to good use in the war. Other qualities informed his leadership style: He listened and took advice, and he allowed others to take the spotlight. He possessed a purity of purpose; the mission was everything.

In retrospect, he also might have been fortunate in his enemies. The British had might on their side, but their leaders suffered from a chronic inability to understand their foes. Too often, British generals were arrogant, complacent, and even lazy, believing the

American army was merely a troublesome rabble, easily disposed of. That they could still believe this after years of battle is a credit to the power of their self-delusion.

The bedrock of Washington's leadership was his patriotism. He accepted leadership as a solemn duty to his homeland. For all its frailties, he fully believed in the promise of the nation he was helping to create, and this conviction saw him through the hard years. He might have said that failure was not an option. But though anyone could clearly see and even list Washington's qualities as a leader, even those closest to him were unable to pierce the final layer, to really know what went on inside him. For a general, practicing caution and reserve was understandable and valuable, but perhaps there is a simpler explanation: he was no different on the inside than he was on the outside.

Power for its own sake was never important to Washington. He was happy now to set aside the role of commander and take his place among the people of Virginia, where he belonged. The closer he got to home, the more his thoughts turned to family. His first sight of the Potomac told him he didn't have far to go. Arriving at Mount Vernon on Christmas Eve, he dismounted into Martha's happy embrace, amid shouts of glee from their grandchildren.

Unburdened for the first time in years, he suddenly felt the weight of exhaustion. "I feel as a wearied traveler must do," he confessed, "who after treading many a painful step with a heavy burden on his shoulders, is eased of the latter, having reached the haven to which all the former were directed, and from his house top is looking back and tracing with an eager eye, the meanders by which he escaped the quicksands and mires which lay in his way, and into which none but the All Powerful Guide and Dispenser of human events, could have prevented his falling."

He was quietly exhilarated by the prospect of being a homebody. "I am retiring within myself," he wrote to Lafayette six weeks after his arrival at Mount Vernon, portraying himself as a man at peace. His delight in his new status is plainly expressed in that letter.

> At length my dear Marquis I am become a private citizen on the banks of the Potomac, and under the shadow of my own vine and my own fig tree, free from the bustle of a camp and the busy scenes of public life, I am solacing myself with those tranquil enjoyments, of which the soldier who is ever in pursuit of fame, the statesman whose watchful days and sleepless nights are spent in devising schemes to promote the welfare of his own and perhaps the ruin of other countries . . . and the courtier who is always watching the countenance of his Prince, in hopes of catching a gracious smile, can have very little conception.

This man, so acclaimed, maintained that he was happiest just to be a farmer and to be in the company of his family. Well into midlife he and Martha continued to be devoted to each other and interested in sharing their lives. Martha's warmth, sociability, and bright intellect held enduring appeal for Washington. Others in the bustling household recognized that she was the center of their lives.

Unfortunately for his plans, the world wasn't willing to let him go. For one thing, Mount Vernon hummed with a constant flow of visitors, friends and strangers alike, who filled Washington's time, dined at his table, and showered him with their attentions. It was not only all-consuming; it was expensive. And he could barely ride off his property without being swept into public ceremonies of reverence and gratitude. To all this was added, writes biographer Douglas Freeman, "another of the prices of being a national hero, the price of correspondence that became more nearly intolerable with each post."

He wanted none of it. He had plenty to take care of at home. After eight years of poor stewardship by a distant cousin, Lund

Washington, Mount Vernon was in desperate need of attention—both the land itself and the income derived from it.

People would have been astonished to learn how tight the financial situation was at Mount Vernon. Washington had accepted no salary for his eight years of service, and the expenses on his properties had mounted. A casual visitor would have thought that he had all the money in the world. However, by 1785, he was struggling, and the extra burden of feeding his adoring fans was unwelcome, though he was always gracious.

In addition to the press of constant visitors, there was a lively family scene and new family responsibilities. After Jacky's death, the Washingtons had adopted two of his four children, to ease the burden on his widow. George and Martha treated Nelly and "Wash" (George Washington) as their own children, showering them with love. Washington relished the fatherly role, just as he had with Patsy and Jacky. They also took in Martha's niece, Fanny.

Beyond his local concerns, Washington was consumed with worry about the state of the nation he had fought so hard on the battlefield to bring forth. A postwar recession had driven the states into separate bunkers, battling each other for economic superiority through taxation and fees levied on outsiders. It was a mess. As the historian Eric Burns put it, "No sooner did Americans stop fighting the British than they started fighting one another."

During the war, Congress had printed paper money instead of trying to raise taxes from the colonies—an effort that surely would have failed, given the antitax fervor so prevalent. As paper money depreciated late in the war, Congress began requisitioning funds and supplies from the states, but it was a futile effort. Many states ignored the requisitions because Congress had no power to make them pay. The situation grew worse after the war, when the matter of paying war debts seemed to lack urgency. With debts sky high, a movement rose in favor of maintaining paper money—something

Washington opposed, believing if specie (hard currency) was scarce, the problem could not be solved with paper. Meanwhile, the nation was rapidly becoming destitute.

The national good didn't seem to be a factor. The Articles of Confederation gave the federal government no authority to levy taxes, to raise an army, or even to protect the nation's shores from incursions. Meanwhile, individual states were collecting impossibly high taxes to pay their own war debts. Although Congress had the authority to make treaties, the states were not obliged to abide by them. Nor could Congress exercise a strong hand in the commercial realm. Other nations continued to treat the United States as a poor stepchild, and it had little muscle in trade wars. Those battles had to be fought—ineffectively—by individual states. What little leverage a state like New York could muster, for example, would be overwhelmed by Britain's superiority in trade.

On winter nights Washington would sit before the fire with his longtime friend and neighbor George Mason, now in his sixties, sipping Madeira and discussing the country's woes. Their bond had survived the colonial era and the fight for independence into the postwar period. Now in their senior years, Mason plagued with gout and Washington with rheumatism and painful teeth, they faced the grim reality that their glorious experiment was faltering.

It was becoming increasingly clear that the freedoms and powers delivered to the states in the Articles of Confederation had created a competitive morass, lacking any strong national framework. Once again, America was in jeopardy, and Washington saw the difficulty of bringing the states around to the idea of national authority. But it had to be done. "The Confederation appears to me to be little more than an empty sound, and Congress a nugatory body; the ordinances of it being very little attended to," he agonized to James Warren, a Massachusetts patriot and state delegate, whose father had been one of the first casualties of the war. It grieved Washington that so many had sacrificed so much for so frail a union.

The Confederation gave Congress little authority to do much of national importance. It could not coin money or properly form and execute a budget, make treaties for the good of national security or the economy, or declare war if that was called for. The unanimous consent of the states was needed to decide important issues, and this was nearly impossible to achieve, absent a sense of national purpose in the body. All attempts at amending the Articles of Confederation to boost solvency failed; these, too, required unanimous consent.

Pennsylvania's Robert Morris, superintendent of finance, had one of the hardest jobs in America. Revenue was desperately needed, and a tariff on imports was proposed twice. (They were dubbed the Impost of 1781 and the Impost of 1783.) In 1781, every state except Rhode Island approved the amendment. In 1783, the holdout was New York. The amendment never passed.

The United States was supposed to exhibit a new form of government that would be the envy of the civilized world. Instead, the government was ineffectual, hardly living up to the grand revolutionary rhetoric that created it. A strong antifederalist sentiment was stirring, and in some corners, there was even talk of returning to the embrace of England. From his post there, John Adams wrote to John Jay, "There are persons in this kingdom sufficiently insane to say, that they will bring America to petition to come again under the government of this country; they will distress them till they break their faith with France, and then, say they, 'We will spurn them.'"

Washington also wrote to Jay, in disgust. "What a triumph for the advocates of despotism to find that we are incapable of governing ourselves. . . ."

So much regional dissent led some to believe that the country should be split into four separate nations: Eastern, Middle, Southern, and Trans-Allegheny (west). Another proposal called for three nations—Eastern, Middle, and Southern. The very idea outraged Henry Knox, who delivered a blistering objection: "The vile state governments are sources of pollution, which will contaminate the American name for ages—machines that must produce ill, but cannot produce good; smite them in the name of God and the people."

A violent uprising in Massachusetts, called Shays' Rebellion after Daniel Shays, a farmer who was one of its leaders, was a tipping point for the simmering unrest. Shays had fought in the war and now, deeply in debt, struggled to keep his farm afloat. The rebellion formed around the economic plight of people like Shays, who were increasingly weighed down by debts, old and new, and protested the injustice of high state taxes. Ironically, their complaints were similar to those that sparked the revolution against Great Britain, but now the grievances were localized.

What began in late 1786 as a farmers' revolt spread to the wider population, and as the situation grew more alarming, the Continental Congress tried to formulate a response. After the war, Congress had moved its headquarters to New York City, abandoning a Philadelphia beset by disruptions from disgruntled veterans seeking back pay, and from outspoken early abolitionists. But the new setting gave Congress no better way to address the rebellion; it simply lacked authority to organize a federal force. This was a gaping hole in the operating blueprint for a nation, leaving it impotent to react to violent internal upheaval.

It fell to the Massachusetts military to settle the uprising.

A frustrated Knox wrote to Washington that the thirteen independent states were turning against each other, but he didn't believe that high taxes were the real reason. That claim, he said, "is as far remote from truth as light from darkness." Most of the instigators, he said, paid nothing or little in taxes. He thought they were rebelling because they saw weakness in government.

Washington responded: "Good God! who besides a Tory could have foreseen, or a Briton predicted them! Were these people wiser than others, or did they judge of us from the corruption and depravity of their own hearts? The latter I am persuaded was the case, and that notwithstanding the boasted virtue of America, we are far gone in everything ignoble and bad . . ."

Noting that there were "combustibles" in every state that might be sparked into fires, Washington suggested that Great Britain might have a hand in the uprisings. "That she is at this moment sowing the seeds of jealousy and discontent among the various tribes of Indians on our frontier admits of no doubt, in my mind. And that she will improve every opportunity to foment the spirit of turbulence within the bowels of the United States, with a view of distracting our governments, and promoting divisions, is, with me, not less certain," he wrote. Most tribes had favored Britain during the war, viewing American expansionist aspirations as a threat and believing that British rule offered them greater protection. Washington viewed the tribes' preference as a fertile avenue for British troublemakers; he was well aware that Great Britain still wielded tremendous power on the continent, in Canada to the north and the West Indies to the south.

In November, Washington reached out to Benjamin Lincoln in Massachusetts, with whom he'd maintained a close relationship after the war. Lincoln was a trusted source of information and had been on the front lines defending the state during the uprising—a role for which he later earned a commendation from the Massachusetts General Court.

"Are your people getting mad?" Washington asked.

Lincoln responded bitterly: "[You ask] 'Are your people getting mad?' Many of them appear to be absolutely so, if an attempt to annihilate our present constitution and dissolve the present government can be considered as evidence of insanity." He saw little probability that "the dignity of government [could be] supported without bloodshed. When a single drop is drawn, the most prophetic spirit will not, in my opinion, be able to determine when it will cease flowing."

Lincoln recognized the unpatriotic purpose behind Shays' uprising—no less than a complete abdication of the national will, fought for in battle and inscribed in the Articles of Confederation. They were willing to cast all that aside, without caring about the consequences for all.

Washington could not stay out of the thick of it. His correspondence became even more voluminous, as letters flew back and forth between the general and his most trusted advisors and old colleagues.

Increasingly, Washington was impressed by the unassuming young James Madison. Slight, prematurely balding, and socially awkward, Madison was nonetheless an intellectual giant. Both in Congress and in the Virginia House of Delegates, Madison had always proved to be astute and hardworking, one of the most dedicated representatives Washington had observed. In his quiet diligence, Madison would risk invisibility were it not for the genius and the powerful logic of his ideas.

Madison's closest friend was Jefferson, whom he'd met in 1776, when he was a twenty-five-year-old newcomer to the House of Delegates. Jefferson was Madison's physical and social opposite—six-foot-two to Madison's five-foot-four and elegant, he was charismatic and worldly in a way that the sickly and often morose Madison could never hope to emulate. But they were intellectually compatible and bonded strongly. As the historian Lee Wilkins noted, "Both needed a political confidant, a man whose intellectual prowess and vision matched his own."

As friends do, Madison and Jefferson shared details of their private lives. Widowed in 1782, when his wife, Martha died,

Jefferson tried to advise the young Madison on his hapless love life and played matchmaker when Madison expressed interest in a vivacious young woman named Catherine ("Kitty") Floyd, the daughter of a New York delegate. They had met in the last years of the war while Madison was serving in the Continental Congress in Philadelphia. Hampered by both his retiring personality and the proprieties of the time, Madison conducted a courtship mostly through Kitty's parents. But when he wrote her a letter attempting to set a wedding date, she dumped him in favor of another suitor.

Madison shared his heartbreak with Jefferson, who tried to reassure him that "the world still presents . . . many other resources of happiness, and you possess many within yourself." It was good advice, and perhaps Madison took it. Things turned out well in the end, as biographer Lynne Cheney notes: "As grave an error as it usually is to read history backward, perhaps in this instance one might be forgiven for observing that if he had married Catherine Floyd, there would have been no Dolley Madison." (Not until 1794 did Madison meet Dolley Payne, who would make up for everything he lacked in social graces.)

But Madison's chief focus was on the nation. He was regularly sending the alarm that "the existing Confederacy is tottering to its foundation." His point was simple, clear, and easy for anyone to understand: "No money is paid into the public treasury; no respect is paid to the federal authority. Not a single state complies with the requisitions [by Congress], several pass over in silence, and some positively reject them."

In November 1786, Washington sent Madison an urgent and uncharacteristically emotional message: "Let prejudices, unreasonable jealousies and local interest yield to reason and liberality." He implored Americans to look beyond the present day to the national character. "Wisdom and good examples are necessary at this time to rescue the political machine from the impending storm."

Alexander Hamilton had prospered as a New York lawyer after the war. A dedicated federalist in a city where there remained unresolved hostilities between patriots and Tory loyalists, he tried to straddle that line.

He was becoming one of the most eloquent spokesmen in the emerging nation. In 1784, Hamilton began to publish a series of letters under the pen name Phocion (a statesman of ancient Athens). These would later form the basis for the Federalist Papers, a series of popular essays on federalism, which was a collaboration among Hamilton, Madison, and Jay.

In *A Letter from Phocion to the Considerate Citizens of New-York On the Politics of the Day*, Hamilton offered a defense of loyalists, who were widely abused and sometimes disenfranchised in the postwar years.

Nothing is more common than for a free people, in times of heat and violence, to gratify momentary passions, by letting into the government, principles and precedents which afterwards prove fatal to themselves. Of this kind is the doctrine of disqualification, disfranchisement and banishment by acts of legislature. The dangerous consequences of this power are manifest. If the legislature can disfranchise any number of citizens at pleasure by general descriptions, it may soon confine all the votes to a small number of partisans, and establish an aristocracy or an oligarchy; if it may banish at discretion all those whom particular circumstances render obnoxious, without hearing or trial, no man can be safe, nor know when he may be the innocent victim of a prevailing faction. The name of liberty applied to such a government would be a mockery of common sense.

In a second Phocion letter, he cautioned, "The world has its eye upon America."

In May 1786, Hamilton was named commissioner to a conference scheduled to be held in Annapolis that September for the purpose of reaching agreement on regulating trade and commerce. The conference drew a paltry attendance, with only five states represented—Virginia, Delaware, Pennsylvania, New Jersey, and New York. As a collaboration among the states it was a dismal failure, but the commissioners did manage to accomplish one significant feat: unanimously agreeing to a national convention of the states to commence in Philadelphia on the second Monday in May 1787. The Constitutional Convention would receive an endorsement from Congress for the purpose of revising the Articles of Confederation. But it would become much more than that.

Selecting slates of delegates would require the compliance of the states. Jumping in early, Virginia met in late November, wholeheartedly approving the convention and naming its slate of delegates. In early December, Washington received a message from Virginia governor Edmund Randolph, informing him that the Virginia General Assembly had named him to helm the Virginia delegation. Randolph's letter read as a desperate appeal:

By the enclosed act you will readily discover that the Assembly are alarmed at the storms, which threaten the United States. What our enemies have foretold, seems to be hastening to its accomplishment; and cannot be frustrated but by an instantaneous zealous & steady union among the friends of the federal government: To you I need not press our present dangers. The inefficiency of Congress you have often felt in your official character: the increasing languor of our associated republics you hourly see: and a dissolution would be I know to you a source of the deepest mortification.

I freely then entreat you to accept the unanimous appointment of the General Assembly, to the Convention at Philadelphia. For the gloomy prospect still admits one ray of hope, that those, who began, carried on and consummated the revolution, can yet rescue America from the impending ruin.

Randolph believed that Washington's presence at the convention was necessary to lend gravitas and urgency. He was the most widely known and revered American, and his involvement would instantly elevate the convention in the eyes of the population and state leaders.

Madison agreed. He knew that having Washington at the head of Virginia's delegation would send a clear message about the convention's legitimacy. He encouraged Washington to attend, yet, as much as Washington feared "anarchy and confusion," he hedged about traveling to Philadelphia, enumerating the conflicts presented by his obligations on the home front. He had many reasons not to go; above all, he sought retirement and thought others should take their turn at the helm. In retrospect, this was one of the most critical moments in the nation's founding, for if Washington had bowed out then, he might never have returned to public life.

Randolph was wily. He chose to set the matter aside, hoping to wait out Washington. He knew the man well. The general was the perennial reluctant candidate who ultimately did his duty, and Randolph gambled that he would answer the call once more. As it sank in with Washington that his legacy of victory would be worthless if the prize was demolished, Randolph believed, he would agree to attend the convention. He sought ways to call upon the deep-seated patriotic spirit that had brought Washington to the cause in the first place.

Madison joined Randolph in plotting to secure Washington's attendance, keeping his name in the public eye. "Randolph and Madison played Washington like expert fishermen," noted historian Pauline Maier. Patience was their supreme virtue in this matter.

Madison was sympathetic to Washington's desire to retire, but he wrote to him expressing his "wish that at least a door could be kept open for your acceptance hereafter, in case the gathering clouds should become so dark and menacing as to supersede every consideration, but that of our national existence or safety."

Knox too weighed in, noting that "your presence would confer on the assembly a national complexion, and . . . would more than any other circumstance induce a compliance to the propositions of the convention."

Washington wasn't yet persuaded, but he was wavering. He began to contemplate whether his absence could be considered a dereliction of the duty he owed to the nation. He imagined what others would say about him if, in his absence, the convention failed to achieve its necessary result. Not only that: Could his own conscience withstand it?

After the long war, he was feeling his age. Painful rheumatism sapped his energy, making it difficult even to ride out to survey his lands. He was wearied of the celebrity his wartime leadership had brought and exhausted by the constant flow of visitors to Mount Vernon. He was also grieving the loss of his younger brother John Augustine, who died suddenly in January 1787. The two were close, and Washington agonized over the loss of "the intimate companion of my youth [and] the most affectionate friend of my ripened age."

And just six months earlier, he had lost Nathanael Greene, his most trusted officer during the war. Washington was so heartbroken by Greene's death that he could hardly bear to speak of him. Learning that Greene had died in financial distress, he made an offer to his friend's estate: if the family and executor thought it proper, he would take on the care of Greene's son (his namesake, George Washington Greene)—give him a good education and help him get settled in the profession of his choice. It turned out that the family had already accepted a similar offer from Lafayette.

Greene epitomized the plight of so many good and brave soldiers. His contribution to the American victory was unchallenged, yet he was left in ruin after the war. He not only failed to retrieve from Congress money owed to him, but also he was personally burdened with the expense of uniforms purchased for his men. In September 1784, he wrote to his brother Jacob, "My situation is truly afflicting! To be reduced from independence to want, and from the power of obliging my friends, to a situation claiming their aid."

When his youngest daughter died in infancy of whooping cough, Greene struggled to pay the modest price of a baby coffin. After burying her, he took Caty and their five children to live at Mulberry Grove plantation in Savannah, Georgia, which the state had gifted him after the war. It might have represented a fresh start. Instead, the lifelong New Englander struggled to get his bearings. The derelict property was a burden. His correspondence was full of despair. One day he was walking on his land under a blazing sun and suffered sunstroke. He died the next day, on June 19, 1786, at the age of forty-four, never having found his way out of the darkness.

This fact pained Washington most of all. Further, he knew that Greene's story was not unusual among those who served under him so bravely. The plight of many veterans then—as now—was distressing. Praised as heroes in battle, they were neglected in peacetime—many, like Greene, struggled in vain for years to recover the pay owed them.

The sad death of his most beloved general touched Washington in a way that was deeper than mere nostalgia. What did he now owe the nation?

What did it mean to fulfill the mission he had begun?

After long reflection, on April 9, Washington announced that he'd decided to attend the convention.

Elated, Knox wrote to Lafayette, "General Washington's attendance at the convention adds, in my opinion, new luster to his character. . . . Nothing but the critical situation of his country would have induced him to so hazardous a conduct. But its happiness being in danger, he disregards all personal considerations."

In a sense, Washington's decision was a formality, though a significant one. He was already fully engaged in the efforts of a tenacious trio—Knox, Jay, and Madison—to craft the outline of a prospective national government. Of their proposals, Madison's had the most heft. He would turn out to be the background conductor of the Constitutional Convention, shaping the movements, controlling the flow. Although he wouldn't always prevail, Madison's voice was the gathering's steady beat.

Seventy-four delegates were chosen to represent twelve states. Rhode Island opted out: an antifederalist spirit in its state legislature prevailed, rejecting the whole point of the convention, and the legislature declined to send representatives.

Not all seventy-four delegates would attend the convention. Only thirty made it for the complete period; fifty-five attended portions of the hearings. Some legendary figures among the most thrilling voices of the Revolution were missing. Thomas Jefferson was serving as minister to France and John Adams as minister to England—although Adams, never content to remain unheard, would publish a lengthy treatise on the front page of the *Pennsylvania Mercury* every Friday during the convention. Patrick Henry, an antifederalist, simply refused to attend. (When asked why he didn't go to the convention and help create a good constitution, Henry just said, "I smelt a rat.") Likewise, Samuel Adams was opposed to the federalist direction of the convention and would not attend.

To Washington, some delegates were more than just fellow legislators. They were former comrades in arms, who had been with him at the most critical moments of the war. Five delegates had been at Valley Forge—Hamilton, New York; Thomas Mifflin,

Pennsylvania; David Brearley and Jonathan Dayton, New Jersey; and William Pierce, Georgia. Pierce and Hamilton had also been at Yorktown, as had William Richardson Davie, North Carolina; and James McClurg, Virginia.

As noted in the Prologue, the delegates were slow to gather in Philadelphia, pushing back the start of the convention for weeks. Only Virginia and Pennsylvania were fully in attendance on the published opening day of May 14. This annoyed Washington greatly: he hadn't made the difficult trip to sit on his hands. But Madison suggested they use the delay to their advantage, so while waiting for enough delegates to make a quorum, the Virginia delegates held daily meetings for two or three hours at Mrs. House's boardinghouse at Fifth and Market, where some were staying. Then they walked over to the State House to meet other delegates and new arrivals. In particular, the Virginians found common cause with members of the Pennsylvania delegation.

One of these, James Wilson, forty-five, is often considered a counterpart to Madison. He too had been a longtime worker in the fields of the republic. A native Scot, he had come to the United States in early adulthood and earned a law degree. He had represented Pennsylvania in the Continental Congress and was a signer of the Declaration of Independence. Tall and severe, his heavy glasses giving him a somber air, Wilson was capable of sentimentality when it came to their purpose, later writing, "After the lapse of six thousand years since the creation of the world, America now presents the first instance of a people assembled to weigh deliberately and calmly, and to decide leisurely and peaceably upon the form of government by which they will bind themselves and their posterity."

Some might dispute his depiction of the body as calm or even peaceable in its debates. Impassioned arguments were waged over the key issues defining the nation.

As delegations continued to arrive, it became evident that sides were forming. One, championed by Madison, called for scrapping the Articles of Confederation and building a new constitution from scratch. Another thought they should confine their work to updating the Articles. Washington rebuked one delegate who suggested that they take care not to do too much, lest they overstep what the people wanted: "If to please the people, we offer what we ourselves disapprove, how can we afterwards defend our work? Let us raise a standard to which the wise and the honest can repair. The event is in the hand of God."

A dustup threatened when Pennsylvania delegates suggested that larger states should have a greater vote than smaller states. The Virginia delegates put down the effort, rightly fearing that it would lead to "fatal altercations" between large and small states—but the debate previewed a greater flare-up later.

Once the convention officially began, the delegates sat grouped by state at tables covered with green baize (similar to the fabric used on pool tables) and arranged in a semicircle. Each state would have one vote in the proceedings—a fair balance that could nonetheless be frustrating to individual delegates. For example, Hamilton was an avowed federalist, while his fellow New York delegate Robert Yates was just as passionate about states' rights. They canceled each other out until the third delegate, John Lansing, arrived. He sided with Yates, to Hamilton's dismay.

At the front of the room on a raised dais was the polished, high-backed chair designed for the president of the convention. Knox had warned Washington that he would almost certainly be elected its president, and this turned out to be the case. Washington was nominated by Robert Morris and unanimously elected. He took his seat with an air of humility, thanking the delegates but mentioning his lack of experience—after all, he had been at war during the other major gatherings, including the creation of the Declaration of Independence and the Articles of Confederation.

Seated in front of Washington and also facing the others was Madison, who was taking notes of the proceedings—a task he would fulfill throughout the four months of the convention. The idea of keeping such a daily record had been Madison's, who saw it as a sacred purpose. After the convention, he kept his notes, edited them over time, and vowed that they would not be made public until the last delegate had died. That turned out to be Madison himself, in 1835. He left the latest revisions to his wife, Dolley, who made sure they were published along with his other papers. The State Department first published them in 1840.

Although other delegates also took notes, Madison's record became anointed as the official version. It's fair to ask how accurate his account is. During those decades when the notes were in his possession alone, he was known to tinker with them. He was set on telling a nation's story, not just recounting the bare facts of what occurred each day at a meeting. Before the era of recorded speech, history was captured by those whose pens were the most fluent and whose ideals were the most persistent. From the outset, Madison acted as a shepherd of the new government—guiding and manipulating it to its best destiny, as he saw it. Biased or not, we owe Madison a debt of gratitude for giving us the only thorough daily account of the convention.

On Monday, May 28—with a quorum achieved and a president and secretary installed—the real work of the convention would begin.

Chapter Ten

The Scaffold of a Republic

Had the Framers gathered in Philadelphia in May 1787 been able to look into the future, and observe the reverence with which they would be regarded 236 years later, would they have been astounded? Not that they didn't have an abundance of ego, coupled with a strong belief in divine guidance. But they didn't consider themselves infallible. Although mostly prosperous and well educated, they were a mixed bag, from many walks of life. Sixty-five percent of those attending the Constitutional Convention were lawyers. They were a political elite charged with representing all of their countrymen. They were also pragmatic men, focused on a set of issues that were foundational to whether this new form of government would survive and last.

These issues included the balance of power between the states and the federal government, a matter so contentious that it prompted some of the greatest patriots to boycott the convention. A related concern was whether or not to create a "bill of rights," which supporters argued was essential to prevent the United States from becoming a despotic state on the model of Great Britain.

The convention's original mandate was not to write a new constitution but to revise the Articles of Confederation, making them more responsive to the needs of the people. However, a discrepancy of purpose quickly arose, as some leading delegates pushed for a new constitution, while others demanded they stick to amending the original brief. Perhaps the latter group imagined they could get by with minor tweaking, but some delegates, like those from Virginia, who had thoroughly studied the Articles of Confederation, found fatal flaws. It was like intending to remodel a house with minor upgrades but finding rot when the walls were opened. This would remain a core debate throughout the convention.

Stripped down to basics, the Framers' intent might be described this way: To create a system of government that would prevent tyrannical authority (such as they had experienced under King George's rule) yet would be well organized and responsive to the will of the people. To share power effectively between the federal government and the states, and within the federal government to institute a system of checks and balances between branches of government—again, precluding any one body from gaining authoritarian control. The Constitution would "constitute" a promise between the national government and the citizens that the people would chart the course of government, rather than government imposing a course that the people would be forced to follow. It was a bold new idea—a form of representative government known as a republic. It was not, strictly speaking, a democracy, which federalists like Madison viewed as a free-for-all. In the Federalist Papers, he would address the distinction, writing that "democracies have ever been spectacles of turbulence and contention; have ever been found incompatible with personal security or the rights of property; and in general have been as short in their lives as they have been violent in their deaths. . . . A republic, by which I mean a government in which the scheme of representation takes place, opens a different prospect and promises the cure for which we are seeking."

Madison and his cohorts, working feverishly before the start of the convention, were homing in on a system of proportionate representation within a federal government composed of three branches—legislative, executive, and judicial—but the details would be hotly debated. The nature of this representative government was not just a question of federal vs. state control but of how the votes would be apportioned among the states. The Articles of Confederation gave each state, large or small, an equal vote. Smaller states liked this method; larger states believed that a fairer allocation would be based on population numbers.

One of the most difficult challenges was to define the nature of the executive branch without sliding into monarchial territory. What should be the limitations on the president, how long would his term run, how would he be elected—and, again, how would the states be fairly represented in that election, given their population differences? This debate would come up again and again.

Remarkably, the convention took only four months to settle all these matters before sending the Constitution to the states for ratification. Their fellow countrymen didn't venerate the Framers the way future generations did and do. They recognized them as flawed architects of a shaky structure, and most of the Framers would have agreed. Writing the constitution of a new nation was more like working at a forge than building a cathedral: loud, hot, and messy.

The men who took their seats in the East Room of the State House at 10:00 a.m. on May 28 carried an air of gravity. This was not a festive occasion; there was little of the lighthearted camaraderie one might have expected from a reunion of comrades. There were familiar faces in the room, but some were strangers to each other. Trust wasn't automatic. Expectation vied with trepidation; they knew that their decisions in the coming weeks could potentially make or break America.

Many of those present, including Washington, believed that the nation was on the brink of civil war, which would lead to complete dissolution of the union. All recognized that the divisions so prominent in the land were also present in their gathering.

The preceding day, Washington had attended services at St. Mary's Roman Catholic Church, near the State House. St. Mary's had been a patriots' haven during the war, and the Continental Congress as a body had attended services there four times—one of those on the eve of Philadelphia's fall to the British. Washington's attendance on the eve of the momentous convention had great import therefore, and was noted in *The Pennsylvania Herald*:

> On Sunday last his Excellency General Washington accompanied by a number of respectable members of the protestant and dissenting churches attended divine service at the catholic chapel. The anthem and other solemn pieces of music performed on this occasion were admirably adapted to diffuse a spirit of devotion throughout a very crowded congregation, and to give effect to our excellent sermon delivered by the Rev. Mr. Beeston.

Historian Edward J. Larson speculated that Washington's decision to attend a Roman Catholic mass was calculated. "Washington had an instinctive sense of theater," Larson wrote. "He spoke more through actions than words. And now he was acting on behalf of the nation."

Benjamin Franklin's arrival at the State House on Monday morning was greeted with fanfare. He had not attended the opening on Friday—bad weather, aching bones—but now he made an entrance worthy of his stature. He was borne aloft in a sedan chair, brought from Paris, by four burly prisoners from a jail across the street, and settled in with, according to Benjamin Rush, a "transcendent benevolence," which he displayed throughout the convention.

The other delegates filed around him. Two more states had arrived since Friday: Massachusetts and Connecticut.

Washington took his seat at the head of the gathering, in his imposing chair with its carved liberty symbols, and called the convention to order.

The first day was devoted to establishing rules, including two of special note. The first regarded secrecy, which was considered an essential element of the proceedings. Although complete transparency might be desirable in theory, it would fall apart in practice. In a nation taut with tension, nothing could be gained by airing the arguments blow by blow, as they were occurring. The delegates even posted guards at the doors and drew shutters over the windows, making the room stifling during an exceptionally hot summer to come. Even so, since newspapers abhor a vacuum, long and colorful accounts of the proceedings were published without much regard for accuracy.

As head of the gathering, Washington in particular took the secrecy rule to heart. When it was discovered early on that an unknown delegate had left a copy of a crucial document lying unattended, Washington erupted in a fit of temper, reminding his colleagues of what they could expect if their deliberations became fodder for the press. He slammed the document on the table, pointedly asked the culprit to claim it, and left the room. It was never claimed.

The second significant rule concerned how the delegates voted. Each state would receive one vote, and the process was somewhat open-ended: "The House may not be precluded, by a vote upon any question, from revising the subject matter of it when they see cause." In other words, no vote was final until the end. Much changing of minds would go on as the convention unfolded.

Preliminaries over, the convention took up its real business on Tuesday, May 29. The process it would use to build the Constitution's framework became immediately clear when Edmund Jennings Randolph rose to speak. Randolph, the governor of Virginia, was essentially the front man for Madison and his cohorts, who included members of the Pennsylvania delegation. Over the course of many hours, Randolph outlined the so-called Virginia Plan.

The handsome, thirty-three-year-old governor stood tall, his dark hair unpowdered, his eyes piercing under heavy brows. He began with a self-deprecating remark, apologizing that it was he, rather than a member of longer standing, who was opening the discussion. Getting to the point, he suggested that their mission was straightforward: to determine what properties the new government should possess, to examine the defects of the Articles of Confederation, to openly face the danger of the country's current situation, and to come up with a remedy. He then proceeded to elaborate on the Virginia Plan, offered by his state's delegation and primarily written by Madison.

The plan consisted of fifteen resolves, and many of its basic tenets are recognizable to this day. The resolutions called for a strong federal government, made up of three branches, the legislative, executive, and judicial. It proposed a legislature (or Congress) of two houses, not unlike the British system of a higher and lower chamber. He proposed that representatives to serve in the "first branch" would be elected by the people of the states for a period of three years. Members of the "second branch" would be elected by the national House of Representatives. (This was later amended, giving to state legislatures the power to elect members of the upper house.)

This scheme rested on the belief that "the people" could be trusted only up to a point. If they were given free rein to elect all the representatives, who knew what kind of unseemly group would end up in Congress? In the days of revolution, the loudest voices in the room moved the population toward a national purpose, but such an unruly spirit would hardly be suitable for running a country.

Randolph went on to stipulate that, under the Virginia Plan, the number of representatives of both branches of the legislature would be apportioned according to population. This proposition instantly inflamed the gathering

The Articles of Confederation gave all the states equal representation. In the proposed system, smaller states would have less power. By the counts existing at the time, states with populations under two hundred thousand included South Carolina, New Jersey, New Hampshire, Rhode Island, Delaware, and Georgia. The larger states, with populations between two and five hundred thousand, were Virginia (the largest), Massachusetts, Pennsylvania, Maryland, Connecticut, New York, and North Carolina.

On the question of a chief executive, the Virginia Plan proposed that a national executive be chosen by the national legislature for a period of seven years. This, too, quickly became controversial. If the legislature had the power to pick a chief executive, there would be no separation of powers, and the balance again would tilt toward the larger states.

The proposed third branch of government would be a national judiciary composed of one supreme tribunal (the Supreme Court, though that term wasn't used) appointed by the second branch of the legislature, along with lower courts.

A detail tucked into the resolutions that further diminished the power of the states (Madison's goal) gave the legislative branch veto power over state laws. This idea, too, immediately sparked dissent.

By the time Randolph was done, the day's end was near, and the delegates were weary. But then came a rustle of activity at the South Carolina table, where its two members, cousins both called Charles Pinckney, were seated. The eldest, Charles Cotesworth Pinckney, had fought bravely in the Southern campaign of the war. His much younger cousin had also fought but was considered an unserious youth. It was he who unexpectedly rose to speak, as Madison stared him down, trying to mask his disdain.

The Pinckney Plan wasn't that different from the Virginia Plan, though the ratio for representation was extremely high—one representative per one thousand people. He insisted that each state ought to have a weight in proportion to its importance—a declaration that surely set the small states fuming.

It hardly mattered. The convention managers were not about to pay homage to these outliers. Although the Pinckney Plan was sent for consideration to the body, it would soon be dismissed, and the original document was not preserved for history.

When the dust of the long day settled, it was clear that the underlying conflict, staked out through Randolph's resolutions, was the tension between power given to the states and the separate powers of the national bodies.

A steady rain beat against the shuttered windows as Washington announced that the convention would meet as a Committee of the Whole, starting the next day, to discuss the resolutions on the table. The Committee of the Whole allowed for the entire body to engage in open debate. It was based on an old English measure that permitted the semblance of egalitarianism—a way to let the common folk have a voice. It was a practice used frequently in America's state legislatures. While the Committee of the Whole was in session, Washington came down from his president's seat and joined his fellow Virginians at their table. Nathaniel Gorham, a mild-mannered delegate from Massachusetts, was elected chairman of the committee, and he took Washington's seat.

This Committee of the Whole discussion lasted two weeks. Even though he sat among his compatriots for the discussion, Washington felt that, as president, he needed to avoid the appearance of bias, and he made no speeches from the floor.

To begin, Randolph rearticulated the chief components of the Virginia Plan with some changes, stating that a "merely federal" government was not enough. What was needed was a more powerful "national government, consisting of a supreme legislative, executive and judicial."

There was silence. No one spoke.

The words "national" and "supreme" echoed in the room. "Federal" they understood. This new description felt ominous. George Wythe from Virginia ventured, "From the silence . . . I presume that gentlemen are prepared to pass on the resolution?"

Not so fast. What was this *national* government Randolph was proposing? What were *supreme* branches of government? The terms struck a nerve, sounding to some members like an elevation in federal authority at the expense of the states.

Washington had long worried about this push-pull between national and state sovereignty. As he'd written to Madison the previous year: "Thirteen sovereignties, pulling against each other, and all tugging at the federal head, will soon bring ruin on the whole." He questioned how thirteen states could coexist without a strong national government. But in this room, any slight to state power struck a sensitive nerve. Was it possible to have both state authority and national authority at the same time?

Pinckney immediately wanted to know if it was Randolph's intention to do away with state governments. This wasn't what they were there for, he argued, and such a change in purpose was a concern, especially for smaller states.

Pennsylvania's Gouverneur Morris rose to offer reassurance. (Not to be confused with Robert Morris, Washington's host; Gouverneur was a family name, not a title.) The handsome Pennsylvanian who walked with a wooden leg after a carriage accident could turn on a persuasive charm. He emphasized that the distinction between a "merely federal" and a national, supreme government was simply that the latter provided a more comprehensive organizational structure. He argued that in any community there must be only one final, supreme power. You couldn't find that power in the states; it must be in the nation. And he declared that if the federal government and the states clashed, the states must yield. But this was not at all acceptable to the states' rights proponents, and the debate continued.

Roger Sherman, representing Connecticut, had just arrived at the convention that day, and he threw himself into the fray. Like Washington, Sherman had not been educated in elite schools; his simple and direct manner, bordering on vulgarity, was widely mocked by the snobs in the room. However, no one doubted his stature and service: he was a long-standing member of the Continental Congress and one of the drafters of the Declaration of Independence and the Articles of Confederation. Sherman might have been unpolished, but he was a natural intellect and didn't hesitate to speak forcefully before the convention. One of his colleagues noted that he was "an able politician, and extremely artful in accomplishing any particular object;—it is remarked that he seldom fails."

Sherman was firmly opposed to the plan to write a new constitution. He believed that their task should be limited to revising the Articles of Confederation. Under the Articles, each state had a single legislative chamber, and its vote in national matters carried equal weight with those of larger states. In a representative system like the one now proposed, the smaller states might have very little say.

But the convention had entered new territory, no longer merely debating the Articles of Confederation but forging a new conversation about national identity. The United States of America had always been conceived as a federal union composed of states. But the central question underlying the current debate was more profound: Would this nation remain a confederation of states, or would it be a nation of all the American people? And how would those people be protected and represented?

The convention voted to accept Randolph's resolve regarding a national government, though the matter would be revisited in the months to come. However, it seemed that most of the delegates had quickly accepted the idea of a new constitution, not just a repair of the Articles of Confederation.

By the end of Wednesday, Madison may have felt satisfied that his national government concept was gaining support. But it was still early days, and though there was a quorum, the gathering had not even reached a satisfactory level of representation. New Hampshire, New Jersey, Maryland, and Georgia were still missing—along with Rhode Island, which would not be coming at all.

Those who favored states' rights bristled at the idea that Congress, under Madison's plan, would have veto power over state laws. That measure would ultimately be defeated. But the question of how to handle representation persisted for some time—a thorny issue capable of bringing down the convention. Madison was unwavering in insisting that an equal vote for each state might have made sense for the confederacy but not for a republic, which rested on a representative government *of the people*.

By that Wednesday evening, Washington was no doubt tired. He chose to dine at home and catch up on his correspondence. In addition to a letter to Jefferson (cited in the Prologue), he wrote to his nephew George Augustine Washington, who was serving as farm manager in his absence, and told him to expect a longer absence: "As there is not the smallest prospect of my returning before harvest—and God knows how long it may be after it—I enclose you the observations I made at last harvest, to be practiced on the ensuing one; because I think it will be found better than the old—at any rate it may be tried."

He most likely wrote to Martha as well, as they were frequent and loving correspondents. What a shame that such a personal and perhaps emotional account is lost to history.

In the ensuing days, the convention turned to the question of how the lower and upper houses should be chosen. It was proposed that the lower house be elected by the people directly and the upper house be appointed by state legislatures—not by Congress. To Madison's chagrin, this motion passed unanimously.

Delaware's John Dickinson was an old hand at these discussions, having been there since the early days of drafting the Articles of Confederation. He offered this image: "Let our government be like that of the solar system. Let the general good be the sun and the states the planets, repulsed yet attracted, and the whole moving regularly and harmoniously in their respective orbits." This dynamic vision of interrelationship—of states "repulsed yet attracted," connected yet independent—became foundational to the republic. Although difficult to fully define and express, the idea would arise repeatedly during the convention, always with a threat in the air that the smaller states might bail if dissatisfied with their level of representation.

Another vigorous debate was waged over whether to give the national executive an absolute veto power over legislation. Both Hamilton and Wilson argued that there would be no danger of such a power being abused. Hamilton pointed out that even the British king had not exercised it since England's Glorious Revolution of 1688.

True, replied Franklin, with sarcastic bite, but then the king hardly needed a veto, so effective was the system of bribes and emoluments bestowed on members of Parliament. "The first man put at the helm will be a good one," he said—no doubt referring to Washington, whose name was already on everyone's lips. "Nobody knows what sort may come afterwards."

The fact that a group of leaders in 1787 could feel assured that power would never be abused long into the future assumed much about the character of men (and women) not yet born, or circumstances not yet imagined.

George Mason, in an agony of frustration over the extent to which his fellows were willing to give away power to a strong executive, argued that they were effectively creating a monarchy—one more dangerous than Britain's because it would be elected but equally capable of corruption. He proposed a different veto system, which would allow the executive to suspend a law until it was revised; his objections would then need to be overruled by a greater majority than before.

The convention ultimately agreed to a version of Mason's proposal, which gave the executive limited veto power, subject to override by a two-thirds majority in both houses. In the original idea, the executive and the judiciary would jointly exercise the veto, but this was scrapped in the interest of separation of powers, a principle that would become a cornerstone of the republic.

The Framers saw the potential for corruption and collusion around every corner. For example, the Virginia Plan originally proposed that the chief executive be appointed by the legislature. But then wouldn't the executive be tempted to pander to the legislature during his first term to win its support for a second term? Some suggested that this problem could be solved by limiting the executive to one term in office—say, of seven years. But a single-term executive office would defeat the fundamental idea of free elections and reelection.

Many thought that the chief executive should be elected by the people, though there was strong sentiment in the body against wide-open democracy. Some delegates openly expressed contempt for "the people," declaring them poor judges of proper government. Hadn't they already experienced it in their states? "The worst men get into the legislatures," pronounced Elbridge Gerry of Massachusetts.

Another proposal would have given the executive and the judiciary joint veto power over legislation in a so-called Council of Revision. But this, it was feared, would essentially drag the judiciary into the job of creating legislation, which it then would have power to veto. Commingling power in this way was a threat to separation of powers, and it did not stand.

Washington kept his eye on the central question, which he articulated in a letter to Lafayette in early June: "Whether we are to have a government of respectability under which life, liberty, and property secured to us, or whether we are to submit to one which may be the result of chance or the moment, springing perhaps from anarchy, confusion, and dictated perhaps by some aspiring demagogue who will not consult the interest of his country so much as his own ambitious views."

Over the convention's early weeks, the opposing sides came into focus. Favoring a strong national government were Madison, Wilson, Franklin, Gouverneur Morris, Randolph, the Pinckneys, Mason, Gerry, and Hamilton. (Washington also supported this side, although he remained neutral while sitting in the president's chair.)

On the states' rights side were Roger Sherman, William Paterson, David Brearley, Luther Martin, Gunning Bedford Jr., John Dickinson, Pierce Butler, Oliver Ellsworth, John Lansing Jr., and Robert Yates.

The delegates often gathered informally during their time off, as people at conventions do. Some delegates were staying at the Indian

Queen, a tavern and lodge on Fourth Street between Market and Chestnut. Others were spotted having dinner there. Backroom deals, or attempts at them, were almost certainly made.

Washington accepted many invitations to dinner, tea, or other genteel social gatherings, as his diary reported, and occasionally was seen dining with other delegates. For the most part, however, he was perfectly circumspect, the picture of neutrality and secrecy. This extended even to his personal diary. Barely a word of the convention's activities or his own opinions seeped into it, as if to keep secrets from himself. He felt the burden of his position and stature. He knew that if he weighed in from his raised seat, others would take it as a higher judgment.

An unexpected development occurred just as the convention was settling into a rhythm. On Friday, June 15, William Paterson of New Jersey rose to propose that the convention scrap the Virginia Plan altogether and replace it with his New Jersey Plan. Paterson was a native of Ireland, whose family moved to the United States when he was a young child. A lawyer who had served in the provincial congress and as attorney general in New Jersey, he was among the most outspoken of the small-state voices. His proposal was a shot across the bow against Madison's plans, stating that the Articles of Confederation should be amended, not enlarged. The plan jolted the delegates with the threat that they could be back where they started from.

Formulated as nine resolutions amending the Articles of Confederation, the New Jersey Plan offered other eyebrow-raising deviations from the Virginia model: a single legislative body elected by one vote per state, more than one chief executive elected by Congress, and a weaker national government.

Dickinson angrily blamed Madison's intransigence for this new standoff. Madison, he said, had been so hostile to the small-state interests that he had forced their hand. He needed to understand one thing, said Dickinson: "We would sooner submit to a foreign power than submit to be deprived of an equality of suffrage in both branches of the legislature and thereby be thrown under the domination of larger states."

However annoyed some delegates might have been by Paterson's introduction of this new wrinkle, the convention duly began to debate the two plans on the following day as a Committee of the Whole. Back and forth they went, with no satisfaction before adjourning. The next day was Sunday, and they planned to pick up the debate on Monday.

Alexander Hamilton had other plans, however. The passionate federalist arrived at the State House on Monday morning, smack in the midst of the debate. He'd grown tired of being outvoted by New York's other two delegates. He had mostly remained quiet in dissent, but now, like a warrior girded for battle, chose to break his silence in dramatic fashion, as he perceived the convention leaning away from federalism.

For six hours, Hamilton detailed his own plan: an inconsistent jumble of ideas highlighted by a couple of claims that set the room on edge. Democracy, he said, would never work as "the people are turbulent and changing; they seldom judge or determine right." Then he made what most consider a major blunder, declaring that "the English model is the only good one. It is the best in the world." He went on to describe a potential hybrid (as well as an oxymoron): a monarchy elected by the people.

Hamilton's lengthy oration is barely remembered, apart from this unfortunate piece. It is telling that the delegates essentially ignored him and never brought up his proposals for discussion. As Connecticut delegate Dr. William Samuel Johnson wrote in his notes, Hamilton's speech "has been praised by everybody but supported by none." If indeed there was any praise, it was muted. Hamilton was thought to have embarrassed himself, and his enemies leaked that he was proposing to establish a monarchy.

The convention moved on. After Hamilton's diversion, the debate between the Virginia and New Jersey plans continued; when put to a vote, an amended Virginia Plan received enough votes for adoption. Certain concessions were included: for example, a two- rather than three-year term for the lower house, and an agreement not to use the term "national" government. The resolution now referred to "the government of the United States."

Washington returned to his chair, and for a time the convention seemed to meander around technical details and side issues, as if avoiding the looming issue that might tear it apart: the still unresolved matter of how to apportion representation in the two houses of Congress. For days, the debate lingered over the roles and terms of congressional representatives and how much they should be paid—if anything.

Pinckney thought senators should not be paid at all; in fact, they should be wealthy! Franklin didn't think that any government officials should be paid. Madison, ever the pragmatist, warned that if patriotism were the only motivation offered, they might find people indifferent to the prospect of serving in government. Many of the Framers, including Madison, seemed to believe that wealth was a barrier to corruption—that the poor were more susceptible to misbehavior and trading favors. In any case, the Convention ultimately agreed that all members of Congress should be paid.

On June 27, Edward Rutledge of South Carolina made a motion to open discussion on the issue that so divided the delegates—large states against small. The former governor of his state, Rutledge was known as a man who wouldn't back down from a fight.

Worried about the debate devolving into warfare, Franklin suggested that they hold prayers every morning. "The longer I live, the more convincing proofs I see of this truth—that God governs on the affairs of men," he said gravely. "And if a sparrow cannot fall to the ground without his notice, is it probable that an empire can rise without his aid?" To this Hamilton snapped that the convention didn't need any "foreign aid." Everyone was on edge.

On a motion to give each state an equal vote in the upper house (the Senate), the vote was five states for and five states against, with one state (Georgia) divided. An appeal was made to Washington to encourage New Hampshire's delegates, still absent but en route, to get there as soon as possible. (It was assumed that New Hampshire would side with other small states.) The appeal was rejected by a vote.

Without a tie breaker, the vote stalled. Franklin sagely suggested a compromise. "The diversity of opinions turns on two points," he summarized. "If a proportional representation takes place, the small states contend that their liberties will be in danger. If an equality of votes is to be put in place, the large states say their money will be in danger." It was a succinct description of their plight. So, what to do about it? Franklin offered another metaphor: "When a broad table is to be made, and the edges of the planks do not fit, the artist takes a little from both, and makes a good joint. In like manner here, both sides must part with some of their demands."

In other words, compromise.

Charles Cotesworth Pinckney proposed that a committee be formed with one representative from each state to try and reach such a compromise. The convention agreed: the members of the committee were elected by ballot and scheduled to issue a report on July 5. Franklin was among those on the committee. Elbridge Gerry of Massachusetts was elected its chair.

"The fate of America was suspended by a hair," Gouverneur Morris would say of the moment. On the eve of the anniversary of American independence, a sober gathering recessed to await a compromise they hoped they could live with.

CHAPTER ELEVEN

WE HAVE A CONSTITUTION

The eleventh anniversary of the Declaration of Independence—
July 4, 1787—found the elected committee wrestling with its most
difficult questions. Two opposing plans were on the table, and the
delegates circled each other warily. In that stifling room at the State
House, the future of the nation was at stake, while outside its
windows, mobs of revelers celebrated the birth of independence
with joyful parades, fireworks, and cannonade salutes.

Most of the delegates set aside their work to take part in the
celebration. The State House yard was the site of a rousing military salute, and other formal observations took place around
town. Washington joined a gathering of militiamen at the German
Lutheran Church for a tribute. Abundant toasting occurred in
taverns all over the city.

Later, with fireworks still booming outside, Washington sat and
read a letter from Hamilton, who had left the convention to travel
back to New York. It wasn't optimistic, even given Hamilton's current dark mood.

In my passage through the Jerseys and since my arrival here I have taken particular pains to discover the public sentiment and I am more and more convinced that this is the critical opportunity for establishing the prosperity of this country on a solid foundation. I have conversed with men of information not only of this city but from different parts of the state; and they agree that there has been an astonishing revolution for the better in the minds of the people. The prevailing apprehension among thinking men is that the Convention, from a fear of shocking the popular opinion, will not go far enough. . . .

A plain but sensible man, in a conversation I had with him yesterday, expressed himself nearly in this manner. The people begin to be convinced that their "excellent form of government" as they have been used to call it, will not answer their purpose; and that they must substitute something not very remote from that which they have lately quitted. . . .

I fear that we shall let slip the golden opportunity of rescuing the American empire from disunion, anarchy and misery. . . .

Once again, Hamilton seemed to be suggesting that old oppressions were preferable to the current upheaval. Washington's tolerance for Hamilton's hotheadedness was great, but his negativity, when they should be pulling together, was frustrating. He had further reason to be worried about what was happening in the whole New York delegation. Not just Hamilton but also the remaining two delegates, Yates and Lansing, left the convention, effectively ending the state's participation. What this augured for New York's eventual ratification of a proposed constitution was unknown.

Reflecting back on the Declaration of Independence, Washington recognized that the challenge a decade earlier was different. Then they were writing the poetry of a revolution. Now they needed to construct the prose of a peace. And they needed to hold together to do it.

On July 5, as workers swept the detritus of the Independence Day revelry from the streets, the "compromise committee" delivered its proposal. Elbridge Gerry introduced the session by noting that there was still disagreement among the committee members and that their proposal was conditional. It was hoped that the full body might sort out the differences. This was becoming a theme of the convention. Those in the modern era who view the Constitution *as written* to be sacrosanct should realize that the deliberations that brought it into being were, like the democratic process itself, rife with dispute.

The compromise committee recommended that the lower house of representatives should have one representative per forty thousand inhabitants, with the enslaved counted as three-fifths of a person (five slaves being the equivalent of three free men). In the upper house, each state would have an equal vote. (There was a debate about whether each state should have more than one senate representative, and it was decided by unanimous vote to make the number two.)

The lower house was conceived as a nod to democracy, while the upper house, the Senate, was envisioned as the more stable deliberative body. At breakfast with Jefferson after the convention, Washington offered a colorful analogy. He asked Jefferson, "Why did you pour that coffee into your saucer?" Jefferson replied, "To cool it." Washington said, "Even so, we pour legislation into the senatorial saucer to cool it."

The debate over the compromise committee's announcement was fierce.

Gouverneur Morris was outraged. "This country must be united," he raged. "If persuasion does not unite it the sword will." Washington wrote to Hamilton in New York, expressing a sense of futility rare for him: "I *almost* despair of seeing a favorable issue to the proceedings of the convention, and do therefore repent having had any agency in the business."

Despite the furor, the convention hobbled along through the subsequent days. It worked out certain details, deciding that apportionment of taxes should be based on representation in the lower house and that what we today call "the power of the purse" should rest with that body.

Washington appointed a special committee of five to settle on a specific number of lower house representatives. That number, based on the limited population information available, was set at fifty-six members, divided proportionately among the states. When no agreement could be reached, a new committee, consisting of one representative from each state, met to review the numbers. It proposed sixty-five representatives. There is little question that some horse trading went on in that committee.

The report landed with a thud on an anxious body and was immediately subjected to sharp attacks. First of all, it was noted that the Southern states overall had fewer representatives. Delegates from small Southern states accused the Northern states of overestimating their numbers and underestimating Southern population figures. For example, they challenged the "generous" calculation of three representatives for New Hampshire while noting that the populations of North Carolina, South Carolina, and Georgia were growing rapidly.

The detractors were somewhat soothed by the agreement that representation would be reevaluated regularly through census-taking of free whites and Blacks, subject to the three-fifths calculation. Then Pinckney proposed a solution that shocked everyone: "that blacks be included in the rule of representation equally with the whites." His argument was that slaves were not persons but property, and slave labor was just as productive as free labor. Giving them equal weight in apportionment would affirm the significance of wealth as a central principle to the governing of a nation. It would also give the Southern states a substantial boost in representation.

Mason was first on his feet. Enslaved people might be valuable, he agreed, but "I cannot regard them as equal to freemen and cannot vote for them as such." Pinckney's proposal didn't go anywhere, but it exposed a fundamental issue with the three-fifths rule. It felt a lot like turning over a rock to find a wriggling mass beneath it.

The convention struggled to make it clear that designating slaves as three-fifths of a person was not in any way a moral declaration. The three-fifths ratio was already being used for revenue purposes, based on a 1783 amendment by the confederation. At this convention, counting enslaved laborers to raise the population of certain states appealed to some of the large-state crowd because it would give them allies in the South. Madison, for one, was concerned that, without this accommodation, the smaller Southern states such as South Carolina and Georgia would not earn a proportion of representatives equal to the larger Northern states, and that this might jeopardize prospects for ratification. Of course, his home state of Virginia, with a population of slaves larger than any other state's, would also be a beneficiary of this rule.

However, the effort to justify the three-fifths accommodation as merely practical was hypocritical at best. To consider enslaved people as property for purposes of ownership, but human for purposes of improving state representation, didn't sit well at all with some delegates.

Massachusetts's Elbridge Gerry, a fervent abolitionist, jumped into the debate. He asked why Blacks, who were property in the South, should count toward representation any more than cattle and horses did in the North.

Gouverneur Morris, who also opposed slavery, was equally indignant. "Upon what principle is it that the slaves shall be computed in the representation? Are they men? Then make them citizens and let them vote. Are they property? Why then is no other property included?" Their strong words carried little weight, however, as a third of the delegates were slave owners, and most others seemed to want to settle the matter and move on. Ultimately the reason was pragmatic. Those who might have wanted to tackle slavery probably recognized that it was a nonstarter and could crash the entire project. Or maybe it was simply indifference. Slavery had yet to become a compelling issue for white Americans, a fact reflected in the delegates to the convention.

Incidentally, free women *were* included in the population counts, even as women were denied the right to vote, among other civil rights. There is no mention of women in the Constitution at all. Did this simply not occur to the Framers, or was the status of women considered so settled that it wasn't an issue?

John Adams was not present at the Constitutional Convention, but when he was serving at the Continental Congress in Philadelphia, in 1776, Abigail had written to him, "I desire you would remember the ladies, and be more generous and favorable to them than your ancestors. Do not put such unlimited power into the hands of the husbands. Remember all men would be tyrants if they could." In response, Adams teased her, calling her saucy for bringing it up. "Depend upon it," he wrote truthfully, "we know better than to repeal our masculine systems." And so it was left. Women were ignored at the convention.

The fight continued in the following days, bitter and sometimes brutal—a proxy for the whole topic of slavery. It skirted the core questions of whether the enslaved were people (human beings) or property (wealth). Sitting silently during the debate, Dickinson scribbled in his notebook: "Acting before the world, what will be said of this new principle of founding a right to govern freemen on a power derived from slaves?" It also touched on another core question—whether representation would be based (at least in part) on wealth. In a late compromise, mention of "wealth" was removed as part of the calculation for representation.

The apparent settlement of this thorny issue only exposed further grievances among the smaller states. Not everyone was sold on proportional representation. Maryland's Luther Martin had preferred the old system of one legislative house with an equal vote for all states and was unhappy that the convention had moved so far away from this model. Suddenly, late in the day, small-state delegates were joining Martin to flex what muscle they had. They recognized that the apportionment scheme was leaving them short of equity with larger states, in what appeared to be a permanent state of disadvantage.

In the opposite camp, Madison and other large-state delegates were still pushing for proportional representation in both houses, the Senate as well as the lower house (to be called the House of Representatives). A note on the proceedings by Madison makes this clear: "It must be kept in view that the largest states particularly Pennsylvania and Virginia always considered the choice of the second branch by the State Legislatures as opposed to a proportional representation to which they were attached as a fundamental principle of just government."

On July 16, the convention finally voted on the compromise. The dual system of representation it proposed called for the number of seats in the House of Representatives to be determined in proportion to population—that is, the total white male population and three-fifths of Blacks. In the Senate, all states would have an equal number of votes—two per state. The compromise was adopted by one vote—the slimmest of margins for such a crucial vote.

Among those left deeply dissatisfied were the original creators of the Virginia Plan, who felt that the larger states were ill-served by the compromise. The Virginians believed passionately in proportional representation for all—meaning, in both houses. Edmund

Randolph rose to offer a shocking suggestion; as Madison recorded it, "He wished the convention might adjourn, that the large states might consider the steps proper to be taken in the present solemn crisis of the business."

Randolph stated plainly what was obvious to all: that such a narrow majority was a shaky platform on which to uphold such a defining matter. The large states needed a chance to reflect on their next move, and the small states should take the same opportunity, he suggested.

But his proposal only inflamed the gathering. Some delegates took it to mean a permanent adjournment, and he hurriedly insisted that he meant it to be only temporary. He quickly backed away from the idea and resumed his seat.

A few days later, hoping to move things along in the public view—and maybe remind the delegates what they were there for—Franklin arranged a strategic press leak to the *Pennsylvania Packet and Daily Advertiser*. On July 19, this item appeared: "So great is the unanimity, we hear, that prevails in the Convention, upon all great federal subjects, that it has been proposed to call the rooms in which they assemble—Unanimity Hall."

It would be more accurate to say that, despite a glaring *lack* of unanimity, the delegates were nevertheless forging ahead into another contentious issue—the process of selecting a chief executive. As discussed earlier, having the executive chosen by the legislative branch was fraught with the danger of collusion, which could be precluded only by requiring a one-term limit. Yet many saw the very idea of reelection as fundamental to the character of the office.

Other options were discussed. The executive could be elected directly by the people. He could be chosen by state legislatures. He could be selected by some system of electors.

At one point, election by the people, favored by Madison, began to gain momentum. But opposition from the small states was strong.

A popular vote would have the effect of giving more power to larger states, and it was assumed that people would naturally vote for candidates from their own states. Other objections were based on fear of what the people might do, if given a free hand. Mason expressed the view, held silently by others, that "it would be as unnatural to refer the choice of a proper character for chief Magistrate to the people as it would to refer a trial of colors to a blind man."

Every option was soon abandoned for its flaws. So, too, were recommendations about length of service, which ranged from four to twenty years. "We seem to be entirely at a loss," Gerry grumbled.

Finally, Madison stepped forward and summarized the various proposals, concluding that only two had legitimate promise: appointing a system of electors or election by the people—his favored choice. The delegates were in no mood to listen to Madison, however, and the debate continued. Some outlandish suggestions were offered, such as one by the normally sensible James Wilson, for a lottery to select fifteen congressmen who would then choose the president.

Now Mason took his shot, proposing a chief executive elected by Congress to serve a single seven-year term. Perhaps the delegates were exhausted, because they voted for Mason's proposal. Notably, Virginia was divided, as both Washington and Madison voted no. This would not be the final word in any case.

Deciding about the judiciary was equally difficult. Should judges be chosen by the executive or elected by the legislature? The subject of giving the executive and the judiciary a joint veto power again came up and again was rejected. One compelling issue was whether national laws would bind the states; the convention ultimately agreed to a measure retrieved from the New Jersey Plan: "that the legislative acts of the United States" would be the supreme law of the land and would bind individual states.

A committee of five known as the Committee of Detail was assigned to prepare a first draft of the Constitution. Its members were Rutledge of South Carolina, Randolph of Virginia, Wilson of Pennsylvania, Oliver Ellsworth of Connecticut, and Nathaniel Gorham of Massachusetts. All but Gorham, who was a merchant, were lawyers. Their draft report was due August 6, and the rest of the convention would be in recess until that date.

Drafting a manuscript is always a tricky proposition, as any author will tell you. A draft by its nature is a work in progress, with revisions expected. Yet it is also a bold task, especially when it reflects an effort to put into words something resembling a consensus. The Committee of Detail would draft a constitution based on elements of existing plans and documents, including the Articles of Confederation and the Virginia Plan. The drafters were required to be dedicated to their task while not getting too attached to their product. Rested from its break, the delegates would have plenty of energy to tear apart the draft, if they chose.

Looking back on the committee's task, it seems daunting. These men had to take a stab at speaking in a common voice, even as debates remained; at putting themselves in their fellows' shoes even when the fit didn't seem right. When they presented their work to the convention, it would be the first time the delegates would be able to see their collective work spread out before them.

Four days before the recess, New Hampshire's two delegates finally arrived—just in time to sit and wait. John Langdon, who had served as speaker of the New Hampshire house as well as the state's chief executive, put up the money for himself and Nicholas Gilman to travel to the convention, after the state refused to pay. Gilman, who had served sporadically in the Continental Congress, said little during the remainder of the convention. Langdon, however, was a vigorous participant in the later debates. To the surprise of many, he turned out to be a supporter of a strong national government.

• • •

The break was welcome. While the Committee of Detail did its work, Washington accepted an invitation from Gouverneur Morris to go fishing. Washington was an avid fisherman; he had also made a successful business of harvesting fish from the Potomac River. And Washington no doubt enjoyed the company of the ebullient ladies' man Morris. The two men had not always been close but grew closer during the early weeks of the convention, as Morris aligned himself with Madison (and by default Washington).

One reported incident from those early days might have derailed the relationship. The tale may be apocryphal, but it seems to nail the players accurately. One day Morris was boasting that he was afraid of no one. Hamilton bet him dinner and wine for the company that he would not dare to walk up to Washington and slap him on the shoulder, while wishing him a good morning. Morris took the bet and did the deed; as he delivered the friendly slap, Washington turned and gave him a freezing stare, putting him in his place. Morris later reported that he'd never won a bet that cost him so much.

Now they were on friendlier terms. Morris had invited the Virginian to his brother-in-law's bucolic farm, with its well-stocked trout stream, north of Philadelphia. Best of all, from Washington's perspective, the farm was close to Valley Forge, which he had not visited since that fateful winter a decade earlier. The day after their arrival, Washington rode to the campsite, where he found the ruins of his army's winter ordeal.

He had never seen the area in the lush warmth of summer, and his mind must have flitted back to the chilling cold and hunger. It was hard to believe that this beautiful spot had been a place of such agony. But Valley Forge had delivered more than suffering in the end. Thanks to von Steuben, it had produced a newly skilled and disciplined army that marched out in the spring with fresh confidence that the war could be won. Surely he would always think of Valley Forge in that way.

Riding back to join Morris, he saw some farmers working in a field of buckwheat and stopped to chat with them. Washington was always curious about agricultural techniques. He knew little of the value of buckwheat and now learned that this delicate grain, which must be quickly harvested between the hottest sun of summer and the early frost, was an excellent source of nutrition for cattle and livestock. There is no indication that the friendly farmers knew who they were speaking to.

Washington enjoyed the respite, and he returned to Philadelphia in good spirits, only to find a distressing letter from Lafayette. His friend wrote that America's name was on the decline overseas: "Her dignity is lowering, her credit vanishing, her good intentions questioned by some, her future prosperity doubted. Good God! Will the people of America, so enlightened, so wise, so generous, after they have so gloriously climbed up the rugged hill, now stumble in the easy path?"

Jefferson, writing from Paris, struck a more positive note:

I remain in hopes of great and good effects from the decisions of the assembly over which you are presiding. To make our states one as to all foreign concerns, preserve them several as to all merely domestic, to give to the federal head some peaceable mode of enforcing their just authority, to organize that head into Legislative, Executive, and Judiciary departments are great desiderata in our federal constitution. Yet with all its defects, and with all those of our particular governments, the inconveniencies resulting from them are so light in comparison with those existing in every other government on earth, that our citizens may certainly be considered as in the happiest political situation which exists.

On August 6, the Committee of Detail submitted a printed rough draft to the delegates for consideration. It included a preamble and twenty-three articles: two articles as an introduction, seven related to Congress, one to the executive, one to the judiciary, and twelve on provisions related to interstate operations, state guarantees, the admission of new states, ratification and amendment processes, and housekeeping matters such as oaths.

In this draft, the preamble, taking its cue from the Articles of Confederation, began with a list of the thirteen states:

> We the People of the States of New Hampshire, Massachu-setts, Rhode Island and Providence Plantation, Connecticut, New York, New Jersey, Pennsylvania, Delaware, Maryland, Virginia, North Carolina, South Carolina, and Georgia, do ordain, declare and establish the following Constitution for the Government of Ourselves and our Posterity.

The preamble was later rewritten by Gouverneur Morris, whom Madison would generously dub "the penman of the Constitution." That version is known by heart to schoolchildren and adults alike to this day. Instead of focusing on the *states*, it elevated the *people* and the union.

> We the People of the United States, in order to form a more perfect Union, establish justice, insure domestic tranquility, provide for the common defense, promote the general wel-fare, and secure the blessings of liberty to ourselves and our posterity, do ordain and establish this Constitution for the United States of America.

In his fascinating account of how the preamble came to be, historian Richard Brookhiser notes that Morris's choice of "We the

People" was his creative contribution, condensing what he took to be a consensus of thought. Later, during ratification, this question would lead to a spirited debate between Henry and Madison.

"Who authorized them to speak the language of 'We the People,' instead of 'We the States'?" Henry demanded.

Madison replied, "Should all the states adopt it, it will be then a government established by the thirteen states of America, not through the intervention of the legislatures, but by the people at large." Madison said, "In this particular respect the distinction between the existing and the proposed governments is very material. The existing system has been derived from the dependent derivative authority of the legislatures of the states; whereas, this is derived from the superior power of the people."

As the delegates settled in for what would be more than a month of review and editing, Washington heard from Henry Knox, who had determined that it was finally proper to share his views. Knox pronounced himself "satisfied with the result of the convention [presumably in advance], although it is short of my wishes and of my judgement."

He used the opportunity to report on a family tragedy. "Mrs. Knox and myself have recently sustained the severe affliction of losing our youngest child of about eleven months old, who died on the 11th of a disease incident to children cutting their teeth in the summer season. This is the third time that Mrs. Knox has had her tenderest affections lacerated by the rigid hand of death."

Washington was moved by Knox's letter and by the fact that he would take time to write in the midst of his grief. He responded quickly. Circumspect as always, he declined to comment on the progress of the Convention, except to say, "I wish a disposition may be found in Congress—the several States Legislatures—and the community at large to adopt the government which may be agreed on in Convention; because I am fully persuaded it is the best that can be obtained at the present moment, under such diversity of ideas as prevail."

He also offered heartfelt sympathies to his friend—and the best advice he knew how to give, having suffered many losses in his own life. Assuring Knox that he and his wife had the fortitude to overcome any trial, he soberly reflected, "Nature, no doubt, must feel severely before *calm* resignation will overcome it."

Max Farrand, who published the Constitutional Convention records in 1913, is the most commonly referenced guide to events. His notation regarding the final editing sessions seems a perfect description of the human process and will sound familiar to anyone who has tried to forge consensus in a mixed group. "It was a trying and wearisome task," he wrote. "Since the adoption of the great compromise and the protection of the interests of the small states in the senate, many of the opposition had been won over and were now working in harmony with those who were in favor of establishing a strong national government." Because of this major agreement, it became a point of contention when certain delegates kept debating matters that the majority deemed "trivial." The majority's response? It "rode roughshod over the few in the minority."

Imagine a discussion covering every single issue that might come up in the forming of a government—not only how to choose representatives, the chief executive, and the judiciary but how to pay them, what their powers and duties were, the limits on their terms, how to remove them if necessary, what constituted treason, how to admit new states, war powers, restrictions on foreigners recently arrived, how to apportion taxes, the extent and limits of commerce (both interstate and international), how to make amendments, and on and on, right down to the process of ratifying this constitution.

Compromise remained the word of the day. And what is compromise but agreeing at times to vote against one's desires in order to reach a higher goal? Those who would define *freedom* as the right to cling to every precious principle dear to one's heart could not form a nation—especially not this one. The key was to decide together which principles were sacred and—no small detail— would make a nation governable.

Earlier agreements fell by the wayside as the convention reconsidered the most critical matters. Some delegates grew weary of the constant back and forth, as resolutions were made one day and upended the next. But as messy as it seemed, the process actually worked.

A "Committee on Postponed Parts" was named to address the jumble of unresolved issues. It was a powerful group: Madison from Virginia, Rufus King from Massachusetts, Sherman from Connecticut, Gouverneur Morris from Pennsylvania, and John Dickinson from Delaware. David Brearley from New Jersey was the chair. Brearley, his state's chief justice, had been a hardworking and quiet delegate throughout the convention.

Probably the most important item on Brearley's agenda was resolving how a president was to be elected. Earlier, Mason had quickly won approval of his proposal that a chief executive be chosen by Congress for a single seven-year term. But this was again under review, with Dickinson arguing that the people would not accept a chief executive if they had no vote.

The committee members were open to a discussion, and Madison led them in figuring out a workable system of electors that would be chosen by a vote of the people. Each state would have a number of electors equal to the number of its members of the Senate and the House combined. Each elector would cast two votes for president. The person gaining the greatest number of electoral votes would become the president; whoever had the second-highest vote total would be the vice president. A four-year term was settled on, with no limit to the number of terms a president might serve. (The two-term limit was not established until 1951, with the ratification of the Twenty-Second Amendment.)

The Framers' presumption was that state electors would vote according to the will of the people expressed in the popular vote, but this isn't specified in the Constitution. Effectively, voters are not voting for candidates but for slates of electors. As we've seen in recent years, the winner of the popular vote is not necessarily the winner in the Electoral College. Some states require their electors to reflect the popular vote.

When completed, the new Constitution emerged as a compact document, consisting of a preamble and seven articles. Articles one through three focused on the three branches of government—legislative, executive, and judicial. The next four concerned ways in which the states would interact with the federal government.

Toward the end of the process, Washington inserted himself into the public discussion for the first time, to propose that congressional representation be fixed at one per every thirty thousand (rather than forty thousand) people—thus providing a greater level of representation. His motion passed.

Near the end, as well, the moral dimension of slavery finally came to the forefront, when George Mason made an objection to the slave trade. It was ultimately a symbolic gesture, as the Southern states made it clear that they would not accept a constitution that limited their right to import slaves. The final outcome was that convenient compartmentalization often used since: leave it to the states. Delegates continued to bicker about how to tax "such persons" (they strived not to use the word *slave*) and whether the matter could be revisited at a future date. These were technicalities. They also agreed to a clause that freedom seekers must be returned.

Finally, they took up the process of ratification. It was agreed that the Constitution would be presented to Congress and then sent to conventions in each of the thirteen states for ratification. The approval of at least nine states would be required.

In his biography of Benjamin Franklin, Walter Isaacson observed Franklin's frustration with the imperfections of this new constitution. And yet "with the wisdom of a patient chess player and the practicality of a scientist, Franklin realized that they had succeeded not because they were self-assured, but because they were willing to concede that they might be fallible."

Some within the convention could not accept such fallibility. They feared that the rights of the people would be abused by the government as it was designed. Over the final weeks, Mason grew increasingly unhappy with a constitution that seemed to "fix an Aristocracy," which he deemed "worse than absolute monarchy."

Along with Gerry, he tried to ameliorate this, proposing a preface to the Constitution that would serve as a bill of rights. This, he believed, would be true to their original purpose, hammered out in the early days. How could they not spell out the individual rights that a government could not violate? What of the individual freedoms essential to the society they were aspiring to create? Mason announced that he would sooner chop off his right hand than approve the Constitution as it stood. But the proposal for a bill of rights was rejected by the delegates. For this reason, Mason, Gerry, and Randolph all refused to sign the Constitution.

At the convention's final session on September 17, the Constitution was read aloud and entered into history. Franklin then made his move, handing a paper to Wilson to read aloud. It was an elaboration of Franklin's inner thoughts—the conscience of a signer.

I confess that there are several parts of this Constitution which I do not at present approve, but I am not sure I shall never

approve them: For having lived long, I have experienced many instances of being obliged, by better information, or fuller consideration, to change opinions even on important subjects, which I once thought right, but found to be otherwise. It is therefore that the older I grow, the more apt I am to doubt my own judgment, and to pay more respect to the judgment of others. . . .

Much of the strength and efficiency of any government, in procuring and securing happiness to the people depends on opinion, on the general opinion of the goodness of that government, as well as of the wisdom and integrity of its governors. I hope therefore that for our own sakes, as a part of the people, and for the sake of our posterity, we shall act heartily & unanimously in recommending this Constitution . . . wherever our influence may extend, and turn our future thoughts and endeavors to the means of having it well administered.

He then appealed to all present—even those with remaining objections—to put them aside in the interests of unanimity.

Washington gave no speech. He maintained his reserve to the end. But for the first time, his diary that day was exceptionally revealing of events—if not of how he felt about them.

Monday 17th.

Met in Convention when the Constitution received the unanimous assent of 11 states and Col. Hamilton's from New York (the only delegate from thence in Convention) and was subscribed to by every member present except Govr. Randolph and Col. Mason from Virginia and Mr. Gerry from Massachusetts. The business being thus closed, the members adjourned to the City Tavern, dined together and took a

cordial leave of each other—after which I returned to my
lodgings, did some business with, and received the papers
from the secretary of the Convention, and retired to meditate
on the momentous work which had been executed, after not
less than five, for a large part of the time six, and sometimes
seven hours sitting every day, Sundays and the ten days
adjournment to give a committee opportunity and time to
arrange the business, for more than four months.

Through it all, Washington had been a steady presence, overseeing the business of the convention from his chair. He was not
an orator like Hamilton or an intellectual like Madison. He didn't
rise to express moral indignation, as many delegates did. People are
often surprised by the absence of quotes attributed to Washington
during the proceedings. Douglas Freeman observed that "his largest contribution was not his counsel but his presence. . . . Letters
from members seldom mentioned him among those at the forge
where the Constitution was hammered out, blow on blow."

But this reticence in no way diminished Washington's stature,
Freeman argued. In fact, it heightened his influence. "Outside the
Convention the reverse was true. In giving the body prestige and
maintaining public confidence in it while deliberations dragged
slowly, Washington had no peer . . ."

As he prepared to head for home, Washington was no doubt
experiencing many emotions, chief among them hope. He believed,
as he wrote to Lafayette—in a letter he attached to a copy of the
Constitution—that the convention's achievement was "little short
of a miracle." This Constitution, he added, was "now a child of
fortune, to be fostered by some and buffeted by others. What will
be the general opinion on, or the reception of it, is not for me to decide, nor shall I say anything for or against it. If it be good, I suppose
it will work its way good. If bad, it will recoil on the framers."

CHAPTER TWELVE

THE PEOPLE DECIDE

Washington was in a hurry. After four and a half months away from home, he could not wait to get back to Martha and the family. He was eager to set foot on his land again, to pursue his farming passions. He was in such a hurry that he nearly made a fatal mistake. Approaching a bridge at Head of Elk (Elkton), Maryland, in heavy rain, he insisted on sending his overloaded carriage across despite the dangerous conditions. Fortunately, he and his companion, Virginia delegate John Blair, got out first, because the bridge collapsed under the weight of the carriage. Thanks to workers from a nearby mill, who rushed to the rescue, the horses and carriage were saved. But it was a close call.

Afterward, recalling how his terrified horses teetered on the edge of their doom, he might have appreciated the analogy to the nation's current condition. The kind of representative government they were proposing was threatened by a dangerous storm out in the country. Its survival would rely on a public groundswell of support, yet every day would bring news of contention as the states began their review. Public opinion wasn't always easy to discern, but the loudest voices carried sway. Once again, federalists and antifederalists faced off, only this time it was more than rhetoric. Ratification was at stake.

A story later made the rounds that, after the convention, Franklin was approached by a woman in the yard of the State House. "Doctor, what have we got—a republic or a monarchy?" He replied, "A republic, if you can keep it." Naturally, some people dispute that this ever happened. It's too perfect. But it does point to one of the chief questions of those early days. From the very start, before the republic was endorsed, there was doubt about whether it could be kept.

Many were confused about exactly what form of government they were being asked to approve. The current atmosphere did not seem to resemble the fervor of the nation's early days, when people were forming political organizations and militias to fight their common enemy. Romantics liked to remember those days as thrilling, inspiring, and effective. They chose to forget just how chaotic and ungovernable the nation was after the war—the reason the Constitutional Convention was called for in the first place.

It was the chaotic aspect of raw democracy that led the Framers to craft the proposed government as a republic. In fact, it had been operating that way, through representatives, for a long time. In a representative government, democracy is achieved—and each voting member of the public has a say—in a collective way. In other words, the people, the ultimate authority in a democracy, allow authority to be exercised on their behalf by chosen representatives.

The Constitution abolished any semblance of hereditary rule. The public had to get used to the democratic mindset, internalize the idea of an equal voice for all, and learn to trust that the representative system was fair.

But first people had to accept that this was the direction they wanted to go. After receiving a recommendation from the Confederation

Congress and being sent to the states, the ratification of the Constitution would be a test of government "by the people." Rather than having state legislatures vote on ratification, the process involved establishing state ratifying conventions whose delegates were elected by popular vote.

Before a single convention had been seated, there were already public disputes about aspects of the Constitution, which was being published in newspapers throughout the country. Happy as he was to be home and out of the direct line of fire, Washington could not help becoming embroiled in the debate. It consumed him. Martha gently remarked that all talk around their household during that time was of politics, a topic she was disinterested in. She tried to stay out of it as her husband was drawn in more deeply.

Writing to Knox on October 15, Washington outlined the essential questions that the people must answer. The following is a summary of his outline.

1. Is the Constitution which is submitted by the Convention preferable to the government (if it can be called one) under which we now live?

2. Is it probable that more confidence will, at this time, be placed in another Convention (should the experiment be tried) than was given to the last? and is it likely that there would be a better agreement in it?

3. Is there not a Constitutional door open for alterations and amendments, and is it not probable that real defects will be as readily discovered after, as before, trial? and will not posterity be as ready to apply the remedy as ourselves, if there is occasion for it, when the mode is provided?

There is ample evidence that he would have answered the first question with a hearty affirmative. There was broad agreement that the Articles of Confederation, as they stood, were ineffective, and that the nation was in chaos. The convention had grown out of the need to fix the most glaring problems.

To the second question, he'd give a resounding no. He felt they must seize the momentum of the Constitutional Convention to build confidence in the proposed government. The urgent need for a constitution far outweighed the disputes about individual points. Going back to the drawing board was not an answer and might stall the process permanently.

Which led to the third question. Yes, he believed that a door was open for alterations and amendments. Those who belabored the Constitution's imperfections could rest assured that it wasn't written in stone. These alterations could come soon, in their own time (as indeed they did), or could be left to future generations. Washington felt assured of this, but not everyone shared his confidence. The antifederalists worried that if a bill of rights was not ratified as part of the Constitution, it never would be.

The divide forming in the country was encapsulated in a failing friendship. No longer did Washington and his old friend George Mason sit by the fire and talk as brothers. It was not in Mason's nature to be a flamethrower—far from it. Being an outlier made him deeply uncomfortable, and being at odds with his good friend was especially painful. But his conscience would not permit him to simply fall into line.

After the convention, Mason accelerated the debate by putting his objections in writing. His "Objections to This Constitution of Government" detailed sixteen serious problems with the document. The first among them was the absence of a declaration of rights.

Mason's ally in this campaign was Patrick Henry. The two resolved to fight ratification in Virginia. In October, Henry sent a painfully polite letter to Washington, containing a stinging repudiation.

> I was honored by the receipt of your favor together with a copy of the proposed federal constitution, a few days ago, for which I beg you to accept my thanks. They are also due to you from me as a citizen, on account of the great fatigue necessarily attending the arduous business of the late convention.
>
> I have to lament that I cannot bring my mind to accord with the proposed Constitution. The concern I feel on this account, is really greater than I am able to express. Perhaps mature reflection may furnish me reasons to change my present sentiments into a conformity with the opinion of those personages for whom I have the highest reverence. Be that as it may, I beg you will be persuaded of the unalterable regard and attachment with which I ever shall be dear sir your obliged and very humble servant.

The flattery was so dense that it nearly masked the letter's substance, Henry's rejection of the Constitution. Some found it hard to discern Henry's true motivations. Madison didn't trust him a bit, believing that Henry had a larger purpose—perhaps the creation of a Southern Confederacy.

The disputes during the convention, and before that in the Continental Congress, usually presented properly and with parliamentary regard, paled in comparison to the uproar that marked the ratification process. Mason's public "Objections" didn't help. But others were skeptical.

The first stop in the Constitution's journey was New York, where it was presented before Congress, accompanied by a letter from Washington:

In all our deliberations we kept steadily in our view, that which appears to us the greatest interest of every true American, the consolidation of our Union, in which is involved our prosperity, felicity, safety, perhaps our national existence. This important consideration, seriously and deeply impressed on our minds, led each state in the Convention to be less rigid on points of inferior magnitude, than might have been otherwise expected; and thus the Constitution, which we now present, is the result of a spirit of amity, and of that mutual deference and concession which the peculiarity of our political situation rendered indispensable.

Mason and other opponents hoped that the Constitution would stall in Congress and never make it to the states. When discussion was opened there, Mason and Randolph spoke. Then Virginian Richard Henry Lee, with elaborate oratorical flourish, called for the addition of a declaration of rights. He spoke at length, proposing various amendments, and though they did not pass, Lee's speech was a harbinger of troubles to come.

The obvious question, looking back on this battle, was why it had not been avoided. Madison's stubbornness in rejecting a bill of rights at this early stage of the ratification process can seem inexplicable. Why did a man so grounded in the principles of this new nation refuse to consider this option? Was it mere expediency? Did he fear that any delay to craft amendments would upset the consensus to send the Constitution forward? Madison's deeper fear seems to have been that enemies of the Constitution were using the bill of rights argument to mask other issues. He worried that concessions on one matter would lead to unraveling other decisions. He may have thought it best to get the Constitution ratified, and then propose a bill of rights from safer ground.

The antifederalists thought they might have one more card to play. The original charge to the convention was not that it write a constitution, but that it amend the Articles of Confederation. Congress might reject the Constitution on this technicality. This was wishful thinking, and Congress brushed it aside and unanimously agreed to pass on the Constitution "to a convention of Delegates chosen in each state by the people" for ratification.

It's not that supporters of the Constitution were free from doubts. We've already seen admissions of the Constitution's flaws by Washington, Franklin, Hamilton, and even Madison. But for Hamilton, Madison, and John Jay, the priority was to move ahead while the opportunity presented itself, in full expectation of making changes in the form of amendments once the Constitution was ratified. Under the pseudonym Publius, the three began publishing essays in New York newspapers. Eighty-five essays appeared between October 1787 and May 1788; they would become known as the Federalist Papers.

Although Madison denied any affiliation with the essays and did not even tell his friend Jefferson that he was involved, he is known to have written many of them. One in particular, No. 10, appearing on November 22, 1787, argued in favor of a stable republic, capable of protecting the rights of all, even those with little power. He presented a case against factions led by charismatic leaders who often stood their ground on one issue or another, which created dissension and caused the whole citizenry to suffer.

In No. 37, Madison defended the process that brought the Constitution into being, and the result, in the strongest terms:

> The real wonder is that so many difficulties should have been surmounted, and with an unanimity almost as unprecedented as it must have been unexpected. It is impossible for any man of candor to reflect on this circumstance without partaking of the astonishment. It is impossible for the man of pious reflection

not to receive in it a finger of that Almighty Hand which has been so frequently and signally extended to our relief in the critical stages of the revolution.

Washington, of course, was almost universally admired, and those who hoped for a quick ratification were not above promoting him as the standard bearer. Word soon spread across the land that, once the Constitution was approved, none other than the general himself would assume the post of chief executive.

Washington himself said nothing about this, but he and Martha felt the inevitability of public life looming in their future. They didn't seek it and didn't want it. Martha, never a fan of politics, was content in her lively home and her family responsibilities. Washington was never happier than at home, managing his lands and talking about agricultural techniques. He was certainly free to remain there. But, having done so much to launch the ship of state, he felt he could not abandon the helm mid-journey. Sometimes it seemed as if the entire nation assumed that he would become its first chief executive—a notion that the federalists did nothing to discourage. They wanted people to believe that they would rest safely in the capable hands of the Commander.

Gouverneur Morris wrote Washington at the end of October, pressing hard on his friend's importance to the process.

I have observed that your name to the new Constitution has been of infinite service. Indeed I am convinced that if you had not attended the Convention, and the same paper had been handed out to the world, it would have met with a colder reception, with fewer and weaker advocates, and with more and more strenuous opponents. As it is, should the idea prevail that you would not accept of the presidency it would prove fatal in many parts.

He went on to urge Washington, in the strongest terms, to stand for president, openly stating that only he could lead this still-fractured nation. But Washington recognized that there was a long way to go before things were settled. The Constitution had many enemies, and they were growing louder.

According to *The Framers' Coup*, by Harvard Law professor Michael J. Klarman, the antifederalists would sink to any level to win their way, including publishing phony letters and doctored documents. The fight was particularly brutal in Pennsylvania, the birthplace of the Constitution.

The antifederalist papers were various writings from the Founding Fathers who opposed the Constitution. Among the most prominent, written under the pseudonym "the Centinel," were a series of lengthy diatribes published in the Philadelphia *Independent Gazetteer*. Among their opening salvos was a direct, offensive attack on Washington:

> It is to be lamented that the interested and designing have availed themselves so successfully of the present crisis, and under the specious pretense of having discovered a panacea for all the ills of the people, they are about establishing a system of government, that will prove more destructive to them, than the wooden horse filled with soldiers did in ancient times to the city of Troy; this horse was introduced by their hostile enemy the Grecians, by a prostitution of the sacred rights of their religion; in like manner, my fellow citizens are aspiring despots among yourselves prostituting the name of a Washington to cloak their designs upon your liberties.

Washington was so outraged by this slander that he sat down and wrote an indignant response. It was probably inflammatory, but we'll never know. When he sent it to his half-brother Augustine, asking if he should publish it, Augustine promptly destroyed it.

In the minds of the Constitution's opponents, the argument boiled down to whether the people really did have the power to determine their own destiny, and whether that power included tossing the Constitution and writing a new one that they liked better. Washington understood politics, as little as he cared for it. He had often observed in the military that minor troublemakers could have an influence far beyond their numbers.

The opponents of the Constitution seemed to give little thought to the real-world consequences of failing to ratify it. How could a new convention be chartered, and where would it find its delegates? Would the two sides, battle-scarred and divided, be as judicious and open to compromise as the original Framers? Meanwhile, would minor confederacies form under their own constitutions, as individual states banded together? Civil war was not out of the question, and bad actors from abroad would happily join in. In sum, failure to ratify the Constitution would signal to the world that the young United States was not ready to stand on its own. The prospect of a new convention, Washington mused, would create "more heat, and greater confusion than can well be conceived."

The ratification process—with nine states needed to ratify—was intensely contested in some states; others had an easier time. Delaware was the first to ratify, on December 7, confirming the observation that smaller states were generally happy with the way power was balanced between the national government and the states—especially the concessions they won on representation in the legislative branch. Delaware was quickly followed in December by Pennsylvania, New Jersey, Georgia, and Connecticut.

The absence of amendments guaranteeing individual freedoms continued to be a sticking point, and it appeared to be a dealbreaker for Massachusetts. At the January convention in Boston, the cradle of American patriotism, delegates debated their concept of "popular liberty," by which they meant the fundamental rights of a free people. Every provision of the Constitution had to pass the "popular liberty" test. In the spirit of democracy, the sessions were open to the public, and nearly a thousand people typically packed the hall. The importance of this decision had finally taken hold, and people were viewing the debate in terms of what it would mean for them personally and practically.

Debate on each article continued through January. Massachusetts governor John Hancock, elected president of the convention, was suffering from a severe case of gout and unable to attend for most of that time. As Hancock lay in his sickbed and fretted about the future, Sam Adams, his old friend and fellow patriot from the earliest days, sat with him. The men had been on the outs in recent years, but now they quietly talked about what could be done to bring the antifederalists around. They kept coming back to the matter of amendments; both agreed that if concessions were made on this front, they could give the Constitution their full support.

And then, like a vision from the past, Paul Revere rode to the rescue. According to Sam Adams biographer William Vincent Wells, Revere arrived at Hancock's bedside to deliver resolutions in support of the Constitution, which had been agreed to by the skilled workingmen (mechanics) of Boston in a meeting at the Green Dragon Tavern.

"How many mechanics?" Adams asked.

"More, sir, than the Green Dragon could hold," Revere replied.

"And where were the rest?"

"In the streets, sir," said Revere.

"And how many were in the streets?" Adams asked.

"More, sir, than there are stars in the sky."

Hearing this, Hancock rose from his bed and was helped to the convention, where he presented what would become the Massachusetts Compromise: in exchange for ratification, it required assurance that amendments would be quickly proposed. He and Adams had penned ten such amendments, and these would help form the basis for what eventually became the Bill of Rights. Massachusetts ratified based on this promise, and Maryland and South Carolina followed soon after.

Now only one state more was needed for the ratification to take effect. All eyes were on New Hampshire and Virginia.

Despite Virginia's pivotal role in creating the Constitution, Washington recognized that it would be a challenge to secure ratification in his state. He urged Madison to stand for delegate. Reluctantly, Madison agreed to leave New York and travel to Virginia to join the fight in person once again.

He was uncomfortable in the role of politician, embarrassed by electioneering. His previous elections to the Virginia legislature and the Continental Congress had been secured without this process. Now he found himself atop a platform in the open air, arguing for a place in the ratification convention. He need not have worried; he was easily elected. But so were three formidable opponents: Mason, Henry, and Randolph.

The Virginia convention opened in Richmond on June 2, long after many states had already completed ratification. Half mad with fury, Henry summoned the worst possible predictions about the fate of the nation if the Constitution was ratified. In the hellscape he imagined, all liberties would be swept away by the forceful arm of the federal government—and the president at its head would lead an army against the people.

He was particularly incensed, as noted earlier, by the preamble's phrase "We the People." He argued that it should be "We the States"—that the contract was between the nation and the states, not individuals. In a passionate plea from the floor, he likened the "We the People" construct to a monarchy: "Mr. Chairman . . . Is this a monarchy, like England—a compact between prince and people, with checks on the former to secure the liberty of the latter? Is this a confederacy, like Holland—an association of a number of independent states, each of which retains its individual sovereignty? It is not a democracy. . . ."

All along, Henry had relied on the support of Randolph, one of the Framers who had refused to sign the Constitution. But suddenly Randolph rose to challenge him. Changing sides without notice, he now argued, "What harm is there in consulting the people on the construction of a government by which they are to be bound? Is it unfair? Is it unjust? If the government is to be binding on the people, are not the people the proper persons to examine its merits or defects?" He then announced that he would support the ratification by Virginia of the Constitution.

Henry was so angered by Randolph's defection that observers thought there would be a physical fight. Mason, too, seemed shaken, but he and Henry stood firm against what Henry called "a relinquishment of rights."

Madison remained calm and logical, the cool center amid all this heat. Point by point, he described and defended each article of the Constitution. He never wavered, despite bouts of illness so severe that they took him out of commission on some days. Once he was forced to stop in mid-speech and leave the room. But he always returned, and his voice ultimately rose above all the dissent. Finally, on June 25, the convention voted eighty-nine to seventy-nine for ratification.

It was a great victory, though not the decisive one, as it turned out. Four days earlier, New Hampshire became the ninth and decisive state to ratify, ensuring the Constitution's adoption.

Physically and emotionally spent by the ordeal, Madison faced a long trip back to Congress in Manhattan. But Washington, who had heard while visiting his mother in Fredericksburg that Madison was ill, intervened. He wrote to Madison, counseling that he rest before returning.

> **Relaxation must have become indispensably necessary for your health, and for that reason I presume to advise you to take a little respite from business and to express a wish that part of the time might be spent under this roof on your journey thither. Moderate exercise, and books occasionally, with the mind unbent, will be your best restoratives. With much truth I can assure you that no one will be happier in your company than your sincere and affectionate servant . . . Go. Washington**

Madison took him up on the offer and visited Mount Vernon. They celebrated July 4 together with renewed optimism, and though Washington felt the burden of what lay ahead for him, they found joy in their accomplishment. The Constitution had been ratified, with ten states approving.

Only New York, North Carolina, and Rhode Island remained. In New York, a standoff between Hamilton and Governor George Clinton came to symbolize the root conflict in the state. Clinton was infuriated by Hamilton's outspokenness, especially the veiled insults in his not-so-anonymous writings, and declared the Constitution "a monster with open mouth and monstrous teeth ready to devour all before it." Hamilton was contemptuous of Clinton, whom he regarded as a corrupt politician interested only in preserving his own power.

Hamilton's essays during this period represented a sustained effort to refute opposition to the Constitution as thoroughly as possible. He preached the stability of a well-formed government and the flexibility of a free nation, and hinted at amendments by saying, "There ought to be a capacity to provide for future contingencies."

New York's convention began on June 14 in Poughkeepsie, before nine states had solidified the ratification. Clinton was elected chairman, and he had his antifederalist supporters in line. The pro-Constitution delegates were an imposing group—Hamilton, Jay, and Robert R. Livingston.

There is no question that Hamilton saved the day. Biographer Ron Chernow called his performance "an exhilarating blend of stamina, passion, and oratorical pyrotechnics." Over a period of six weeks, he rose again and again to explain and argue each clause. His stamina in this endeavor was unmatched, and his renowned charisma was on full display. He preached and seduced, and he did not shy away from calling out his opponents in the strongest terms.

Clinton believed that the United States was so large and complex that no single government could accommodate it. This defeatist premise was a nonstarter for Hamilton, who argued that a united nation already existed in its basic culture and practices.

And on it went, until one day the convention was shocked by the news that New Hampshire had ratified the Constitution. Even though his prize had been lost, Clinton made no move to stop fighting. Hamilton speculated to Madison that Clinton wouldn't give in unless Virginia ratified.

So, as New York's convention deteriorated into rhetorical blows (and nearly physical ones), Hamilton awaited word from Virginia. It came on July 2, via messenger: Virginia had ratified. Emotional, Hamilton stood on the floor and read Madison's letter aloud. After that, the convention seemed willing to accept a deal similar to the one struck in Massachusetts: ratification with the promise of amendments. The vote on July 26 was tight—thirty to twenty-seven—but it was done, and Hamilton was hailed as a hero.

North Carolina finally ratified on November 21, 1789, attaching its own "Declaration of Rights." Rhode Island didn't follow until May 29, 1790. Dubbed "Rogue Island" by the press, the state had been truculent throughout the entire process, beginning with its failure to participate in the Constitutional Convention. Long after the Constitution was adopted, Rhode Island's governor told Congress that his state was still operating out of the Articles of Confederation until they received satisfactory proof that their rights and tax bases would be protected. It was a dangerous game, ending finally when the powers that be in Newport threatened to secede from the state if it didn't get its act together.

While the federalists prevailed in the ratification process, the antifederalists gained important concessions. In Massachusetts, New York, and Virginia, the vote for ratification was contingent on the later addition of a bill of rights. The antifederalist population would continue to watch the government with a wary eye and participate as the loyal opposition. And it would always be thus. The balancing act of democracy is never comfortable, and the practice of compromise demands that opposing parties get a fair say.

Washington was understanding and conciliatory toward his fellow citizens who had mounted such a vigorous campaign against the Constitution. He expressed those feelings in a letter to Benjamin Lincoln that June. "By folly and misconduct . . . we may now and then get bewildered, but I hope and trust that there is good sense and virtue enough left to bring us back into the right way before we shall be entirely lost."

He might have privately longed for the citizenry to be in absolute agreement on the principles and practices of the new government—as we still long for such agreement today—but he understood that the bravery underlying this new form of government could not expire at its founding. It would take courage to govern a diverse and outspoken people.

Mount Vernon could be idyllic, no matter the season, and as late summer moved into fall in 1788, Washington took special care to cherish every moment, lovingly overseeing his family and his lands. In the wider country, the states were beginning the process of choosing electors for a November presidential election, and his fate was now in the hands of others.

Martha's true desire for their future was no secret: she hoped that they would "grow old in solitude and tranquility together." Clearly, this was not to be. In a letter to her niece Fanny is a hint of her frustration with the plotting about her husband's future: "We have not a single article of news but politics which I do not concern myself about." It's likely that she concerned herself greatly but chose not to fight her husband's destiny.

Because it was the first, the presidential election of 1789 was one of a kind. There was no campaign as such. Between December 15, 1788, and January 10, 1789, each state chose its presidential electors, their methods varying. For example, in Virginia, people voted for electors by district (Washington rode to Alexandria to cast his vote), while in New Jersey, the governor and his appointees made the selection. Each elector had two votes—the original system devised to give smaller states a semblance of equality.

The Electoral College convened on February 4, 1789. Ten states cast votes. North Carolina and Rhode Island had not yet ratified the Constitution, so they were unable to weigh in. New York inexplicably failed to pass legislation regarding the appointment of its eight electors, so it also missed the chance to take part. Each elector received two votes. When the votes were counted, Washington had received sixty-nine—a unanimous result. John Adams came in second with thirty-four votes and was elected vice president.

Charles Thomson, the secretary of Congress, was dispatched to bring the news to Mount Vernon. One imagines his tall, stately figure approaching the estate—a visitor who was expected and somewhat dreaded. Washington accepted the result, and two days later he was headed for New York. He wrote a melancholy entry in his diary:

About ten o'clock, I bade adieu to Mount Vernon, to private life, and to domestic felicity and, with a mind oppressed with more anxious and painful sensations than I have words to express, set out for New York in company with Mr. Charles Thompson, [sic] and Colonel Humphreys, with the best dispositions to render service to my country in obedience to its call, but with less hope of answering its expectations.

Martha stayed behind. After Washington departed, she wrote a morose letter to her nephew John Dandridge, revealing her true feelings. "I am truly sorry to tell that the General is gone to New York," she wrote. "When, or whether he will ever come home again God only knows." She and Nelly, ten, and Wash, eight, would join him in New York in mid-May; at that point Martha would assume the duties of First Lady, which she once described as akin to being "a state prisoner."

The president-elect's eight-day journey to New York became something of a processional, as Washington was welcomed with great fanfare along the way. He was feted by friends and neighbors at Wise's Tavern in Alexandria and greeted by crowds as he passed through Baltimore and into Delaware.

The liveliest welcome was in Philadelphia, a city whose post-convention spirit had not abated. Washington was, in a sense, an adopted son, and Philadelphians celebrated him with all their might, amid cannon fire and pealing church bells. The *Pennsylvania Gazette* reported that the numbers of citizens who "filled the doors, windows and streets [were] greater than on any other occasion we ever remember."

A dinner was arranged at the City Tavern, the convention delegates' favorite haunt, and many toasts were offered, punctuated by
artillery and a band. Washington spent that night at the home of
Robert Morris.

Traveling on through Trenton, the site of one of his greatest
victories, Washington was astounded by the dramatic welcome. An
arch had been built over the bridge at Assunpink Creek, painted
with these grand words: "The Defender of the Mothers will also
Defend the Daughters." As he began to ride across the bridge, a
group of women and young girls, dressed in white, appeared before
him singing, as girls with baskets scattered petals in his path:

> Welcome, mighty Chief! once more
> Welcome to this grateful shore! . . .
> Virgins fair, and Matrons grave,
> Those thy conquering arms did save, . . .
> Strew, ye fair, his way with Flowers,
> Strew your Hero's way with flowers.

Finally, he reached the wharf in Elizabethtown, across from
New York, where a forty-seven-foot presidential barge, decked out
in patriotic bunting, awaited. It began its journey accompanied by
six other barges carrying members of Congress and other dignitar-
ies. The festive flotilla was accompanied by music, including one
song set to the tune of "God Save the King."

> Hail, thou auspicious day!
> For let America
> Thy praise resound.
> Joy to our native land!
> Let every heart expand,
> For Washington's at hand.

Notably, this version of uncertain origins seems to have been spontaneous to the day. Decades later, in 1831, Samuel Francis Smith would pen more permanent lyrics to the tune—the verses we know as "My Country 'Tis of Thee."

Washington was emotional about the reception, the journey across the waters recalling so many memories. As he later wrote:

The display of boats which attended and joined us on this occasion, some with vocal and some with instrumental music on board; the decorations of the ships, the roar of cannon, and the loud acclamations of the people which rent the skies, as I passed along the wharves, filled my mind with sensations as painful (considering the reverse of this scene, which may be the case after all my labors to do good) as they are pleasing.

At last, Washington was delivered to his temporary home, Franklin House, at No. 3 Cherry Street, near the East River, where guests were entertained for hours with wine and punch. He would stay there for five days, with barely a moment to himself in that time.

At sunrise on April 30, artillery sounded from Fort George at Bowling Green. At 9:00 a.m., bells began ringing from the city's churches every half hour.

At 12:30, a military escort arrived at Franklin House to collect Washington, who was modestly dressed in a plain brown broadcloth suit. He stepped into his carriage, which set off for Federal Hall, accompanied by a large procession. There were congressional representatives, the ministers of France and Spain, and countless citizens who had turned out to witness the momentous occasion. A full military parade followed, five hundred strong, including a troop of horses, artillery, two companies of grenadiers, a company of light infantry, and a company of Scottish Highlanders in traditional dress.

Arriving at Federal Hall, Washington was escorted to the Senate Chamber, with its high arched ceiling and stately windows, where he was presented to both houses of Congress. John Adams led him to his chair. Adams had accepted his role of vice president graciously, tamping down the ego that made taking second place difficult for him. At fifty-three, he had spent many years abroad feeling neglected and even forgotten. Now he would take his seat at the center of the new government.

Prone to pessimism and worry, Adams approached his new role with more trepidation than elation. He might not have known that his doubts were shared by none other than Washington, who constantly feared that he was not up to the task before him. Adams did know that his life would improve when Abigail arrived in early summer, and this was equally true for Washington. Martha's presence would make life easier.

Washington's plain suit was embellished for the occasion with a dress sword and silver buckles on his shoes. Brown broadcloth was apparently the style of the day: Adams wore it too. He led Washington out to the balcony. Below them, a throng of ten thousand roared its approval.

Washington's friend Robert Livingston, now chancellor of New York State, stepped forward to administer the oath of office. With his right hand on a Masonic Bible, procured for the occasion, Washington spoke the words of the presidential oath for the first time in its history:

I do solemnly swear that I will faithfully execute the office of President of the United States, and will, to the best of my ability, preserve, protect, and defend the Constitution of the United States. ["So help me God" was added later.]

Washington was not an orator. The timbre of his voice was low and slow, with a slight hiss from his poorly fitted dentures. But he wanted to give an address after he took the oath of office, to put his stamp on the next four years. He knew that the nation was still divided, and he wanted the inauguration to be a unifying moment. As most American citizens could not witness it for themselves and would only read accounts days or weeks later, he planned that his address would tell them where they were headed and reassure them about his intentions.

Back at Mount Vernon, Humphreys had helped him write a lengthy speech. The draft, seventy-three pages long, contained hefty recommendations for governance.

Madison took one look and scrapped it, creating a much shorter speech, unladen with policy recommendations. It was only fourteen hundred words, and given Washington's slow-paced diction, would have taken around fifteen minutes to deliver.

The significance of the moment was tremendous, even as the air of the orator was understated. He stood before them in his brown suit, no crown upon his head. It was the point when any hint of a monarchy fully receded, and the government of the people took power.

It's obvious that Washington had unity in mind, as if his words could reach out and bring all sides together. By reminding them that they were a people uniquely formed under divine providence, he could help them transcend their differences.

His words were humble.

No people can be bound to acknowledge and adore the invisible hand which conducts the affairs of men more than the people of the United States. Every step by which they have advanced to the character of an independent nation, seems to have been distinguished by some token of providential agency.

And later:

> The sacred fire of liberty and the destiny of the republican model of government are justly considered, perhaps, as deeply, as finally, staked, on the experiment entrusted to the hands of the American people.

For the critics of federalism, the most satisfying line in the address was its single policy recommendation, proposing the adoption of constitutional amendments. (Behind the scenes, Madison was introducing the necessity he had known was coming.)

> I shall again give way to my entire confidence in your discernment and pursuit of the public good; for I assure myself that whilst you carefully avoid every alteration which might endanger the benefits of an united and effective government, or which ought to await the future lessons of experience, a reverence for the characteristic rights of freemen and a regard for the public harmony will sufficiently influence your deliberations on the question how far the former can be impregnably fortified or the latter be safely and advantageously promoted.

Washington then announced that, during his entire career in public service, he had never taken compensation for his work, and he intended to continue that practice. He concluded with yet another appeal to the Almighty:

> . . . the benign Parent of the Human Race in humble supplication that, since He has been pleased to favor the American people with opportunities for deliberating in perfect tranquility, and dispositions for deciding with unparalleled unanimity on a form of government for the security of their union and the

advancement of their happiness, so His divine blessing may be equally conspicuous in the enlarged views, the temperate consultations, and the wise measures on which the success of this Government must depend.

After Washington finished speaking, the procession headed for St. Paul's Chapel nearby for a Divine Service and Te Deum, celebrated by the Episcopal bishop of New York, who also served as chaplain to the Senate.

Afterward, Washington joined Livingston at the latter's home to watch the fireworks light up the skies. He was back at Franklin House by ten o'clock, and might have spent the late hours contemplating his new position. The nation had its president, and Washington had his lonely mission. He would begin work on the next day, the first of May, 1789.

Massachusetts congressman Fisher Ames, who would become a reliable documenter of the nation's early years, recorded a vivid account of Washington's demeanor that day and the impact he made on Congress. "Time has made havoc upon his face," he noted. "That, and many other circumstances not to be reasoned about, conspire to keep up the awe which I brought with me." He found the scene touching, the mannerisms of their new president affecting. "His aspect grave, almost to sadness; his modesty, actually shaking; his voice deep, a little tremulous, and so low as to call for close attention." Ames reported that he was not the only member of Congress who was openly moved.

PART FOUR

THE LIVING REPUBLIC

Chapter Thirteen

THE FIRST TERM

Washington had been in office for several months before Congress got around to deciding on his official title. Although the word "president" had been used in the interim, it was not considered a formal title. That determination had yet to be made. A committee in the Senate debated the issue for some time, with Vice President John Adams a much-interested party. The House review was more democratic, designating the chief executive's title as simply "the President of the United States." But the senators were looking for something grander. Urged on by the vice president, who was president of the Senate, the committee landed on: "His Highness, the President of the United States of America and Protector of the Rights of the Same." Quite a mouthful, but even shortened to His Highness, it didn't sit well.

In the House, Madison watched this exercise with disgust and wrote about it to Jefferson. Weighing in from France, Jefferson replied caustically, "The president's title as proposed by the senate was the most superlatively ridiculous thing I ever heard of. It is a proof the more of the justice of the character given by Doctor

Franklin of my friend [referring to Adams]: 'always an honest man, often a great one but sometimes absolutely mad.'" Jefferson, now embroiled in the early months of the French Revolution, suggested that Americans should be mindful of their long fight for freedom.

Adams's argument for more elevated titles did not endear him to many of his colleagues. Perhaps his years as minister to Great Britain had distanced him from populist and egalitarian trends that had so influenced the ratification process. In sum, the ratification debate centered on a fear that a strong federal government could slip into a monarchial-style form of rule. Now here was the vice president, tossing around grandiose, kingly titles.

Senator William Maclay of Pennsylvania, no fan of Adams and something of a watchdog against the slightest hint of excessive power, kept a diary of life in the early Senate, which is among the only surviving records. Maclay, a witty and incisive orator and scribe, recorded his disdain for lofty titles, comparing the impulse to elevate America's leaders to the collapse of republicanism that brought down Rome.

In the end, democratic impulses won out, and the Senate agreed with the House on the title President of the United States.

Adams was disappointed and could not help but think himself misunderstood. They were all feeling their way, trying on this governmental system they had devised in theory and now had to put in practice—inventing the US government as they went along.

The first president–vice president pairing was a case study in opposites. Physically the two men couldn't have been more different: Washington tall and stately with a reserved manner and serene blue eyes, and Adams short and stocky with mobile features. Their personalities were contrasting, too—Washington remote and Adams by turns fiery and self-involved.

Washington the Southerner and Adams the New Englander were representative of the cultures and concerns of their places of origin, and many Americans appreciated the fairness of having a mixed North–South team, rather than two Southerners or two New Englanders in those offices.

Although generally acknowledged to be intellectually brilliant, Adams often let his emotions get the better of him, and his acerbic comments made him hard to take. He was respected, though not especially beloved. As Maclay uncharitably described his affect, "When he is at loss for expressions (and this he often is, wrapped up, I suppose, in the contemplation of his own importance) . . . [he] suffers an unmeaning kind of vacant laugh to escape him."

Adams was miserable in those early days, alone and missing Abigail and feeling beset on all sides. Worst of all, the president, with whom he might have forged a partnership, was as remote as ever. Only when Abigail finally arrived, in late June, did he begin to settle in. Happily, Abigail was easily accepted, especially by Martha, and the Adamses soon were making regular appearances at the Washington table and settees.

When he first took office, Washington found the social obligations overwhelming. Americans took their citizens' government to heart, embracing the idea that the president was one of them, not their better. Many of them thought nothing of dropping by to see him whenever they wanted. Washington wrote to David Stuart, a Virginia politician and friend, that it was nearly impossible for him to get anything done, "for, by the time I had done breakfast, thence 'till dinner, and afterwards 'till bed time, I could not dispatch one (ceremonial) visit before I was called to another."

His private secretary, Tobias Lear, tried to sort things out, but Washington struggled to function amid the bedlam. He wrote that the house was in a "state of the greatest confusion—pulling down—putting up—making better and making worse."

Lear was tenacious, though. He'd been with the Washingtons for a few years, initially as a tutor (recommended by Ben Lincoln) for the grandchildren, then as Washington's personal secretary. In time, he'd become indispensable and as close to the Washingtons as if he were a member of their family. He was devoted, well organized, and determined to overcome the chaos of his boss's life in New York. Eager for Martha to arrive and help settle things, Lear sent word through nephew George Augustine that her favorite seafood was in abundance in the capital: "Oysters and lobsters make a very conspicuous figure upon the table, and never go off untouched. Tell Madam Washington this."

The urgent matter of the president's public levees had to be settled before he was consumed by the clamoring masses. It was decided that the doors would be open each week for two hour-long gatherings of men, one on Tuesday and one on Friday. Once Martha arrived, the Friday reception was changed to a more informal three-hour social hosted by the First Lady, with women as well as men in attendance. Coffee, tea, and cake were served in the cooler months, and lemonade and ice cream when it got warmer.

Observing Washington at these gatherings, Abigail Adams had nothing but praise for the president: "He is polite with dignity, affable without formality, distant without haughtiness, grave without austerity, modest, wise, and good."

Martha had barely settled into life in New York when her husband suffered an alarming medical scare. Washington's condition was agonizing—what he described as "a very large and painful tumor on the protuberance of my thigh," which made it difficult to walk or sit. (The "tumor," which was a subcutaneous anthrax, was actually located on his buttock; the report of its location on the thigh was probably an attempt to preserve dignity.)

It was serious—large, deep, and infected. There was only one treatment possible, the complete excavation and removal of the mass. It was a harrowing prospect in an era before anesthesia.

On June 17, two doctors, Dr. John Bard and his son, Dr. Samuel Bard, arrived to perform the operation. The son began to cut, Washington remaining silent and unflinching. With no end in sight, Bard paused, not knowing if he should go on, but his father urged him: "Cut away—deeper, deeper still!" The son continued slicing. "Don't be afraid," his father said. "You see how well he bears it."

Once the mass was removed, Washington's recovery was in question for some time. According to the younger Dr. Bard, the infection was "so malignant as for several days to threaten mortification [gangrene]." At one point, Washington demanded that the doctor give an honest opinion about his chances of survival, telling him in a calm, steady voice, "Do not flatter me with vain hopes; I am not afraid to die, and therefore, can bear the worst." Dr. Bard told him he was right to worry, yet he was hopeful. Washington's recovery took weeks, and the effects of the illness lingered for months. During that time he summoned his reserves of strength for the important task at hand. Every action was stamped with destiny in those early days.

Some of Madison's congressional colleagues might have preferred a delay on the question of amendments to the Constitution, once ratification had been achieved. Most federalists still didn't see the point, and few relished another lengthy battle. But Madison considered the bill of rights a congressional priority. And he had promised his fellow Virginians that amendments would be considered in the first Congress.

Madison had become a true believer in a bill of rights. Although he had voiced strong reservations during the convention about the need for amendments, the ratification process had convinced him. He was well aware that several states, including his own, would not have ratified the Constitution without the promise of amendments. Two states, Rhode Island and North Carolina, had still not voted for ratification, presumably waiting for action on amendments.

On May 4, Madison rose to announce that he planned to introduce the topic of amendments on May 25. His announcement had an immediate effect, as passionate forces within the new Congress were already angling for a different solution. The next day, the antifederalist Virginian Theodorick Bland, a friend of Patrick Henry, presented a petition from a faction of Virginians calling for a second constitutional convention. Bland proposed that this new convention address "the defects of this Constitution that have been suggested by the state conventions, and report such amendments thereto, as they shall find best suited to promote our common interests, and secure to ourselves and our latest posterity, the great and unalienable rights of mankind."

This was a direct slap in the face to Madison, and it was followed a day later by a second petition, from New York representative John Laurance, also promoting a new convention. In the coming days, both congressmen would push for the matter to be taken up by the whole Congress.

Madison argued that they were out of order. According to the Constitution, Congress was bound to call for a new convention only if two-thirds of the states made a petition, which clearly had not happened.

Back and forth they went, but Madison's reference to the Constitution proved to be the final word. Out of respect, however, the petitions were entered into the record and kept on file.

The path was now clear for Madison's discussion of constitutional amendments. When he rose on June 8 to deliver the speech of his lifetime, he had confidence that he was well prepared for the moment.

He began with an apology.

> If I thought I could fulfill the duty which I owe to myself and
> my constituents, to let the subject pass over in silence, I most
> certainly should not trespass upon the indulgence of this
> house. But I cannot do this; and am therefore compelled to
> beg a patient hearing to what I have to lay before you. And I
> do most sincerely believe that if congress will devote but one
> day to this subject, so far as to satisfy the public that we do not
> disregard their wishes, it will have a salutary influence on the
> public councils, and prepare the way for a favorable reception
> of our future measures.

He invoked a spirit of inclusiveness, pointing out that a large
constituency had expressed the desire for amendments.

> It cannot be a secret to the gentlemen in this house, that,
> notwithstanding the ratification of this system of govern-
> ment by eleven of the thirteen United States, in some cases
> unanimously, in others by large majorities; yet still there is a
> great number of our constituents who are dissatisfied with it;
> among whom are many respectable for their talents, their
> patriotism, and respectable for the jealousy they have for
> their liberty, which, though mistaken in its object, is laudable
> in its motive.

Even apart from the desires of the citizenry, Madison acknowledged, there was something far more fundamental about the need
for amendments. To anyone looking into the future, it was clear
that no single, inalterable document could last for the ages. It was
important that the American Constitution, born of a revolutionary

belief in liberty and the democratic rights of a free people, be adaptable to the times.

> But I will candidly acknowledge, that, over and above all these considerations, I do conceive that the constitution may be amended; that is to say, if all power is subject to abuse, that then it is possible the abuse of the powers of the general government may be guarded against in a more secure manner than is now done, while no one advantage, arising from the exercise of that power, shall be damaged or endangered by it.

Fearing that the amendments would be considered less significant, an afterthought to the Constitution, Madison recommended that they be textually incorporated into relevant sections of the main body, not stand apart. This became a troubling distraction as congressmen tried to imagine how and where these alterations might fit, and whether they could be done without undermining the entire Constitution. Roger Sherman of Connecticut was the most outspoken critic of the plan, and in the end, Madison lost that battle. The amendments would appear at the end of the Constitution—a good thing, as this might have opened the door to rampant tinkering with the main document. As time would tell, the status of the Bill of Rights as an independent document would achieve a place in the hearts of Americans approaching the sacred. From then on, all amendments (twenty-seven of them to date) would be separate.

Madison concluded his speech by moving that the proposal be sent to a committee of the whole, so the entire House could debate it in the open. He had barely finished speaking when the objections began, rapid and fierce. How could Congress consider amendments when the government itself was barely formed? James Jackson of Georgia argued, "The Constitution may be compared to a ship that has never yet put to sea—she is now laying in the dock—we have had no trial as of yet; we do not know how she may steer." And even if a discussion of amendments was warranted, why not send the matter to a dedicated committee for a full review rather than consuming the entire body's time?

Others feared that an open discussion of amendments would upset the fragile peace that had been achieved since ratification. No one wanted a repeat of that tempestuous time.

Madison countered with the plain fact that the ratifying conventions of different states had demanded it. Five states had already proposed amendments for congressional review. Congress could not now turn its back on the sincere expectations of the people that had made the new government possible.

After weeks of discussion, the House voted to send the matter to a select committee, composed of one representative from each state—eleven members in all. This had not been what Madison wanted.

A substantial number of representatives continued to believe that the whole exercise was silly—that the freedoms proposed of religion, speech, the press, and so forth were indeed self-evident. Theodore Sedgwick of Massachusetts mocked the process: "They might have declared that a man should have a right to wear his hat if he pleased, that he might get up when he pleased, and go to bed when he thought proper."

After complaining to his friend Richard Peters, who had served in the Continental Congress, Madison was delighted to receive from him a letter containing a lengthy poem, which Peters dubbed "The Wise Cooks and Foolish Guests." It served as a parable for the current congressional dissent:

Eleven Cooks assembled once
To make a Treat of Soup
All knowing—not a Dunce Among the skilful Group.
The Soup was made—delicious! good!
Exclaim'd each grateful Guest,
But some who would not taste the Food,
Declar'd it wanted Zest.
Among those Malcontents were found
Some faulting each Ingredient
While others eager search'd around
To find out some Expedient
With which at once to damn the whole
Not take it in Detail.
They would not sup a single Bowl
Lest more they dare not rail.
At Length the Grumblers all fell out
In Nothing could agree
Not e'en while making of a Rout
of what the Soup should be.
They curse the Cooks & hungry rave
for those of better Skill—
Another Mess some swear they'll have
On which they'll freely swill . . .

Madison's spirits briefly lifted. The poem aptly reflected his own reality. Yet he could not fail to take the criticisms personally, and flinch as he saw his carefully constructed prose stripped apart and rewritten. He felt worn down and found the process "nauseous." His old hypochondria threatened.

Worried that another fight in the states lay ahead, Massachusetts's Fisher Ames expressed his fondest desire: "I wish to have every American think the union so indissoluble and integral, that the corn would not grow, nor the pot boil, if it should be broken."

The amendments first went for review to the House, where their number was pared down to seventeen. They were then passed to the Senate, where the total was further reduced. A joint House and Senate committee took on the task of reconciling the differences before sending the document to the president. On October 2, 1789, Washington signed off, sending the final twelve amendments to the states for ratification. Three-fourths of the states had to approve them.

The ratification process took more than two years. To Madison's immense satisfaction, Virginia had the honor of becoming the tenth and decisive state to ratify, on December 15, 1791. By then, however, the amendments had been further altered. The first two—one revising the formula for congressional representation, the other restricting Congress from changing its pay while in session—were dropped. (A version of the latter would be ratified in 1992 as the twenty-seventh amendment.)

Summarized, the ten amendments in the Bill of Rights included:

1. Freedom of religion, speech, the press, and assembly; and the right to petition the government.

2. The right to bear arms.

3. The right to not have soldiers quartered in a private home.

4. The right to be secure against unreasonable search and seizure.

5. The right to due process, a determination of a grand jury, protection against self-incrimination, and protection against double jeopardy.

6. The rights of the criminally accused to a speedy trial, legal representation, an impartial jury, and other protections.

7. The right to jury trial in civil suits.

8. Protection against excessive bail or fines and cruel and unusual punishment.

9. Enumeration of certain rights in the Constitution does not deny rights not enumerated.

10. The powers not delegated to the nation or prohibited by the Constitution are reserved to the states.

While the creation of the Bill of Rights was a triumph of legislative collaboration, Madison's determination was chiefly responsible for making it happen. It can truly be said that, at the moment when the Bill of Rights was ratified, Madison had rescued the Constitution in his own way. His force of will and eloquence created the opportunity for Washington to preside over a less fractured nation.

Even so, it seemed that, in the early days of the republic, every issue held an exaggerated sense of importance and an accompanying risk of conflict. For example, George Mason had not given up his opposition to the Constitution. If anything, he had only become more strident. He called Madison's amendments "a farce" and accused him of pandering to the people to secure reelection. Ironically, Mason's own work in promoting amendments had laid a foundation in Virginia that ultimately led to Madison's proposal. But Mason viewed the amendments as inadequate. He believed that the Constitution needed large structural changes. Yet he was on the outside, with little power to act.

In June 1789, Mason had extended an olive branch to Washington, although it was wrapped in a patronage request—a position for his son's business partner. He ended his letter, "And should anything occur, in which I can render you any service here, I beg you will command me, without reserve, as I can truly say there is not a man in the world who more sincerely wishes you every felicity." Unfortunately, the president was in the midst of his medical crisis and was unable to respond. It's uncertain whether Washington ever received the message, and Mason received a reply from Lear. He took it as an affront.

In some respects, Mason was a tragic figure. A brilliant man who was at Washington's side as they created a brave framework for action in the early revolutionary days, he had grown incapable of trusting his brethren, seeing deceit and bad faith at every turn. Sadly, his relationship with Washington was never restored.

From his home in Virginia, Mason watched the new government take shape without having a voice in its direction. He was known to snipe about the pomp and formality that went on in New York—the useless ceremonies and high living that he saw as an insult to the nation's nobler purpose. He no doubt cringed to hear, in early 1790, that the Washingtons moved to a larger and fancier residence on lower Broadway, previously occupied by the French minister. It gave them more room to comfortably entertain at their weekly soirées and regular dinners. Mason's harsh judgment ignored what he knew of his friend's character based on their long friendship. Washington was completely disinterested in the trappings of his office and often found them uncomfortable. When possible, he tried to avoid the fanfare that accompanied him everywhere, more interested in meaningful relationships and authentic conversation around his dining table.

In Congress, too, discomfort lingered about the office of the presidency, fueled by the adulation of those who would canonize Washington. Senator Maclay was determined to hold the presidency to democratic principles but often found others blatantly disinterested in doing so.

Maclay detailed a conversation involving Adams, senators Ellsworth and Ames, and himself. Adams and Ellsworth were convinced that the president was immune from any proceeding against him. He was, in effect, above the law.

Maclay put a question to the others that might perk up modern ears: "Suppose the President committed murder in the street. Impeach him? But you can only remove him from office on impeachment [you say]. Why, when he is no longer President you can indict him. But in the meantime he runs away. But I will put up another case. Suppose he continues his murders daily, and neither House is sitting to impeach him. Oh, the people would rise and restrain him [you say]. Very well, you will allow the mob to do what legal justice must abstain from."

Adams dismissed Maclay's suggestion, protesting that such a scenario would be nearly impossible. As evidence, he pointed out that there had been hundreds of crowned heads in the past two centuries in Europe, with no instances of them committing murder.

"Very true, in the retail way, Charles IX of France excepted," Maclay replied. "They generally do these things on a great scale. I am, however, certainly within the bounds of possibility, though it may be improbable."

New York senator Philip Schuyler (a former general in the Continental Army and Hamilton's father-in-law) joined the conversation, and Maclay put the question to him. "I am not a good civilian, but I think the President a kind of sacred person," Schuyler replied.

Maclay was satisfied that his point was proven. The thread of monarchial sentiment was still strong in America's leadership.

• • •

Like many strong leaders, Washington favored an advisory council of diverse experience and opinions. Disagreements and conflict didn't bother him. They could sometimes illuminate a truer direction.

Washington had practiced this principle of leadership as commander of the Continental Army for his war councils and now sought to repeat it in his cabinet. As detailed by Lindsay M. Chervinsky, Washington usually assembled a war council in the dining room at his headquarters or at a tavern out in the field. He quickly learned that advisors advise but do not decide. It was his job to gather the best opinions available and then choose a course of action. In some cases, he sought written opinions, a way to give everyone—even the less loquacious—a chance to state their case.

As president, Washington resurrected the most effective elements of those war councils. His choices were among the most elite and well-qualified men in the nation. The original cabinet consisted of four men: Alexander Hamilton as secretary of the treasury, Thomas Jefferson as secretary of state, Henry Knox as secretary of war, and Edmund Randolph as attorney general.

The president's cabinet is not mentioned in the Constitution, but Article II, Section 2, provides that the president "may require the opinion, in writing, of the principal officer in each of the executive departments, upon any subject relating to the duties of their respective offices."

An innocuous passage, which seems obvious. Of course, the president should consult the department heads for their opinions. Inevitably, though, these advisors would attain power in their own right.

Washington was always painfully aware that every organizational choice he made set a precedent. He knew that every executive innovation would be heavily scrutinized, often through the prism of how it compared to the British monarchy. (After all, the Brits had had a cabinet, whose mischievous designs had created hardships in America.) So he began the process carefully and not until after his term was firmly underway.

His first selection was for the treasury. Congress had agreed to a department of the treasury, but many were leery of its function. Washington had always known he'd need a particularly steady hand in this role. On the way to his inauguration, he'd visited in Philadelphia with Robert Morris, whom he had always trusted, especially on matters of finance. He told him, "The treasury, Morris, will of course be your berth. After your invaluable services as financier of the Revolution, no one can pretend to contest the office of secretary of treasury with you." Morris declined for personal reasons but said, "I can recommend to you a far cleverer fellow than I am for your minister of finance, in the person of your former aide-de-camp, Colonel Hamilton."

Washington was taken aback by this unexpected recommendation. "I always knew Colonel Hamilton was a man of superior talents, but never supposed that he had any knowledge of finance," he said doubtfully.

Morris reassured him. "He knows everything, sir; to a mind like his nothing comes amiss."

Hamilton had big ideas for the financial health of the nation, which he saw as necessarily reliant on the strength of its business elites. He believed that without their support, the system could not achieve greatness. Some within the government preferred to define the United States as an agrarian nation, but Hamilton was focused on its abundant commercial opportunities.

Beneath this optimism, however, Hamilton felt a rising dread over the nation's debt. The states were being crushed by it. Hamilton knew that unless the United States had a strong central financial system—supported in part by federal taxes—which could take responsibility for the debts of the states, it might not survive. The idea was incendiary. States that had already paid their war debts (Virginia being one of them) were outraged at the prospect of being dragged into debt payment for the others. And everybody hated taxes. Bringing a federal system of finance into being would be Hamilton's greatest challenge.

Thomas Jefferson was in his final days in Paris when he learned that Washington had him in mind for a new role. "In the selection of characters to fill the important offices of government in the United States," Washington wrote, "I was naturally led to contemplate the talents and disposition which I know you to possess and entertain for the service of your country." Jefferson at first rejected the idea of serving as secretary of state, having the mistaken impression that the job meant overseeing all domestic matters.

He could not imagine himself in such a position: he was focused on the larger world, particularly the upheaval in France. He had been there at the start of the French Revolution in 1789, just as the US government was beginning, and it had been a tumultuous period both professionally and personally. He had supported the French Revolution—how could he not? He recognized in their struggle the same human quest for freedom and self-determination that had sparked America's revolt. He had collaborated with Lafayette in designing strategies, ultimately to little effect. The storming of the Bastille shocked Jefferson, but he soon came to see that it was a legitimate action. Although there was little he could contribute, he never stopped being on the side of the revolution. He reluctantly sailed for home on September 27, 1789.

He left behind his diplomatic work and the friendships he'd enjoyed but brought home a woman who had become important in his life. Much has been made of Jefferson's relationship with the slave woman Sally Hemings. She had been sent to Paris in 1787 at the age of fourteen to work as a domestic in his household, and over the years she bore him at least six children, four of whom survived to adulthood. Some accounts have characterized it as a romance of equals. It was hardly that, though no one really knows what the lonely widower felt for this woman, or she for him.

The man who wrote that "all men are created equal" operated his plantation and organized his personal life through the labor of hundreds of enslaved people. He sometimes spoke out against the system of slavery but seemed to feel that he had little leverage in altering it. His relationship with the young Hemings began in Paris; when he was preparing to return to the states, she was sixteen and pregnant. Knowing that she had a right to petition for freedom in France, she at first refused to return to Virginia. Jefferson persuaded her with the promise that she would receive "extraordinary privileges" along with freedom for her unborn children.

As he sailed toward America, Jefferson contemplated his home in Monticello and his plans to retire there. But when he landed at Norfolk, Virginia, on November 23, he learned to his shock that Washington had nominated him as secretary of state. Still believing that the role would require him to oversee domestic affairs, he was distressed. He wrote to Washington that "when I contemplate the extent of that office, embracing as it does the principal mass of domestic administration, together with the foreign, I cannot be insensible of my inequality to it: and I should enter on it with gloomy forebodings from the criticisms and censures of a public . . . sometimes misinformed and misled."

To correct Jefferson's mistaken view of the job description, Washington enlisted Madison, depending on the latter's close friendship with Jefferson to be persuasive. Traveling to Monticello, Madison assured Jefferson that his primary occupation as secretary of state would be foreign diplomacy. Simultaneously, Washington wrote to Jefferson that no other man could better fill the role.

Jefferson reluctantly agreed to join the new government, just as Washington had earlier. But no sooner had he arrived in New York than he discovered a troubling trend. As Jefferson began to mingle with the political and business elite, he heard an undercurrent of conversation that sounded undemocratic. "Politics were the chief topic, and a preference of kingly, over republican, government, was evidently the favorite sentiment," he wrote. "An apostate I could not be, nor yet a hypocrite: and I found myself, for the most part, the only advocate on the republican side of the question, unless, among the guests, there chanced to be some member of that party from the legislative houses."

But Jefferson's real conflict was with Hamilton, and the feeling was mutual. Jefferson couldn't stand Hamilton's imperial airs and his thirst for power; both felt un-American to him. Hamilton thought Jefferson pompous and remote, and after five years in France, out of touch with American ways. Joanne B. Freeman, professor of history at Yale University, offers this insight:

> Hamilton was many things that Jefferson was not: aggressive, confrontational, openly ambitious. The same holds true in reverse. Jefferson was many things that Hamilton was not: indirect, somewhat retiring, apt to work behind the scenes. Hamilton thus saw Jefferson as sneaky and hypocritical, someone with wild ambition who was very good at masking it. And Jefferson saw Hamilton as a wildly ambitious attack dog who would hammer his way into getting what he wanted.

With all the drama around Jefferson and Hamilton, other cabinet members have gotten less attention. However, Secretary of War Henry Knox was tremendously influential: a loyal lieutenant to General Washington, he was now to perform that role for the president. Knox came to the job with a wealth of hard-won knowledge about the costs of war. He had experienced firsthand the grievous fate of an army poorly supported by its government, whose pleas for resources and equipment went unanswered. Under the Articles of Confederation, the government lacked power to stand behind its army. This experience made Knox a confirmed federalist and a believer in the necessity of a strong central government.

The final member of Washington's first cabinet was Attorney General Edmund Randolph. Technically, Randolph didn't oversee a department; the Department of Justice wasn't created until 1870, during Ulysses S. Grant's presidency. However, Randolph was a friend of Washington's, had introduced the Virginia Plan at the Constitutional Convention, and was generally respected in the political world. In a letter of September 28, 1789, asking Randolph to consider the role, Washington was full of praise:

> Impressed with a conviction that the due administration of justice is the firmest pillar of good government, I have considered the first arrangement of the judicial department as essential to the happiness of our country and to the stability of its political system; hence the selection of the fittest characters to expound the laws, and dispense justice, has been an invariable object of my anxious concern.

It was the Senate's job to formulate how the courts would operate, from the Supreme Court to the lower courts. The Judiciary Act, passed and signed by Washington in September 1789, put in place the final leg on the stool. Washington was elated, saying, "I have always been persuaded that the stability and success of the national government, and consequently the happiness of the people of the United States, would depend in a considerable degree on the interpretations and execution of its laws." Now that process was firmly in motion.

Washington's nominee for the first chief justice was John Jay, whose formative contribution to American law resonates to this day. At the time, Jay had attained a stature in the new republic that few could match. One of the Founders, a member of the Continental Congress and at one point its president, and former minister to Spain, he was serving as Washington's secretary of foreign affairs when he was appointed. In nominating him, Washington referred to the judiciary as "the keystone of our political fabric." He also nominated five associate justices, forming a high court of six members.

The Supreme Court of the United States met for the first time on February 2, 1790, in New York City, and twice a year thereafter. Like the other branches of government, it would be a work in progress.

Washington dreamed of a federal city. He imagined a place of distinguished and elegant architecture that would rival the great capitals of Europe, especially London. He spent many years dreaming of this capital, and he had a visionary idea about where it might be located—in an area he loved and which, he felt, could rise to such a magnificent challenge.

Washington was happiest not in confined meeting rooms and parlors but out roaming the beautiful American landscape. He was partial, of course, to the Virginia countryside, to which he had a native son's devotion. So, when the subject arose of where the permanent capital of the United States should be located, he quietly lobbied for land along the Potomac. An emerging debate on the subject was mired in partisan biases and age-old tensions between

North and South. How could a Southern capital meet the needs of the North, especially those in the far northeastern states? Conversely, how could the South be satisfied with a Northern capital? Southerners were already unhappy with the temporary location, New York, which was distant from them both geographically and culturally.

Congress was willing to give Washington a say in the location, but this only heightened the conflict. The president's obvious bias for the Potomac blinded many to the actual virtues of the location. Things seemed to reach an impasse—unless a deal could be made.

Who could have guessed that the partners to forge such a deal would be Hamilton and Jefferson?

On June 20, Jefferson invited Hamilton and Madison to a private dinner at his small rented house on Maiden Lane in lower Manhattan. Considering the animosity between him and Hamilton, the guest list was surprising. But self-interest brought them together. Each had something the other wanted.

Hamilton's grand financial plan was stuck in Congress due to a provision that the federal government would assume the states' debts. Southern congressmen objected on the grounds of fairness. Although the Northern states still held enormous war debt, the Southern states had paid off most of theirs. They saw the measure as one more effort to burden them with Northern debt. Northen legislators, for their part, were highly dubious about locating the nation's capital in a Southern state. So, there they were, in Jefferson's modest rental, finding their way to a deal that would give Hamilton his financial plan and the Virginians their capital. As Jefferson described it: "They came. I opened the subject to them, acknowledging that my situation had not permitted me to understand it sufficiently but encouraged them to consider the thing together. They did so."

Jefferson's self-deprecation, so unlike him, was almost certainly a pose to get the others to talk. He reported:

It ended in Mr. Madison's acquiescence in a proposition that the question [i.e., assumption of the state debts] should again be brought before the House by way of amendment from the Senate, that he would not vote for it, nor entirely withdraw his opposition, yet he would not be strenuous, but leave it to its fate.

And then came the carrot:

It was observed, I forget by which of them, that as the pill would be a bitter one to the Southern states, something should be done to soothe them; and the removal of the seat of government to the Potomac was a just measure, and would probably be a popular one with them, and would be a proper one to follow the assumption.

Hamilton agreed, and the Compromise of 1790 was born. On July 16, Congress passed the Residence Act, declaring that the Potomac River site, straddling Maryland (in the North) and Virginia (in the South), would become the nation's capital. No city existed there. The land was empty; the capital, to be named after Washington in the "District of Columbia," was aspirational. The city and the new form of government practiced there would be built together.

In a further compromise to gain support from Pennsylvania congressmen, it was agreed that the government would move to Philadelphia in the interim, for a period of ten years, while the new capital was designed and constructed from the ground up.

In August, Congress passed the Funding Act: Hamilton's financial plan, which included the assumption of state debts.

Although the land along the Potomac had a special place in Washington's heart, it wasn't just hometown pride that motivated his choice. He was also thinking ahead. The nation was expanding westward, and the permanent seat of government needed to accommodate this. He made the case forcefully to Arthur Young, a British agricultural expert with whom he had a regular correspondence.

[The] Potomac River then, is the center of the Union. It is between the extremes of heat and cold. It is not so far to the south as to be unfriendly to grass, nor so far north as to have the produce of the summer consumed in the length and severity of the winter. It waters that soil, and runs in that climate, which is most congenial to English grains, and most agreeable to the cultivators of them. It is the river, more than any other, in my opinion, which must, in the natural progress of things, connect by its inland navigation (now nearly completed 190 measured miles up to Fort Cumberland, at the expense of £50,000 sterling raised by private subscription) the Atlantic states with the vast region which is populating (beyond all conception) to the westward of it. It is designated by law for the seat of the empire; and must, from its extensive course through a rich and populous country become, in time, the grand emporium of North America.

The New York business and political classes were anguished to be losing the seat of government, with all its advantages. They had been elevated by association with the new government, and their city shone in a favorable light. Now it would take second place to its nemesis, Philadelphia, and ultimately to some anonymous southern acreage on the Potomac. Still, New Yorkers pulled together a respectful sendoff for Washington.

If New York's farewell was solemn, Philadelphia's exuberant welcome in November 1790 was the opposite. The city's bells rang to herald the president's arrival, and its citizens felt that they knew him from his time there in war and during the convention. They had always believed that their city—the birthplace of the Declaration of Independence and the Constitution—was the rightful seat of national government. No doubt, many figured that there was a fair chance that government would remain there. Ten years was a long time.

The Washingtons were pleased with their accommodations in Philadelphia: they rented Robert Morris's beautiful three-story brick home in the center of the city, which they knew well from prior visits. Its public rooms were spacious and attractive, and there was space for a servants' quarters, stables, and a large garden. The Washingtons would live there with their grandchildren and the Lears. Tobias Lear had married his longtime love Mary "Polly" Long in 1790. The couple moved into the Philadelphia house with the Washingtons, and their son, Benjamin Lincoln, was born there in March 1791.

There was some difficulty concerning the enslaved workers the Washingtons brought from Mount Vernon. By law in Pennsylvania slaves could claim freedom after six months' residency. Not wanting to lose theirs, the Washingtons hit on a devious solution: they rotated them through Philadelphia so that none stayed for the required six-month period. The decision was revealing. Although they reportedly treated their enslaved workers well, the Washingtons didn't want to take the chance that they might seek their freedom. Deep down, men like Washington and Jefferson, whose quest for freedom and self-determination had been the great cause of their adult lives, still could not see it for the enslaved—or if they did see it, could not summon the will to act.

During this period of transition, the government was operating fully, including the cabinet, though they'd still held no formal meetings. That would happen for the first time on November 26, 1791, in Washington's private study at the president's house in Philadelphia.

By then, however, the conflict between Hamilton and Jefferson had flared up again. The most serious dispute was over the question of a central bank. Hamilton imagined the "Bank of the United States" as a fundamental stabilizing force for the nation, but the nation was divided on whether such an institution was desirable or even constitutional.

Washington was hearing negative reviews from his closest advisors. Randolph and Jefferson both deemed the bank unconstitutional, Jefferson pointing out that the Constitution did not give Congress the power to create such an entity. Madison also objected on the grounds of unconstitutionality.

Standing alone in the inner circle, Hamilton fought for his bank. He argued that, by its very nature, the government had this authority, as long as the Constitution did not explicitly preclude it.

Hamilton ultimately prevailed, and Congress chartered the Bank of North America on February 25, 1791.

By then, Washington had been persuaded that a national bank was constitutional. But he was growing increasingly troubled by the contentious relationship between the two men upon whom he most relied. He had tried, mostly in vain, to curb their animosities. Finally, he put his thoughts on the need for unity into a strongly worded letter to Jefferson:

> How unfortunate, and how much is it to be regretted . . . that whilst we are encompassed on all sides with avowed enemies and insidious friends, that internal dissension should be harrowing and tearing our vitals. The last, to me, is the most serious—the most alarming—and the most afflicting of the two. And without more charity for the opinions and acts of one another in governmental matters . . . I believe it will be difficult, if not impracticable, to manage the reins of government or to keep the parts of it together: for if, instead of laying

our shoulders to the machine after measures are decided on, one pulls this way and another that, before the utility of the thing is fairly tried, it must inevitably be torn asunder. And, in my opinion the fairest prospect of happiness and prosperity that ever was presented to man, will be lost—perhaps forever!

He wrote in a similar vein to Hamilton. Neither man took the admonishment especially to heart. Washington wasn't telling them anything they didn't already know, and each was convinced that he was right.

The rift between the two men, arising from their deeply embedded core beliefs, seemed impossible to heal, and the atmosphere was tense with their conflict. As Jefferson would later describe that period, "Hamilton and myself were daily pitted in the Cabinet like two cocks."

The conflicts in his cabinet added to the weight of Washington's responsibilities, as he turned sixty and approached the final year of his term. War in Europe and rising tensions at home with some Indian tribes did not ease his mind. Meanwhile, Congress was still arguing about apportionment; legislation it passed on this issue provoked his first presidential veto.

Would he consider a second term? He wanted to return home, and the failing health of George Augustine, whom he'd left as caretaker of Mount Vernon, made this path seem even more desirable.

Martha begged him to retire. She worried about his health and the strains and burdens of a second four years. She longed to be home with him, surrounded by family, again enjoying their happy domestic life. She'd never liked her public role, finding it by turns oppressive and boring. She had mostly abstained from complaining, out of respect for her husband, but she imagined the joy of packing up their house and heading south. She hoped that they might have some years together away from the public obligations.

Washington was torn about the decision and began sending out feelers to those closest to him about his wish to retire. To a man, his cabinet and Madison tried to talk him out of it. The timing couldn't be worse, they argued. Although the government had survived infancy intact, its growing pains became more severe each year. Continued conflicts between the North and South were especially worrisome. "North and South will hang together if they have you to hang on," Jefferson told him. Washington might have wondered if the right time would ever come.

Even with his advisors united in favor of his serving another term, Washington still wasn't convinced, until he received an appeal from a very private source. Martha excepted, Elizabeth Willing Powel was as close as any woman had ever been to Washington. Wealthy, patriotic, and engaged in the struggle, Elizabeth and her husband, Samuel, had been friends of the Washingtons since before the Revolution, and their bond had strengthened over time. The Powels' home in Philadelphia was a haven of relief and comfort as well as intellectual stimulation: Elizabeth's salons were attended by all the great names of the era, and she was present during the Constitutional Convention.

Mrs. Powel and Washington had a special connection. She always knew how to reach him by going to the heart of the matter. For this reason, perhaps only she was capable of uttering the strong words that would point up for him the unmistakable duty of a second term.

Your resignation would elate the enemies of good government and cause lasting regret to the friends of humanity. The mistaken and prejudiced part of mankind, that see through the

medium of bad minds, would ascribe your conduct to unworthy motives. They would say that you were actuated by principles of self-love alone—that you saw the post was not tenable with any prospect of adding to your fame. The Antifederalist would use it as an argument for dissolving the Union, and would urge that you, from experience, had found the present system a bad one, and had, artfully, withdrawn from it that you might not be crushed under its ruins—that, in this, you had acted a politic part.

Bowing once more to his duty and perhaps fortified by Mrs. Powel's letter, Washington left his name in the running.

Already the nation was taking on a different character, one that deeply troubled Washington. There had always been factions—federalist, antifederalist; North, South—but these now solidified into what he viewed as a new and dangerous scourge: political parties. The election of 1792, which took place between November 2 and December 5, was complicated by this phenomenon. The same rules applied as in the first election—an early version of ranked-choice voting, where the highest vote-getter became president and the second-highest vice president. Each elector cast two votes. Washington, running under no party affiliation, received 132 votes—or one vote from each elector. It was his second unanimous victory.

The runner-up position—vice president—was complicated by emerging party loyalties. Adams had the support of the Federalist Party, but nipping at his heels was New York governor George Clinton, Hamilton's nemesis, representing the nascent Democratic-Republican Party. Adams won seventy-seven votes in the Northeast and in some mid-Atlantic states but didn't receive a single vote in Virginia, North Carolina, Georgia, or Kentucky (carved off from western Virginia and admitted to the Union only that June). Clinton received fifty votes, winning New York and several Southern states. Lesser candidates received the remaining votes.

While Adams's vote total was enough for reelection, the partisan division was an omen of things to come. Never again would the government be free of partisan politics.

With his new term set to begin on March 4, 1793, Washington asked his cabinet to advise on what kind of inaugural event would be appropriate the second time around. Jefferson and Hamilton at first suggested that he simply take the oath privately, but Knox and Randolph believed that a public ceremony before Congress was important to the nation. That's what Washington decided on.

On the morning of March 4, he rode alone to the Senate chamber. In style and manner, he sought to downplay the event and normalize this ritual of government—to make it less like a coronation. As he took the oath, administered by Associate Justice William Cushing, Washington embodied a contrast: between his humble posture, as a servant of the people, and an exalted nation that was changing the course of history.

His address was the shortest in history, only 135 words. Wanting to underscore that he served at the pleasure of the people, Washington again made a sincere vow: "This oath I am now about to take, and in your presence: That if it shall be found during my administration of the government I have in any instance violated willingly or knowingly the injunctions thereof, I may (besides incurring constitutional punishment) be subject to the upbraiding of all who are now witnesses of the present solemn ceremony."

There was no parade. Washington returned to the executive mansion and got back to work.

Chapter Fourteen

The Gift of a Peaceful Transition

Washington's first term was a paragon of peace and unity compared to his second.

Even before the nation had successfully completed its second federal election and its leader took his second oath of office, a shadow had spread over the celebration. Overseas, the country that had been its closest ally, and indeed its savior, during the Revolutionary War was in deep trouble. In the months before Washington's second inauguration, the French Revolution had become more violent and chaotic. Those like Jefferson, who found parallels between the American and French revolutions, had trouble squaring the quest for freedom with the latest events—particularly the beheading of Louis XVI, long a friend to America, in January 1793.

Washington's beloved Lafayette, who had become a military leader after the fall of Bastille, had found himself increasingly on the outs, fleeing in 1792 in the hope that he could return to America. But he was caught and imprisoned in Austria and remained there for five years. He and Washington would never see each other again.

The king's execution accelerated the conflicts in Europe, particularly between France and England, the old combatants. On February 1, France declared war on England, Spain, and the Dutch Republic. The eyes of Europe turned to America, wondering what it would do.

There was strong sentiment in many circles that the United States owed France its support. Surely no one appreciated France's role in the victory over Great Britain more than Washington. But he now believed that his responsibility to the American people demanded that the United States remain neutral. The nation would later pay a price for its policy of neutrality, especially among those who saw it as showing favoritism toward Great Britain at the expense of an American ally.

Complicating the situation was the arrival in Charleston, South Carolina, of French diplomat Edmond Charles Genet. Genet was determined to undermine any efforts of the United States toward neutrality and to "liberate" British Canada and the Spanish Americas. Genet's flaming red hair matched his fiery rhetoric. He was willing to make mischief, even inciting violence that he hoped would turn the tide of American opinion. He hired privateers to seize British ships along the US coast and spoke openly about the proposed alliance between America and France—which, among other things, would involve America paying off a hefty war debt.

While Genet was busy being disruptive, Washington issued a Neutrality Proclamation on April 22, declaring, "The duty and interest of the United States require that they should with sincerity and good faith adopt and pursue a conduct friendly and impartial toward the belligerent powers."

When Genet arrived in Philadelphia and met with Jefferson, he was surprised to find the man who he thought most likely to support his cause instead fuming at his interference. Genet's behavior was so outrageous that it was impossible to defend. Reluctantly, Jefferson joined the rest of the cabinet in demanding that Genet be recalled to France. However, the situation there had become so dire that it was clear Genet would be executed if he returned. Washington and Attorney General Randolph granted him safe haven in the United States, and Genet lived there until his death, causing no more trouble.

Jefferson was growing ever more weary of the constant conflict with Hamilton, which erupted with each new issue. They could not stay in their lanes but continued to interfere in each other's domains without hesitation. Jefferson felt that he'd more than done his duty, writing to Madison, "To my fellow citizens the debt of service has been fully and faithfully paid." He added poetically, "The motion of my blood no longer keeps time with the tumult of the world." He was fifty years old, ready to turn the page on this chapter in his life.

Jefferson was living on a small estate on the eastern bank of the Schuylkill River in Philadelphia. Washington visited him there one day, hoping to convince him to stay at the state department. Jefferson let loose with a string of familiar grievances, chief among them the danger of a swing toward monarchy, which he still believed Hamilton was instigating.

Washington reassured Jefferson that no man was more intent on resisting that inclination than he, noting that "the constitution we have is an excellent one if we can keep it where it is . . ."

Jefferson would stay in his post during the coming months, as the nation grappled with a yellow fever epidemic. But on the last day of the year, he submitted his resignation to Washington; it was accepted graciously and with regret. Washington would nominate Attorney General Edmund Randolph as secretary of state, and would nominate William Bradford, a justice of the Pennsylvania supreme court, as attorney general. Both were confirmed.

Not everyone was sorry to see Jefferson go. Adams, once a close friend, wrote: "a good riddance to bad ware." Adams had been distressed by Jefferson's growing susceptibility to conspiracy theories and panic. Jefferson would retire to Monticello, but Adams would not get rid of him so easily. In two years, Jefferson would return to challenge him for the presidency.

A tax rebellion plagued Washington in his second term—the so-called Whiskey Rebellion. In 1791, to the dismay of the antifederalists, Hamilton had proposed an excise tax on whiskey to help keep the government solvent. Washington approved the idea, and Congress passed the Excise Whiskey Tax, taxing domestic and foreign-made alcohol.

It wasn't exactly a fair system. Larger producers were given substantial tax breaks, leaving smaller producers to carry an unequal burden. This led to violence when a Pennsylvania tax collector was assaulted, tarred, and feathered by a group of tax protesters. He survived the ordeal and identified two of the culprits, but the officer who tried to arrest them suffered a similar fate.

Violent incidents continued, and many distillers simply refused to pay the tax. Matters came to a head in the summer of 1794, when a battle between tax collectors and protesters ended with a tax collector named John Neville shooting and killing a distiller named David Miller. A large mob formed, waving what became known as the Whiskey Rebellion flag, featuring thirteen stars and an eagle. They set fire to Neville's home, but he had already fled.

When the rebellion spread to Pittsburgh, having grown to some seven thousand men, Washington realized that the nation was facing a critical moment in its young life. He knew that mob violence had a life and power of its own. The danger could escalate quickly, with the protesters' anger serving as a surrogate for all the partisan battles that were growing by the day. The government could not tolerate violence; it must act decisively and with strength.

When the rebels did not respond to peaceful overtures, Washington had no choice. As he assembled a federal militia—composed of 12,950 soldiers from several states—he understood what a critical act this was. What would be the impact of a federal force marching into a state of the union? Even as the militia was assembling, Washington prayed he wouldn't have to use it. He hoped that the threat and the mere presence of armed troops would quell the rebellion.

His fondest wish was granted. When the militia arrived at Pittsburgh, it encountered a quiet landscape. The rebels had scattered. Only two men were brought to trial for the rebellion, and both were pardoned by Washington. However, the whiskey tax never succeeded; it continued to be subject to protests and a widespread refusal to pay. It was finally repealed in 1802.

One lesson Washington took from the uprising was a conviction that the nation faced a growing danger in the rise of political societies—in effect, political parties. He believed that they represented a departure from the idea that the United States could be truly a *united* nation. The sole purpose of these emerging societies was to stand in opposition to the federalists. Washington was aware of their influence on the Whiskey Rebellion.

As it turned out, the Whiskey Rebellion was only the beginning. Political societies would grow and increase in influence, representing not only opposition to domestic policies but also international affairs. On the face of it, Washington's criticisms of them seem undemocratic. Why should citizens not be free to organize and debate as they chose? Madison, for one, was appalled by Washington's negative view. It was surely romantic to think that each citizen could have an equitable relationship with his government without organizing into groups. Were not political groups an expression of free speech, one of the key principles on which the nation was founded? Did not Washington see that, by criticizing groups that opposed his own views, he was only boosting the society he personally favored—the federalists? Washington may have appreciated these considerations, but the advent of political societies still troubled him.

Much of his attention was consumed with the crisis abroad. Despite the nation's policy of neutrality, the war in Europe began to impinge on the national good. England refused to abide by the 1783 treaty, which held that neutral commercial ships could not be intercepted. As a result, British ships grabbed and impounded hundreds of American vessels, especially those delivering goods to French territories. If anything was provocative enough to trigger another war with the British, this lawless behavior might qualify.

Washington's advisors and federalist members of Congress proposed that Hamilton be sent as an envoy to negotiate with Great Britain. Washington supported the choice at first, but it was soon scrapped when the other side raised its voice. Hamilton might be a federalist hero, but to the republicans he represented an ideological threat—aside from being a man whose temperament wasn't necessarily suited to diplomacy.

A compromise was found in Supreme Court Chief Justice John Jay, who agreed to perform the service while keeping his job on the court—constitutionally questionable but not particularly troubling to Washington or other leaders. Hamilton himself approved.

The negotiations would be delicate. The United States could not be seen to be siding with Great Britain merely in order to enforce the 1783 treaty. The agreement Jay eventually struck with the British would become a tinderbox that threatened to blow up Washington's last years in office.

Much to Washington's disappointment, Hamilton resigned his post at Treasury early in 1795. He left feeling depressed and unsure whether the United States would last. Only forty, he wondered if his best days were behind him. It didn't help that he was as good as broke and desperately needed to stabilize his family's economic picture. After leaving the government, he continued to be a federalist leader and sometime advisor to Washington.

Unknown to most, Hamilton's personal life was also in an uproar. In 1791, as treasury secretary, Hamilton began an affair with Maria Reynolds, a young married woman and a fellow New Yorker. She told him that her abusive husband had abandoned her and their child for another woman; she didn't know how they would survive. Hamilton gave her a small amount of money, and they also began to be intimate. (Hamilton's wife, Eliza, was out of town visiting her father.)

Soon after the affair began, Hamilton received a visit from James Reynolds, Maria's husband. An unsavory character, Reynolds exacted a heavy price to keep the affair secret: he actually encouraged Hamilton to continue seeing his wife and asked for more money. Whether Maria was involved in this extortion is unknown, but Hamilton ended things after a year.

When Reynolds later was arrested for financial fraud, he appealed to Hamilton to intervene, threatening to reveal his secret. Hamilton refused, and Reynolds told his story to then-senator James Monroe, implicating Hamilton in the fraud as well.

Monroe kept Hamilton's secret for several years, while serving abroad as ambassador to France. But in 1797, after Hamilton had resigned and Monroe had recently returned home, the matter came to light when a Senate clerk lied to a journalist named James Callander about Hamilton being involved in an illegal financial scheme. Callander reported that Hamilton's affair was just a cover for insider trading.

Hamilton blamed Monroe for letting the secret out, and the two had a shouting match that nearly led to a duel. Finally, Hamilton chose an unexpected way to clear his name. He revealed all in a pamphlet of his own, telling the world, "The charge against me is a connection with one James Reynolds for purposes of improper pecuniary speculation. My real crime is an amorous connection with his wife, for a considerable time with his privity and connivance, if not originally brought on by a combination between the husband and wife with the design to extort money from me." The confession cleared Hamilton's name of the fraud but scandalized the public and caused great humiliation to Eliza, who was pregnant with their sixth child. She left him for a time, but they ultimately reconciled.

Washington's second term was a happier time for James Madison, who at age forty-three had finally met a woman who captured his heart and loved him back. Dolley Payne Todd was a beautiful, high-spirited widow, seventeen years younger than Madison. With saucy blue eyes and jet-black hair, Dolley was a head turner, popular and much sought after, but her greatest appeal was her charm and social intelligence. Once he laid eyes on Dolley, Madison was determined to court her, despite his own social awkwardness. Their relationship took place almost entirely through intermediaries, but both managed to communicate their growing attraction. For Dolley, Madison felt a blinding love; for him she felt a great respect. She was convinced that marriage to this important but modest man would be good for both of them, and she was right.

Sadly, Madison's relationship with Washington deteriorated during this time, especially over the Jay Treaty. When the document arrived in Philadelphia, in March 1795, Madison was horrified. In exchange for minor concessions, Britain was essentially allowed to proceed with its current policies; the treaty gave it free rein to seize the cargo of neutral ships and included an especially generous hands-off policy on trade. Madison wrote that it was "so full of shameful concessions, of mock reciprocities, and of party artifices that no other circumstances [other] than the peculiar ones which mark our present political situation could screen it from universal execration."

His disgust was shared by Jefferson, who saw Hamilton's influence in the deal—even if he imagined this—and by many others, who could not abide making concessions with the British, especially given the United States' failure to support France. While the federalists in Congress tried to push though approval of the treaty, republicans stood in opposition.

Washington's position was unwavering: while the concessions were painful, the value of avoiding war with Britain outweighed all other considerations. The treaty would ultimately be ratified, but the relationship between Washington and Madison would never recover.

Washington could have served for life, but as the end of his second term neared, he knew it would be his last. By way of an announcement to the nation, on September 19, 1796, he published a statement that would later be known as his Farewell Address.

This final address to the people, which many believe is Washington's greatest, ran a lengthy 7,641 words. He began to prepare it by consulting material written by Madison back in 1792, when Washington had considered stepping down. However, he did not consult Madison personally, as he'd vowed never to ask his advice again. Instead, he turned to Hamilton, who was more than happy to help craft the prose.

He began with lavish praise for the American people and their system of government, asking them to consider some principles that he believed were important to their "felicity as a people." He spoke at length of what united the nation, praising "the unity of government which . . . is a main pillar in the edifice of your real independence, the support of your tranquility at home, your peace abroad, of your safety, of your prosperity, of that very liberty which you so highly prize." But there would be many efforts to undermine this unity, he warned. He urged the nation to stand guard over this "political fortress."

What were the threats to unity? Washington described the "baneful effects" of parties, which he had long considered to be a pernicious force. While acknowledging a widespread belief that parties in free countries could be "useful checks upon the administration of the government," he cautioned against the constant danger of excess embedded in their very nature. Parties could inflame disagreements, heighten resentments, undermine the government, and enliven a "spirit of mischief" that makes it difficult to govern. "A fire not to be quenched, it demands a uniform vigilance to prevent its bursting into a flame, lest instead of warming it should consume."

Organized factions, he said, could lend an artificial appearance of strength, even when they merely represent certain enterprising minorities within the larger community.

On international endeavors, he urged that the nation should "observe good faith and justice toward all nations; cultivate peace and harmony with all." Countering harsh criticism for his failure to intervene in wars abroad in support of America's friend France, he again defended his policy of neutrality. He proposed that the nation should avoid both "inveterate antipathies" and "passionate attachments" in dealing with other nations. (In reality, the world had already grown too small for the United States to sustain its neutrality. A standoff with France during Adams's first term, and the looming War of 1812, would again force America to take sides in a world conflict.)

He ended with a plea for indulgence for all his flaws and mistakes and expressed his hope that "after forty-five years of my life dedicated to its service with an upright zeal, the faults of incompetent abilities will be consigned to oblivion, as myself must soon be to the mansions of rest."

Washington certainly believed that his message to the nation was urgent. What he couldn't have imagined was how significant it would become to his legacy. Its timeliness has survived the centuries. Since 1896, it has been a practice in the US Senate to read the address aloud on Washington's birthday. A member of each party is designated to do the honors on alternating years.

In the 1796 election, the first to test a government without Washington, a fire indeed threatened to consume the process. The dangers of partisanship were on full display in the heated conflict between Federalist Party candidate John Adams and Democratic-Republican Party candidate Thomas Jefferson. Never again would the nation see a unanimously elected president.

After a bitter campaign, Adams won with seventy-one electoral votes, only three more than Jefferson's sixty-eight. Thus, the presidency was won by one party and the vice presidency by the other. Adams would only serve one term; Jefferson defeated him in the election of 1800.

Adams's election was historically significant, too, because for the first time the executive branch changed hands, and it took place without incident. An observer with a front-row seat to Adams's inauguration described the drama of the handover: "There stood the 'Father of the Country.' . . . No marshals with gold-colored scarfs attended him—there was no cheering—no noise; the most profound silence greeted him, as if the great assembly desired to hear him breathe and catch his breath in their hearts."

Although it was Adams's day, Washington still commanded center stage. In stepping aside, he left the nation his greatest gift of all— the model of a peaceful transition of power. Adams appreciated the gravity of the occasion and also the burden he faced. It was "a solemn scene," he wrote to Abigail, "made affecting to me by the presence of the General, whose countenance was as serene and unclouded as the day. He seemed to enjoy a triumph over me. Methought I heard him say, Ay, I am fairly out and you fairly in! See which of us will be happiest."

Jefferson's reflection was more pessimistic. "The President is fortunate to get out just as the bubble is bursting," he observed to Madison in a bout of cynicism.

Washington would never have put it in such a way, but he certainly had earned an appreciation of the challenges of leading a free country. There was no precedent. The men he'd led in the army had operated under a code of obedience, but the free citizens of the United States owed no man such regard. The mandate for civil leadership was not control but service. This required an inner steel, which he had cultivated throughout his life. He strove not to resent the people for their strong voices, their disagreements, their challenges to him. Every conflict offered a new opportunity to fulfill the national purpose.

No one was more eager to return home than Martha Washington. Although suffering from a bad cold, she helped Lear organize a massive packing project in Philadelphia. Most of their worldly goods accumulated in the executive mansion would be sent by ship (the *Salem*), but their traveling party encompassed two overloaded coaches, with children, aides, slaves, a dog, and a parrot. (Describing the collection of travelers in a letter to Lear after they arrived home, Washington joked, "On one side, I am called upon to remember the parrot, on the other to remember the dog. For my own part, I should not pine much if both were forgot.")

The journey home took a week, slowed by frequent crowds that gathered to catch a glimpse of them. As they drew closer to Virginia, Washington was pleased to linger at a place dear to his heart. To the backdrop of a sixteen-gun salute, he rode by the city of Washington, his vision of the future, and saw that the frame of the new president's house was being constructed. As the carriages continued through Virginia, crowds welcomed the Washingtons, ushering them home.

Once at Mount Vernon, they were overwhelmed by domestic pursuits. The first major task was to clean and repair the property. Martha wrote to Humphreys that they'd found "everything in a deranged [condition] and all the buildings in a decaying state."

Repairs and painting were completed in time for the arrival of the *Salem*, with the shipment of furniture and other possessions from the executive quarters in Philadelphia. By all accounts, they were delighted to be back, Martha giddily writing to Lucy Knox that "the General and I feel like children just released from school."

In retirement Washington immersed himself in the working of his land. Barely a day went by when he was not on his horse, riding to different areas and supervising operations. He would have been ecstatic to be left in peace, but the people of the nation too often came knocking on his door. The Washingtons welcomed strangers, no matter who they were, and felt obliged to invite them to dine and spend the night. Hundreds of people accepted their hospitality in each of the two-plus years of his retirement. On a rare occasion when no visitor came, a note to Tobias Lear hints at their crowded life: "Unless someone pops in, unexpectedly—Mrs. Washington and myself will do what I believe has not been done within the last twenty years by us—that is to set down to dinner by ourselves."

The larger world was ever present in Washington's thoughts and interactions, but only once did it threaten to pull him out of retirement. Rising tensions with France had plagued Adams since the start of his presidency. The Jay Treaty, negotiated during Washington's second term, had inflamed the French government with its appeasements to Great Britain, and the conflict was escalating. Belief was growing that America would be pulled into war with France. An attempt to negotiate by dispatching envoys Elbridge Gerry, Charles Cotesworth Pinckney, and John Marshall to Paris had yielded no results. By July 1798, President Adams was facing a "quasi-war" with French privateers, who were seizing American ships in the Caribbean. After some three hundred American merchant ships and their cargos had been seized, the United States retaliated by suspending repayment of its war debt to France.

Adams was widely expected to ask Congress for a declaration of war. Instead, he surprised everyone with a request to appoint George Washington as commander in chief of a new provisional army. It won unanimous approval. "We must have your name," Adams wrote to Washington, after the fact, "if you, in any case will permit us to use it." Tensions would be soothed, Adams hoped, by the single act of bringing Washington's name back into the forefront.

In a striking response, for a man supposedly in his final retirement, Washington quickly rose to the moment. His answer to Adams was almost ebullient: "I cannot express how greatly affected I am at this new proof of public confidence, and the highly flattering manner in which you have been pleased to make the communication." He added that the call to service had come at a time when his declining years limited the prospect of physical service. Even so, because "everything we hold dear and sacred is so seriously threatened," he had decided to accept the commission. He hosted Secretary of War James McHenry at Mount Vernon to discuss the details.

Knowing that it was unlikely that he would personally be on a battlefield, Washington suggested Hamilton as his second in command. Hamilton was experienced, fit, and he wanted the job. However, Adams balked. He had never thought too highly of Hamilton and let Washington know that he preferred Henry Knox, and as president he had the final word. Washington had made it clear to McHenry that his acceptance of the command was contingent on being able to select his own officers. Either Adams did not know of the stipulation or was ignoring it. In fact, Adams resented that the former president would try to infringe on a presidential prerogative. Ultimately, though, Washington got his way.

During a six-week trip to Philadelphia to help organize the army, Washington labored to construct a framework for the new regiments and their officers. His arrival in the city, accompanied by pealing church bells and crowds coming out to greet him, was eerily reminiscent of earlier days.

Attaching Washington's name to the military buildup may have had the desired effect on the French government. On October 1, Gerry arrived back from Paris with the news that France wanted peace. By early 1799, negotiations were well underway, and the possibility of war faded from the public mind. The Treaty of Amity and Commerce was signed on February 6.

Home at Mount Vernon, during what would be his final year of life, Washington stayed deeply immersed in the politics of the day as a committed federalist. Some even suggested that he come out of retirement to run for president against Adams in 1800. Washington wrote to one of these vocal backers that if he were to run, he would be accused of "inconsistency, concealed ambition, dotage— and a thousand more etceteras."

In 1799, Washington completed his last will, leaving the bulk of his estate to Martha, and writing off debts owed to him by extended family members. He was considerate of the public good and his legacy, setting aside land and stocks for the formation of educational institutions. He left his papers to his nephew Bushrod Washington, who was serving as a Supreme Court justice.

Also in his will, Washington freed William Lee, the enslaved man who had served so faithfully as his valet during the war, and he stipulated that his 122 enslaved workers be freed after Martha's death. He provided financial support for those who could not work.

According to David Humphreys, with whom Washington shared his views for a biography that Humphreys was planning, Washington later in his life expressed regret about slavery: "The unfortunate condition of the persons, whose labor in part I employ, has been the only unavoidable subject of regret. To make the adults among them as easy and comfortable in their circumstances as their actual state of ignorance and improvidence would admit, and to lay a foundation to prepare the rising generation for a destiny different from that in which they were born, afforded some satisfaction to my mind, and could not I hoped be displeasing to the justice of the Creator."

Washington's mortal end came suddenly on December 14, 1799, following a two-day ordeal. Lear, who was at his side through his last suffering, faithfully recorded his observations of what occurred, although it must have been painful for him to bear witness to such a personal and national tragedy.

It started innocuously enough on December 12, a bitter day, with rain, snow, and wind battering the former president as he went about his business, riding out to his farms throughout the day. When he returned to Mount Vernon at 3:00 in the afternoon, flushed and wet, with snow hanging from his hair, Lear urged him to change into warm clothes, but Washington shrugged him off, declaring himself dry beneath his greatcoat and unwilling to inconvenience people by delaying dinner. He dined and then spent the evening happily engaged in his usual activities, with correspondence and conversation with Martha in front of a strong fire. There was no sign that he was anything but perfectly well.

The next morning, he awoke with a cold, but considered it little more than an inconvenience. Heavy snow had fallen overnight, so he didn't go out but worked indoors, complaining only of a sore throat and hoarseness. That evening, he seemed cheerful to Lear, who suggested that he take medication before going to bed. Washington dismissed the suggestion: "You know I never take anything for a cold. Let it go as it came."

But in the middle of the night, he woke Martha, complaining of feeling quite ill. His breathing was labored, and his voice was nearly gone. She would have called for help, but he assured her that it could wait until morning. At that point she called Lear, who rose quickly and, at Washington's request, sent for an overseer to come and bleed him—then a standard treatment for all kinds of ailments. His doctor, Dr. James Craik, who had been Washington's personal physician for many years, was also summoned.

As Washington's condition worsened, Craik called for a second doctor, and the president was treated with various remedies, including a gargle of vinegar, sage, and tea, which he choked on and found suffocating. By now, Washington was convinced that he was dying. He sent Martha to bring him the two wills in his desk. He studied them both and asked that one be destroyed, as it was old and superseded by the most current will. He called for Lear and questioned him about various papers, wanting to know if they were in order.

As the afternoon progressed, Washington became weaker. He knew he was dying and said so repeatedly. Lear attended to him, physically turning him on the bed several times so he would be more comfortable. Washington thanked him fervently and expressed concern that he would be tired by the exertion. Lear assured him that he had no thought but to make him comfortable.

"Well! it is a debt we must pay to each other, and I hope when you want aid of this kind you will find it." (Lear's account of Washington's deathbed eloquence is probably exaggerated, given his swollen throat and difficulty in speaking or drinking.)

At 5:00, when Dr. Craik entered the room, Washington said to him, "Doctor, I die hard; but I am not afraid to go. . . ." He lingered until ten p.m. on the evening of December 14, uttering his final words—"Tis well"—before dying. Martha, sitting at the foot of the bed, had known the end was coming. "Tis well," she repeated sorrowfully. "All is now over. I shall soon follow him! I have no more trials to pass through." Her grief was all-consuming, and she would live only two and a half more years.

A heartfelt and homely service was held at Mount Vernon on the fourth day after Washington's passing, before the news had even reached the far-flung citizens of his nation. His family gathered around the coffin, on which lay his sword and Masonic apron. A small group of military officers and Masons served as pallbearers.

In a larger sense, Washington belonged to the American people by his own choice. When called to their aid, he had always chosen to serve. They had come to rely on him to mirror their aspirations and to show them the promise of their government. As the word of his passing spread, hundreds of mourning ceremonies were held in his honor. Chief among these was the official funeral ceremony in Congress. At noon on December 29, trumpets sounded and bells pealed, and a somber band played Handel's Dead March (from his oratorio *Saul*) as the funeral procession made its way through the streets of Philadelphia to the German Lutheran Church.

According to a newspaper report, the procession was led by a riderless horse, escorted by two marines wearing black scarves. The horse, "trimmed with black—the head festooned with elegant black and white feathers the American Eagle displayed in a rose upon the breast, and in a feather upon the head"—carried an empty saddle, holsters, pistols, and boots reversed in the stirrups. Officers of the federal cavalry stationed in Philadelphia followed behind, accompanied by volunteers from local militia.

Congressman Henry Lee, who had served under Washington as a major general (where he earned the nickname "Light Horse Harry"), was selected to give the eulogy. His words, loving and eloquent, illuminated the character of the man they all so admired:

> First in war, first in peace, and first in the hearts of his country-men, he was second to none in the humble and endearing scenes of private life: Pious, just, humane, temperate, and sincere; uniform, dignified, and commanding, his example was as edifying to all around him as were the effects of that example lasting.

Lee had not been present at Washington's deathbed, but he captured those final moments in uplifting prose, reminding his listeners of Washington's steady, brave nature. "His last scene comported with the whole tenor of his life," Lee said. "Although in extreme pain, not a sigh, not a groan escaped him; and with undisturbed serenity he closed his well spent life. Such was the man America has lost. Such was the man for whom our nation mourns."

The new capitol building in the new city of Washington, due for completion in 1800, featured a burial chamber below the rotunda, meant to hold Washington's body. Today it stands empty, as it has for centuries. For his final resting place, Washington chose to remain at home, where he was close to the earth.

AFTERWORD

In Their Footsteps

George Washington was the original great uniter of the United States. He didn't do it in a showy way. He wasn't known for his oratory. But the steady guidance he provided during the nation's formative years was its essential glue. I would argue that, had a different man been our first president—say, John Adams or Thomas Jefferson—the grand experiment might not have survived its infancy. It required not only the right words on paper in the form of a strong constitution but the right person at the helm to implement them. And the great challenge was to do this not in a dictatorial way but through collaboration—finding common ground.

As we've seen, that was no easy task. In the brief era before political parties emerged to formalize a climate of permanent opposition, the pursuit of common ground was the cornerstone of building the nation. In the early days, when the first stirrings of a democratic spirit were felt—years before the start of the war—the Philadelphian John Dickinson, who would become a Founding Father, wrote "The Liberty Song." Its many verses included these lines:

Then join hand in hand brave Americans all,
By uniting we stand, by dividing we fall . . .

Almost a century later, Abraham Lincoln declared, "A house divided against itself cannot stand." Many times in our most recent history, too, we've heard appeals to find common ground. A popular sentiment, often expressed by political figures, is that there is more that unites Americans than divides us. But why does that sentiment so often feel untrue?

Today, we are scrambling to recapture a sense of unity in a fractured time. After January 6, 2021, I began to hear people asking whether or not our Constitution could survive. It is easy to wonder if we are just too divided to make it through the tumult of our times.

If it's instructive and even comforting to look back to our founding days, it's not because they reflect the purity of our national convictions. Our current crisis feels new to us, but it is as old as the republic. Factionalism, extremism, antigovernment movements, and other challenges have always existed. And those who think we live in an unusually violent time never experienced an era where political battles were settled at gunpoint and insults were resolved by duels.

As president, Washington was the nation's best defense against the divisions that continually threatened. He single-handedly defended or rescued the United States on countless occasions.

Such were his achievements that those around him could be forgiven for wishing he would continue in the presidency beyond two terms. But he made a greater impact by leaving than he would have done by staying. As modeled by Washington, the peaceful transition of power has been one of the hallmarks of our republic.

Throughout our history we have fought a constant battle against factions. Madison and others spoke out against the danger of one or another faction assuming too much power. As we've seen, Washington likewise spoke out against partisanship, which he called the greatest threat to the nation's survival.

The Constitutional Convention, under Washington's leadership, was our founding example of people with differing views finding ways to compromise and reach resolution. The Founders disagreed on many critical issues, and yet they chose to compromise in order to form a government. The alternative was anarchy. In statements around the publication of the Constitution, Washington, Franklin, Madison, Hamilton, and others mentioned its flaws before they praised its importance.

In a letter to Samuel Kercheval in 1816, Jefferson articulated an important concept: "Some men look at constitutions with sanctimonious reverence, and deem them like the arc of the covenant, too sacred to be touched. They ascribe to the men of the preceding age a wisdom more than human, and suppose what they did to be beyond amendment. . . . We might as well require a man to wear still the coat which fitted him when a boy, as civilized society to remain ever under the regimen of their barbarous ancestors."

Today, on the eve of our 250th anniversary (in 2026), some people are calling for a new constitutional convention. Is that a good idea? Is it even possible? No less than Justice Antonin Scalia weighed in on the question in 2014: "I certainly would not want a constitutional convention. Whoa! Who knows what would come out of it?" He had a point. We've only had one constitutional convention in our history—in 1787. A whole new convention could open a Pandora's box of issues.

If two-thirds (thirty-four) of the states ask for a constitutional convention, Congress must act to form one, but once it gets underway, there are few controls in place. Remember, the original convention was tasked simply with editing the Articles of Confederation, and it ended up throwing them out completely in favor of an entirely new constitution. In theory, a modern convention could completely dismantle some of the most treasured elements of American democracy—whether those impulses come from the left or the right. It's a sobering prospect.

But let's say we do have a constitutional convention. How would we approach the debates? Would finding common ground even be remotely possible? Let's look at a fascinating experiment that sought to answer those questions.

In 2020, the National Constitution Center conducted an experiment, designed to learn whether scholars from across the political spectrum could find agreement on certain critical and controversial issues. The center assembled three teams of constitutional scholars representing different philosophies: conservative, progressive, and libertarian. Each team was assigned to rewrite the Constitution from scratch.

In the end, none of the teams chose to rewrite the Constitution—only to reform it. No matter what their viewpoints, the scholars approached the Constitution respectfully—which should comfort those who worry about a constitutional free-for-all.

Each of the three came at the task from a unique perspective. The conservative team, comprising two "originalist" law professors, as well as a political theorist and a philosopher of law, noted that a constitution could not resolve all disputes and isn't designed to do so. It mentioned that "reasonable people of goodwill can and do disagree" and stated that the role of the Constitution was to clearly articulate fundamental principles, which is the source of its power.

The progressive team was composed of three prominent authors and professors of law from Georgetown, Columbia, and New York University School of Law. They took the view that the 1787 Constitution "is not completely incompatible with progressive constitutionalism" but thought that its democratic levers should be strengthened wherever possible. The original document established the structure for a constitutional democracy, but the reality of "robust protections for individual rights" must be extended. The team further noted, "We have in some circumstances provided for explicit protections for equality, liberty, and democratic institutions that were not contemplated by the original document or its amendments."

The libertarian team, whose members were a director of constitutional studies at the Cato Institute, a vice dean at the Goldwater Institute, and a vice dean and professor of law at the Brooklyn Law School, saw the original Constitution as essentially a libertarian document. They joked that maybe all they needed to do was add "and we mean it" to the end of every clause.

"Unfortunately," the libertarians wrote, "many parts of our fundamentally libertarian constitution, particularly those that limit federal power, have been more often ignored or cleverly evaded, than honored, especially by court decisions that have perverted the actual meaning of the document's text. Our task was therefore largely to clarify and sharpen those provisions"— citing, among other examples, federal power grabs as reflected in the Commerce Clause, out-of-control spending, and the "imperial presidency."

What's interesting is that, though the teams came from these three different perspectives, they landed on some pretty significant common ground. All agreed on term limits for the Supreme Court, suggesting eighteen years. Conservatives and progressives agreed that the president should be elected by popular vote through a ranked-choice system, dissolving the Electoral College. And all three teams believed in setting more limits on presidential power— especially with regard to executive orders. They viewed these as too much like making law—something the president doesn't have the power to do. (President Obama, faced with an uncooperative Congress, famously said, "I've got a pen and I've got a phone.")

The extent of presidential power is one of the most crucial and controversial issues facing us today, and the increasing use of executive orders is a big part of the concern. According to the American Presidency Project, Washington issued eight executive orders in two terms. Franklin Roosevelt issued 3,721 in twelve years in office, as he launched the New Deal and led the nation into war.

More recent presidents have typically issued them in the hundreds—364 for Clinton, 291 for Bush, 276 for Obama, 220 for Trump, and 102 (so far) for Biden. These numbers do not include informal measures such as signing statements, which effectively change the execution of laws.

Executive orders are often controversial, since they take up initiatives that would have little chance of getting passed into law in Congress. Lincoln's Emancipation Proclamation was an executive order, as was Trump's travel ban on people from Muslim-majority countries. (The Trump travel ban was repealed by a counter executive order from Biden on his first day in office.)

The American people aren't blind. They see these orders as a workaround to the grueling and often unproductive legislative process. And though it feels a bit monarchial for our taste, legislating by fiat usually wins enough approval from supporters to see it through. Everyone knows it will last only until the next president of a different party comes along.

The Supreme Court is also in the crosshairs of controversy, charged with having become politicized. This fear was the reason behind the Founders declining to set terms for the justices. Lifetime Supreme Court terms "during good behavior" were designed to eliminate any hint of political influence. It is doubtful that this would really be an issue if the term were, say, eighteen years. The Founders also were not entirely secure in their understanding of how the Supreme Court would work or how difficult it might be to find qualified candidates. Hamilton, for one, believed that only a "few men" would qualify for the weighty job of judging the constitutionality of laws and actions. That concern is less valid today.

According to the conservative team, the very arrangement meant to take the Supreme Court out of politics actually created the opposite effect:

> Lifetime tenure for Justices has become a serious problem. Some Justices remain in office longer than they should, and many make tactical retirement decisions to ensure replacements from the same political party. The outcome is that one President may have the opportunity to appoint a significant number of Supreme Court Justices, and others might not appoint any.

And what of Congress? Here, just like the Framers, the teams made a variety of recommendations designed to make both bodies more representative. The most unwieldy and unlikely solution came from the progressive team, which recommended reapportionment for the Senate to more accurately reflect the population disparity between large and small states. This is an argument literally as old as the Framers, and the progressive solution is a variation on an idea rejected at the Constitutional Convention: assigning one senator per state plus additional senators based on population. Based on current calculations, those additional senators would go in particularly high numbers to California, Texas, and Florida, at the expense of smaller states. It didn't fly in 1787, and it's hard to imagine that it would fly today, as it would require the cooperation of the smaller states to have any chance of being enacted. The progressive team did make one interesting recommendation, however: to change the terms for House members from two to four years, thereby suppressing the endless political and fundraising cycle.

The conservative team also singled out the Senate for special attention, lamenting that it was becoming less the sober, deliberative body the Framers imagined and more focused on short-term actions with election advantage in mind. Its recommendations—rein in the filibuster, require physical presence, and institute a pledge to serve the common good—fell into that behavioral category.

The libertarians preferred a return to the appointment of senators by the states but did not actually recommend it, since they felt it had virtually no chance of winning public agreement. Most of its recommendations fell squarely into the "we really mean it" category—such as a reiteration that Congress exercise only the powers granted to it in the Constitution.

The Constitution Center's exercise is appealing because most of us agree that the Constitution isn't perfect. New times might require some tinkering—which is why we have amendments. We should not be intimidated by the Constitution or be afraid to read it from a modern perspective. Even originalists would agree with that; otherwise, there would be no free speech protections for the internet.

From far-off Paris, Thomas Jefferson wrote eloquently to James Madison about the legacy of the Constitution and the need to be vigilant, lest it become "an act of force and not of right." He asked whether one generation has the right to bind another.

> . . . Between society and society, or generation and generation there is no municipal obligation, no umpire but the law of nature. We seem not to have perceived that, by the law of nature, one generation is to another as one independent nation to another. . . . On similar ground it may be proved that no society can make a perpetual constitution, or even a perpetual law. The earth belongs always to the living generation. . . .

The horse race politics of today, intensified by a highly partisan media and social media environment, makes adherence to high-minded principles especially difficult. Washington's warnings have proved to be well founded. Were he alive now, he'd be issuing the same warnings about the dangers of partisanship that he gave to his countrymen in his day. It was his special genius to see into the future.

Washington believed that the best way to attain the common ground necessary to govern was to model that approach, and he mostly succeeded, earning trust across the political and de-mographic spectrums. He challenged citizens to regard national unity as "the palladium of your political safety and prosperity." That which provides security. That which allows the nation to thrive.

Unity is what we crave, even in the midst of our divisions. The lessons of the past can lead us back there. When I visited Inde-pendence Hall, where our government was born, I could viscerally feel the push and pull of ideas, the bitter conflicts, and the break-throughs, all happening under the steady eye of Washington. And I could visualize the ultimate consensus, as the Framers lined up, quills in hand, to sign the new Constitution.

The United States has many great monuments and memorials to our history but there is no place quite like Center City in Philadelphia, where the nation's foundations were laid. They come to life in the Georgian style of Independence Hall, an architectural tribute to the Greeks and Romans; the parklike surroundings and mellow streets with their modest houses and abundant historical markers. Philadel-phia is a special city precisely because America was born there.

The president's chair Washington occupied at the Constitutional Convention is on display at Independence Hall, its rising sun emblem in full view, symbolizing the hopes of the convention. In 1787, as the last of the Framers signed the Constitution, Benjamin Franklin was heard to observe, "I have often looked at that picture behind the president without being able to tell whether it was rising or setting. But now at length I have the happiness to know that it is a rising and not a setting sun."

APPENDIX

Washington's Farewell Address
to the People of the United States

SEPTEMBER 17, 1796

Friends and Fellow Citizens:

The period for a new election of a citizen to administer the Executive Government of the United States being not far distant, and the time actually arrived when your thoughts must be employed in designating the person who is to be clothed with that important trust, it appears to me proper, especially as it may conduce to a more distinct expression of the public voice, that I should now apprise you of the resolution I have formed to decline being considered among the number of those out of whom a choice is to be made.

I beg you at the same time to do me the justice to be assured that this resolution has not been taken without a strict regard to all the considerations appertaining to the relation which binds a dutiful citizen to his country; and that in withdrawing the tender of service, which silence in my situation might imply, I am influenced by no diminution of zeal for your future interest, no deficiency of grateful respect for your past kindness, but am supported by a full conviction that the step is compatible with both.

The acceptance of and continuance hitherto in the office to which your suffrages have twice called me have been a uniform sacrifice of inclination to the opinion of duty and to a deference for what appeared to be your desire. I constantly hoped that it would have been much earlier in my power, consistently with motives which I was not at liberty to disregard, to return to that retirement from which I had been reluctantly drawn. The strength of my inclination to do this previous to the last election had even led to the preparation of an address to declare it to you; but mature reflection on the then perplexed and critical posture of our affairs with foreign nations and the unanimous advice of persons entitled to my confidence impelled me to abandon the idea. I rejoice that the state of your concerns, external as well as internal, no longer renders the pursuit of inclination incompatible with the sentiment of duty or propriety, and am persuaded, whatever partiality may be retained for my services, that in the present circumstances of our country you will not disapprove my determination to retire.

The impressions with which I first undertook the arduous trust were explained on the proper occasion. In the discharge of this trust I will only say that I have, with good intentions, contributed toward the organization and administration of the Government the best exertions of which a very fallible judgment was capable. Not unconscious in the outset of the inferiority of my qualifications, experience in my own eyes, perhaps still more in the eyes of others, has strengthened the motives to diffidence of myself; and every day the increasing weight of years admonishes me more and more that the shade of retirement is as necessary to me as it will be welcome. Satisfied that if any circumstances have given peculiar value to my services they were temporary, I have the consolation to believe that, while choice and prudence invite me to quit the political scene, patriotism does not forbid it.

In looking forward to the moment which is intended to terminate the career of my political life, my feelings do not permit me to suspend the deep acknowledgment of that debt of gratitude which I owe to my beloved country for the many honors it has conferred upon me; still more for the steadfast confidence with which it has supported me, and for the opportunities I have thence enjoyed of manifesting my inviolable attachment by services faithful and persevering, though in usefulness unequal to my zeal. If benefits have resulted to our country from these services, let it always be remembered to your praise and as an instructive example in our annals that under circumstances in which the passions, agitated in every direction, were liable to mislead; amidst appearances sometimes dubious; vicissitudes of fortune often discouraging; in situations in which not unfrequently want of success has countenanced the spirit of criticism, the constancy of your support was the essential prop of the efforts and a guaranty of the plans by which they were effected. Profoundly penetrated with this idea, I shall carry it with me to my grave as a strong incitement to unceasing vows that Heaven may continue to you the choicest tokens of its beneficence; that your union and brotherly affection may be perpetual; that the free Constitution which is the work of your hands may be sacredly maintained; that its administration in every department may be stamped with wisdom and virtue; that, in fine, the happiness of the people of these States, under the auspices of liberty, may be made complete by so careful a preservation and so prudent a use of this blessing as will acquire to them the glory of recommending it to the applause, the affection, and adoption of every nation which is yet a stranger to it.

Here, perhaps, I ought to stop. But a solicitude for your welfare which can not end but with my life, and the apprehension of danger natural to that solicitude, urge me on an occasion like the present to offer to your solemn contemplation and to recommend to your frequent review some sentiments which are the result of much reflection, of no inconsiderable observation, and which appear to me all important to the permanency of your felicity as a people. These will be offered to you with the more freedom as you can only see in them the disinterested warnings of a parting friend, who can possibly have no personal motive to bias his counsel. Nor can I forget as an encouragement to it your indulgent reception of my sentiments on a former and not dissimilar occasion.

Interwoven as is the love of liberty with every ligament of your hearts, no recommendation of mine is necessary to fortify or confirm the attachment.

The unity of government which constitutes you one people is also now dear to you. It is justly so, for it is a main pillar in the edifice of your real independence, the support of your tranquility at home, your peace abroad, of your safety, of your prosperity, of that very liberty which you so highly prize. But as it is easy to foresee that from different causes and from different quarters much pains will be taken, many artifices employed, to weaken in your minds the conviction of this truth, as this is the point in your political fortress against which the batteries of internal and external enemies will be most constantly and actively (though often covertly and insidiously) directed, it is of infinite moment that you should properly estimate the immense value of your national union to your collective and individual happiness; that you should cherish a cordial, habitual, and immovable attachment to it; accustoming yourselves to think and speak of it as of the palladium of your political safety and prosperity; watching for its preservation with jealous anxiety; discountenancing whatever may suggest even a suspicion that it can in any event be abandoned, and indignantly frowning upon the first dawning of every attempt to alienate any portion of our country from the rest or to enfeeble the sacred ties which now link together the various parts.

For this you have every inducement of sympathy and interest. Citizens by birth or choice of a common country, that country has a right to concentrate your affections. The name of American, which belongs to you in your national capacity, must always exalt the just pride of patriotism more than any appellation derived from local discriminations. With slight shades of difference, you have the same religion, manners, habits, and political principles. You have in a common cause fought and triumphed together. The independence and liberty you possess are the work of joint councils and joint efforts, of common dangers, sufferings, and successes.

But these considerations, however powerfully they address themselves to your sensibility, are greatly outweighed by those which apply more immediately to your interest. Here every portion of our country finds the most commanding motives for carefully guarding and preserving the union of the whole.

The *North,* in an unrestrained intercourse with the *South,* protected by the equal laws of a common government, finds in the productions of the latter great additional resources of maritime and commercial enterprise and precious materials of manufacturing industry. The *South,* in the same intercourse, benefiting by the same agency of the *North,* sees its agriculture grow and its commerce expand. Turning partly into its own channels the seamen of the *North,* it finds its particular navigation invigorated; and while it contributes in different ways to nourish and increase the general mass of the national navigation, it looks forward to the protection of a maritime strength to which itself is unequally adapted. The *East,* in a like intercourse with the *West,* already finds, and in the progressive improvement of interior communications by land and water will more and more find, a valuable vent for the commodities which it brings from abroad or manufactures at home. The

West derives from the *East* supplies requisite to its growth and comfort, and what is perhaps of still greater consequence, it must of necessity owe the *secure* enjoyment of indispensable *outlets* for its own productions to the weight, influence, and the future maritime strength of the Atlantic side of the Union, directed by an indissoluble community of interest as *one nation*. Any other tenure by which the *West* can hold this essential advantage, whether derived from its own separate strength or from an apostate and unnatural connection with any foreign power, must be intrinsically precarious.

While, then, every part of our country thus feels an immediate and particular interest in union, all the parts combined can not fail to find in the united mass of means and efforts greater strength, greater resource, proportionably greater security from external danger, a less frequent interruption of their peace by foreign nations, and what is of inestimable value, they must derive from union an exemption from those broils and wars between themselves which so frequently afflict neighboring countries not tied together by the same governments, which their own rivalships alone would be sufficient to produce, but which opposite foreign alliances, attachments, and intrigues would stimulate and imbitter. Hence, likewise, they will avoid the necessity of those overgrown military establishments which, under any form of government, are inauspicious to liberty, and which are to be regarded as particularly hostile to republican liberty. In this sense it is that your union ought to be considered as a main prop of your liberty, and that the love of the one ought to endear to you the preservation of the other.

These considerations speak a persuasive language to every reflecting and virtuous mind, and exhibit the continuance of the union as a primary object of patriotic desire. Is there a doubt whether a common government can embrace so large a sphere? Let experience solve it. To listen to mere speculation in such a case were criminal. We are authorized to hope that a proper organization of the whole, with the auxiliary agency of governments for the respective subdivisions, will afford a happy issue to the experiment. It is well worth a fair and full experiment. With such powerful and obvious motives to union affecting all parts of our country, while experience shall not have demonstrated its impracticability, there will always be reason to distrust the patriotism of those who in any quarter may endeavor to weaken its bands.

In contemplating the causes which may disturb our union it occurs as matter of serious concern that any ground should have been furnished for characterizing parties by geographical discriminations—Northern *and* Southern, Atlantic *and* Western— whence designing men may endeavor to excite a belief that there is a real difference of local interests and views. One of the expedients of party to acquire influence within particular districts is to misrepresent the opinions and aims of other districts. You can not shield yourselves too much against the jealousies and heart-burnings which spring from these misrepresentations; they tend to render alien to each other those who ought to be bound together by fraternal affection. The inhabitants of our Western country have lately had a useful lesson on this head. They have seen in the negotiation by the Executive and in the unanimous ratification by the Senate of the treaty with Spain, and in the universal satisfaction at that event throughout the United States, a decisive proof how unfounded were the suspicions propagated among them of a policy in the General Government and in the Atlantic States unfriendly to their interests in regard to the Mississippi. They have been witnesses to the formation of two treaties—that with Great Britain and that with Spain—which secure to them everything they could desire in respect to our foreign relations toward confirming their prosperity. Will it not be their wisdom to rely for the preservation of these advantages on the union by which they were procured?

Will they not henceforth be deaf to those advisers, if such there are, who would sever them from their brethren and connect them with aliens?

To the efficacy and permanency of your union a government for the whole is indispensable. No alliances, however strict, between the parts can be an adequate substitute. They must inevitably experience the infractions and interruptions which all alliances in all times have experienced. Sensible of this momentous truth, you have improved upon your first essay by the adoption of a Constitution of Government better calculated than your former for an intimate union and for the efficacious management of your common concerns. This Government, the offspring of our own choice, uninfluenced and unawed, adopted upon full investigation and mature deliberation, completely free in its principles, in the distribution of its powers, uniting security with energy, and containing within itself a provision for its own amendment, has a just claim to your confidence and your support. Respect for its authority, compliance with its laws, acquiescence in its measures, are duties enjoined by the fundamental maxims of true liberty. The basis of our political systems is the right of the people to make and to alter their constitutions of government. But the constitution which at any time exists till changed by an explicit and authentic act of the whole people is sacredly obligatory upon all. The very idea of the power and the right of the people to establish government presupposes the duty of every individual to obey the established government.

All obstructions to the execution of the laws, all combinations and associations, under whatever plausible character, with the real design to direct, control, counteract, or awe the regular deliberation and action of the constituted authorities, are destructive of this fundamental principle and of fatal tendency. They serve to organize faction; to give it an artificial and extraordinary force; to put in the place of the delegated will of the nation the will of a party, often a small but artful and enterprising minority of the community, and, according to the alternate triumphs of different parties, to make the public administration the mirror of the ill-concerted and incongruous projects of faction rather than the organ of consistent and wholesome plans, digested by common counsels and modified by mutual interests.

However combinations or associations of the above description may now and then answer popular ends, they are likely in the course of time and things to become potent engines by which cunning, ambitious, and unprincipled men will be enabled to subvert the power of the people, and to usurp for themselves the reins of government, destroying afterwards the very engines which have lifted them to unjust dominion.

Toward the preservation of your Government and the permanency of your present happy state, it is requisite not only that you steadily discountenance irregular oppositions to its acknowledged authority, but also that you resist with care the spirit of innovation upon its principles, however specious the pretexts. One method of assault may be to effect in the forms of the Constitution alterations which will impair the energy of the system, and thus to undermine what can not be directly overthrown. In all the changes to which you may be invited remember that time and habit are at least as necessary to fix the true character of governments as of other human institutions; that experience is the surest standard by which to test the real tendency of the existing constitution of a country; that facility in changes upon the credit of mere hypothesis and opinion exposes to perpetual change, from the endless variety of hypothesis and opinion; and remember especially that for the efficient management of your common interests in a country so extensive as ours a government of as much vigor as is consistent with the perfect security of liberty is indispensable. Liberty itself will find in such a government, with powers properly distributed and adjusted, its surest guardian. It is, indeed, little else than a name where the government is too feeble to withstand the enterprises of faction, to confine each member of the society within the limits prescribed by the laws, and to maintain all in the secure and tranquil enjoyment of the rights of person and property.

I have already intimated to you the danger of parties in the State, with particular reference to the founding of them on geographical discriminations. Let me now take a more comprehensive view, and warn you in the most solemn manner against the baneful effects of the spirit of party generally.

This spirit, unfortunately, is inseparable from our nature, having its root in the strongest passions of the human mind. It exists under different shapes in all governments, more or less stifled, controlled, or repressed; but in those of the popular form it is seen in its greatest rankness and is truly their worst enemy.

The alternate domination of one faction over another, sharpened by the spirit of revenge natural to party dissension, which in different ages and countries has perpetrated the most horrid enormities, is itself a frightful despotism. But this leads at length to a more formal and permanent despotism. The disorders and miseries which result gradually incline the minds of men to seek security and repose in the absolute power of an individual, and sooner or later the chief of some prevailing faction, more able or more fortunate than his competitors, turns this disposition to the purposes of his own elevation on the ruins of public liberty.

Without looking forward to an extremity of this kind (which nevertheless ought not to be entirely out of sight), the common and continual mischiefs of the spirit of party are sufficient to make it the interest and duty of a wise people to discourage and restrain it.

It serves always to distract the public councils and enfeeble the public administration. It agitates the community with ill-founded jealousies and false alarms; kindles the animosity of one part against another; foments occasionally riot and insurrection. It opens the door to foreign influence and corruption, which find a facilitated access to the government itself through the channels of party passion. Thus the policy and the will of one country are subjected to the policy and will of another.

There is an opinion that parties in free countries are useful checks upon the administration of the government, and serve to keep alive the spirit of liberty. This within certain limits is probably true; and in governments of a monarchical cast patriotism may look with indulgence, if not with favor, upon the spirit of party. But in those of the popular character, in governments purely elective, it is a spirit not to be encouraged. From their natural tendency it is certain there will always be enough of that spirit for every salutary purpose; and there being constant danger of excess, the effort ought to be by force of public opinion to mitigate and assuage it. A fire not to be quenched, it demands a uniform vigilance to prevent its bursting into a flame, lest, instead of warming, it should consume.

It is important, likewise, that the habits of thinking in a free country should inspire caution in those intrusted with its administration to confine themselves within their respective constitutional spheres, avoiding in the exercise of the powers of one department to encroach upon another. The spirit of encroachment tends to consolidate the powers of all the departments in one, and thus to create, whatever the form of government, a real despotism. A just estimate of that love of power and proneness to abuse it which predominates in the human heart is sufficient to satisfy us of the truth of this position. The necessity of reciprocal checks in the exercise of political power, by dividing and distributing it into different depositories, and constituting each the guardian of the public weal against invasions by the others, has been evinced by experiments ancient and modern, some of them in our country and under our own eyes. To preserve them must be as necessary as to institute

them. If in the opinion of the people the distribution or modifica-
tion of the constitutional powers be in any particular wrong, let it
be corrected by an amendment in the way which the Constitution
designates. But let there be no change by usurpation; for though this
in one instance may be the instrument of good, it is the customary
weapon by which free governments are destroyed. The precedent
must always greatly overbalance in permanent evil any partial or
transient benefit which the use can at any time yield.

Of all the dispositions and habits which lead to political prosperity, religion and morality are indispensable supports. In vain
would that man claim the tribute of patriotism who should labor
to subvert these great pillars of human happiness—these firm-
est props of the duties of men and citizens. The mere politician,
equally with the pious man, ought to respect and to cherish them.
A volume could not trace all their connections with private and
public felicity. Let it simply be asked, Where is the security for
property, for reputation, for life, if the sense of religious obligation *desert* the oaths which are the instruments of investigation
in courts of justice? And let us with caution indulge the supposi-
tion that morality can be maintained without religion. Whatever
may be conceded to the influence of refined education on minds
of peculiar structure, reason and experience both forbid us to
expect that national morality can prevail in exclusion of religious
principle.

It is substantially true that virtue or morality is a necessary spring
of popular government. The rule indeed extends with more or less
force to every species of free government. Who that is a sincere
friend to it can look with indifference upon attempts to shake the
foundation of the fabric? Promote, then, as an object of primary
importance, institutions 'for the general diffusion of knowledge. In
proportion as the structure of a government gives force to public
opinion, it is essential that public opinion should be enlightened.

As a very important source of strength and security, cherish public credit. One method of preserving it is to use it as sparingly as possible, avoiding occasions of expense by cultivating peace, but remembering also that timely disbursements to prepare for danger frequently prevent much greater disbursements to repel it; avoiding likewise the accumulation of debt, not only by shunning occasions of expense, but by vigorous exertions in time of peace to discharge the debts which unavoidable wars have occasioned, not ungenerously throwing upon posterity the burthen which we ourselves ought to bear. The execution of these maxims belongs to your representatives; but it is necessary that public opinion should cooperate. To facilitate to them the performance of their duty it is essential that you should practically bear in mind that toward the payment of debts there must be revenue; that to have revenue there must be taxes; that no taxes can be devised which are not more or less inconvenient and unpleasant; that thee intrinsic embarrassment inseparable from the selection of the proper objects (which is always a choice of difficulties), ought to be a decisive motive for a candid construction of the conduct of the Government in making it, and for a spirit of acquiescence in the measures for obtaining revenue which the public exigencies may at any time dictate.

Observe good faith and justice toward all nations. Cultivate peace and harmony with all. Religion and morality enjoin this conduct. And can it be that good policy does not equally enjoin it? It will be worthy of a free, enlightened, and at no distant period a great nation to give to mankind the magnanimous and too novel example of a people always guided by an exalted justice and benevolence. Who can doubt that in the course of time and things the fruits of such a plan would richly repay any temporary advantages which might be lost by a steady adherence to it? Can it be that Providence has not connected the permanent felicity of a nation with its virtue? The experiment, at least, is recommended by every sentiment which ennobles human nature. Alas! is it rendered impossible by its vices?

In the execution of such a plan nothing is more essential than that permanent, inveterate antipathies against particular nations and passionate attachments for others should be excluded, and that in place of them just and amicable feelings toward all should be cultivated. The nation which indulges toward another an habitual hatred or an habitual fondness is in some degree a slave. It is a slave to its animosity or to its affection, either of which is sufficient to lead it astray from its duty and its interest. Antipathy in one nation against another disposes each more readily to offer insult and injury, to lay hold of slight causes of umbrage, and to be haughty and intractable when accidental or trifling occasions of dispute occur.

Hence frequent collisions, obstinate, envenomed, and bloody contests. The nation prompted by ill will and resentment sometimes impels to war the government contrary to the best calculations of policy. The government sometimes participates in the national propensity, and adopts through passion what reason would reject. At other times it makes the animosity of the nation subservient to projects of hostility, instigated by pride, ambition, and other sinister and pernicious motives. The peace often, sometimes perhaps the liberty, of nations has been the victim.

So, likewise, a passionate attachment of one nation for another produces a variety of evils. Sympathy for the favorite nation, facilitating the illusion of an imaginary common interest in cases where no real common interest exists, and infusing into one the enmities of the other, betrays the former into a participation in the quarrels and wars of the latter without adequate inducement or justification. It leads also to concessions to the favorite nation of privileges denied to others, which is apt doubly to injure the nation making the concessions by unnecessarily parting with what ought to have been retained, and by exciting jealousy, ill will, and a disposition to retaliate in the parties from whom equal privileges are withheld; and it gives to ambitious, corrupted, or deluded citizens (who devote themselves to the favorite nation) facility to betray or sacrifice the interests of their own country without odium, sometimes even with popularity, gilding with the appearances of a virtuous sense of obligation, a commendable deference for public opinion, or a laudable zeal for public good the base or foolish compliances of ambition, corruption, or infatuation.

As avenues to foreign influence in innumerable ways, such attachments are particularly alarming to the truly enlightened and independent patriot. How many opportunities do they afford to tamper with domestic factions, to practice the arts of seduction, to mislead public opinion, to influence or awe the public councils! Such an attachment of a small or weak toward a great and powerful nation dooms the former to be the satellite of the latter. Against the insidious wiles of foreign influence (I conjure you to believe me, fellow-citizens) the jealousy of a free people ought to be *constantly* awake, since history and experience prove that foreign influence is one of the most baneful foes of republican government. But that jealousy, to be useful, must be impartial, else it becomes the instrument of the very influence to be avoided, instead of a defense against it. Excessive partiality for one foreign nation and excessive dislike of another cause those whom they actuate to see danger only on one side, and serve to veil and even second the arts of influence on the other. Real patriots who may resist the intrigues of the favorite are liable to become suspected and odious, while its tools and dupes usurp the applause and confidence of the people to surrender their interests.

The great rule of conduct for us in regard to foreign nations is, in extending our commercial relations to have with them as little political connection as possible. So far as we have already formed engagements let them be fulfilled with perfect good faith. Here let us stop.

Europe has a set of primary interests which to us have none or a very remote relation. Hence she must be engaged in frequent controversies, the causes of which are essentially foreign to our concerns. Hence, therefore, it must be unwise in us to implicate ourselves by artificial ties in the ordinary vicissitudes of her politics or the ordinary combinations and collisions of her friendships or enmities.

Our detached and distant situation invites and enables us to pursue a different course. If we remain one people, under an efficient government, the period is not far off when we may defy material injury from external annoyance; when we may take such an attitude as will cause the neutrality we may at any time resolve upon to be scrupulously respected; when belligerent nations, under the impossibility of making acquisitions upon us, will not lightly hazard the giving us provocation; when we may choose peace or war, as our interest, guided by justice, shall counsel.

Why forego the advantages of so peculiar a situation? Why quit our own to stand upon foreign ground? Why, by interweaving our destiny with that of any part of Europe, entangle our peace and prosperity in the toils of European ambition, rivalship, interest, humor, or caprice?

It is our true policy to steer clear of permanent alliances with any portion of the foreign world, so far, I mean, as we are now at liberty to do it; for let me not be understood as capable of patronizing infidelity to existing engagements. I hold the maxim no less applicable to public than to private affairs that honesty is always the best policy. I repeat, therefore, let those engagements be observed in their genuine sense. But in my opinion it is unnecessary and would be unwise to extend them.

Taking care always to keep ourselves by suitable establishments on a respectable defensive posture, we may safely trust to temporary alliances for extraordinary emergencies.

Harmony, liberal intercourse with all nations are recommended by policy, humanity, and interest. But even our commercial policy should hold an equal and impartial hand, neither seeking nor granting exclusive favors or preferences; consulting the natural course of things; diffusing and diversifying by gentle means the streams of commerce, but forcing nothing; establishing with powers so disposed, in order to give trade a stable course, to define the rights of our merchants, and to enable the Government to support them, conventional rules of intercourse, the best that present circumstances and mutual opinion will permit, but temporary and liable to be from time to time abandoned or varied as experience and circumstances shall dictate; constantly keeping in view that it is folly in one nation to look for disinterested favors from another; that it must pay with a portion of its independence for whatever it may accept under that character; that by such acceptance it may place itself in the condition of having given equivalents for nominal favors, and yet of being reproached with ingratitude for not giving more. There can be no greater error than to expect or calculate upon real favors from nation to nation. It is an illusion which experience must cure, which a just pride ought to discard.

In offering to you, my countrymen, these counsels of an old and affectionate friend I dare not hope they will make the strong and lasting impression I could wish—that they will control the usual current of the passions or prevent our nation from running the course which has hitherto marked the destiny of nations. But if I may even flatter myself that they may be productive of some partial benefit, some occasional good—that they may now and then recur to moderate the fury of party spirit, to warn against the mischiefs of foreign intrigue, to guard against the impostures of pretended patriotism—this hope will be a full recompense for the solicitude for your welfare by which they have been dictated.

How far in the discharge of my official duties I have been guided by the principles which have been delineated the public records and other evidences of my conduct must witness to you and to the world. To myself, the assurance of my own conscience is that I have at least believed myself to be guided by them.

In relation to the still subsisting war in Europe my proclamation of the 22d of April, 1793, is the index to my plan. Sanctioned by your approving voice and by that of your representatives in both Houses of Congress, the spirit of that measure has continually governed me, uninfluenced by any attempts to deter or divert me from it.

After deliberate examination, with the aid of the best lights I could obtain, I was well satisfied that our country, under all the circumstances of the case, had a right to take, and was bound in duty and interest to take, a neutral position. Having taken it, I determined as far as should depend upon me to maintain it with moderation, perseverance, and firmness.

The considerations which respect the right to hold this conduct it is not necessary on this occasion to detail. I will only observe that, according to my understanding of the matter, that right, so far from being denied by any of the belligerent powers, has been virtually admitted by all.

The duty of holding a neutral conduct may be inferred, without anything more, from the obligation which justice and humanity impose on every nation, in cases in which it is free to act, to maintain inviolate the relations of peace and amity toward other nations.

The inducements of interest for observing that conduct will best be referred to your own reflections and experience. With me a predominant motive has been to endeavor to gain time to our country to settle and mature its yet recent institutions, and to progress without interruption to that degree of strength and consistency which is necessary to give it, humanly speaking, the command of its own fortunes.

Though in reviewing the incidents of my Administration I am unconscious of intentional error, I am nevertheless too sensible of my defects not to think it probable that I may have committed many errors. Whatever they may be, I fervently beseech the Almighty to avert or mitigate the evils to which they may tend. I shall also carry with me the hope that my country will never cease to view them with indulgence, and that, after forty-five years of my life dedicated to its service with an upright zeal, the faults of incompetent abilities will be consigned to oblivion, as myself must soon be to the mansions of rest.

Relying on its kindness in this as in other things, and actuated by that fervent love toward it which is so natural to a man who views in it the native soil of himself and his progenitors for several generations, I anticipate with pleasing expectation that retreat in which I promise myself to realize without alloy the sweet enjoyment of partaking in the midst of my fellow-citizens the benign influence of good laws under a free government—the ever-favorite object of my heart, and the happy reward, as I trust, of our mutual cares, labors, and dangers.

G. Washington.

ACKNOWLEDGMENTS

The US Constitution is the product of a remarkable collaboration. It's fitting that *To Rescue the Constitution*, my sixth book and fifth presidential biography, is also a collaboration—the product of a very successful team effort. For the five presidential books, I have had the great pleasure and real honor to work alongside my coauthor and friend, Catherine Whitney. Catherine is an amazing talent who is a dedicated and enthusiastic partner. She shares my desire to reach below the surface and uncover the meaning of these great leaders' lives for our times. We have worked in sync for five books, and I look forward to our next endeavor. I am very thankful for our collaboration. The second invaluable member of our team, also with me for all five presidential books, is my researcher, Sydney Soderberg, who truly is masterful in her ability to dig up historical treasures in presidential libraries and public documents. I call them the nuggets that make the narrative crackle or sing. It's the little things Sydney finds that provides a wonderful person-in-the-room view that we have been able to bring to these books as we look back at different points in history.

Special thanks to the team at Mariner Books, led by our editor, Peter Hubbard. Peter has shepherded all five presidential books through the process, with his penetrating eye for the significant details of history and his interest in capturing the often-unappreciated aspects of the presidents we write about. Thanks to everyone on Peter's team for helping to craft a solid plan for launching this book, especially: Maureen Cole, Tavia Kowalchuk, Jessica Vestuto, Molly Gendell, Benjamin Steinberg, and Renata DiBiase.

In our research, we received help from many people. I want to give special thanks to those at Mount Vernon and the George Washington Presidential Library. I am especially indebted to Douglas Bradburn, PhD, the president and CEO, for his graciousness and support. I also appreciate the efforts of his team, particularly Julie Coleman Almacy, director of public affairs; Samantha Snyder, reference librarian; and Kevin Butterfield, executive director of library programs.

I would also like to thank my agent, Jay Sures, with UTA and my book agent, Byrd Leavell, also with UTA, who both helped steer the project from the beginning.

Thank you to Fox News for allowing me the leeway to spend time on these projects, and for once again producing a one-hour documentary special about the book scheduled to run around the launch (as they have done for each of the other books).

And special gratitude to my family—my beautiful wife, Amy (who I refer to as my coanchor in life), and my two sons, Paul and Daniel. They have been very supportive of this historical addiction I have developed and have been there even when it meant taking time away from them. When people ask me why I am so drawn to these historical stories, my answer always goes back to my hopes and dreams for my sons and the world I really want for them. We can always learn from where we have been and the leadership that steered our country through difficult times. Understanding our history and its relevance to current times is an important step in creating the future we want for our children.

Finally, from my position in the twenty-first century, which often feels like a battleground of ideas, I owe a debt of gratitude to George Washington, who set in motion the template for living and governing that has guided us for almost 250 years. No one knew better than Washington that protecting our values and striving for unity is a constant process that demands our attention and our devotion.

NOTES

Prologue: Where Are the Delegates?

1 "highly vexacious": George Washington to George Augustine Washington, May 17, 1787, ConSource (Constitutional Sources Project), Records of Proceedings in Convention, https://www.consource.org/document/george-washington-to-george-augustine-washington-1787-5-17/.

2 "the superstructure we have been seven years": George Washington to James Madison, 5 November 1786, Founders Online/National Archives, https://founders.archives.gov/documents/Madison/01-09-02-0070.

3 "We are either a united people": George Washington to James Madison, 30 November 1785, Founders Online/National Archives, https://founders.archives.gov/documents/Washington/04-03-02-0357.

3 "From the high ground": George Washington to John Jay, 18 May 1786, Founders Online/National Archives, https://founders.archives.gov/documents/Jay/01-04-02-0159.

3 "for the sole and express purpose": Report of Proceedings in Congress; February 21, 1787, Avalon Project/Yale Law School, https://avalon.law.yale.edu/18th_century/const04.asp.

4 "The great object": George Washington to the States, 8 June 1783, Founders Online/National Archives, https://founders.archives.gov/documents/Washington/99-01-02-11404.

5 "This journey (of more than one hundred miles)": George Washington to Henry Knox, 27 April 1787, Founders Online/National Archives, https://founders.archives.gov/documents/Washington/04-05-02-0149.

5 "To forsake the honorable retreat": James Thomas Flexner, *Washington: The Indispensable Man* (Boston: Little Brown & Company, 1974), 274.

6 "We will give you as little trouble": Robert Morris to George Washington, 23 April 1787, Founders Online/National Archives, https://founders.archives.gov/documents/Washington/04-05-02-0143.

6 "Mrs. Washington is become too domestic": George Washington to Robert Morris, 5 May 1787, Founders Online/National Archives, https://founders.archives.gov/documents/Washington/04-05-02-0159.

7 "I am summoned": George Washington to Henry Knox, 27 April 1787, Founders Online/National Archives, https://founders.archives.gov/documents/Washington/04-05-02-0159.

8 "This great patriot": Carol Sue Humphrey, *The Press of the Young Republic, 1783–1833* (*History of American Journalism*, 2) (Westport, CT: Praeger, 1996), 8.

10 "what the French call": Benjamin Franklin to Thomas Jordan, May 18, 1787, ConSource, Supplementary Records of Proceedings in Convention, https://www.consource.org/document/benjamin-franklin-to-thomas-jordan-1787-5-18/.

10   "to grow": Catherine Drinker Bowen, *Miracle at Philadelphia: The Story of the Constitutional Convention May to September 1787* (Boston: Little Brown & Company 1966), 18.

10   "Not more than four states": George Washington to Arthur Lee, 20 May 1787, Founders Online/National Archives, https://founders.archives.gov/documents/Washington/04-05-02-0173.

11   "Rhode Island . . . still perseveres": George Washington to David Stuart, 1 July 1787, Founders Online/National Archives, https://founders.archives.gov/documents/Washington/04-05-02-0225.

11   "Much is expected by some": George Washington to Thomas Jefferson, 30 May 1787, Founders Online/National Archives, https://founders.archives.gov/documents/Washington/04-05-02-0188.

Chapter One: A Stroke of Destiny

15   "I am now convinced beyond a doubt": Founders Online/National Archives, https://founders.archives.gov/documents/Washington/03-12-02-0628.

16   "I can assure those gentlemen": George Washington to Henry Laurens, 22 December 1777, Founders Online/National Archives, https://founders.archives.gov/documents/Washington/03-12-02-0611.

16   "We hold these truths": Declaration of Independence, America's Founding Documents/National Archives, https://www.archives.gov/founding-docs/declaration-transcript.

17   "America . . . has ever had": George Washington to Patrick Henry, 27 March 1778, Founders Online/National Archives, https://founders.archives.gov/documents/Washington/03-14-02-0300.

18   "In the progress of time": Henry Cabot Lodge, *George Washington, vol. 1* (Boston: Houghton Mifflin Co., 1889).

18   "Nearly every recent biographer": Wayne Whipple, *The Story-Life of Washington: A Life-History in Five Hundred True Stories* (Philadelphia: The John C. Winston Company, 1911), 1.

20   "less swearing": Alexander Spotswood, *Letters of Alexander Spotswood, lieutenant-governor of the colony of Virginia 1710–1722* (Richmond: Virginia Historical Society, 1882–1885), 28.

21   Ferry Farm was not left standing: David Zax, "Washington's Boyhood Home," *Smithsonian* (September 2008), https://www.smithsonianmag.com/history/washingtons-boyhood-home-7113627/.

21   "I cannot tell a lie": Mason Locke Weems, *The Life of Washington* (Augusta, GA: George P. Randolph, 1806), 8–9.

22   He was encouraged to read: J. M. Toner, M.D., ed. *Washington's Rules of Civility and Decent Behavior in Company and Conversation* (Copied from the original). (Washington, DC: W. H. Morrison, 1888).

24   "grave, silent, and thoughtful": David Ramsay, *The Life of George Washington* (New York: Hopkins & Seymour, 1807), 6.

24   "She was an imperious woman": Lodge, *George Washington, vol. 1*.

25   "a woman of small intelligence": Bonnie Angelo, *First Mothers: The Women Who Shaped the Presidents* (New York: William Morrow, 2000), 420.

25   "The matron held in reserve": George Washington Parke Custis, *Recollections and Private Memoirs of Washington* (Washington, DC: William H. Moore, 1859), 130, https://leefamilyarchive.org/arbadosn/reference/custis/index-2.html.

26   "has not a child": George Washington to Benjamin Harrison, 27 March 1781, Founders Online/National Archives, https://founders.archives.gov/documents/Washington/99-01-02-05144.

27   "He had seen with his own eyes": Douglas Southall Freeman, *George Washington: A Biography*. An Abridgement by Richard Hartwell, New York: Simon & Schuster, 1968, 22.

27   "nothing but a little straw": George Washington, "A Journal of My Journey Over the Mountains began Fryday the 11th of March 1747/8," Founders Online/National Archives, https://founders.archives.gov/documents/Washington/01-01-02-0001-0002.

27   There is an intriguing tale: "Law and Order: How a Founding Father Was Robbed," George Washington's Mount Vernon, https://www.mountvernon.org/blog/2018/12/law-and-order-how-a-founding-father-was-robbed.

28   "fickle and merciless ocean": Voyage to Barbados 1751-52, manuscript. Founders Online/National Archives, https://founders.archives.gov/documents/Washington/01-01-02-0002-0005.

28   "perfectly ravished": Ibid.

28   "strongly attacked": Ibid.

29   "this climate has not afforded the relief": Lawrence Washington to William Fairfax, "The Washingtons in Barbados," Founders Online/National Archives, https://founders.archives.gov/documents/Washington/01-01-02-0002-0004.

Chapter Two: The King's Uniform

31   the only statue in existence: George Washington Statue in Waterford, YourErieRoots.com, https://www.yourerie.com/digital-first/digital-exclusive/yourerie-roots/yourerie-roots-george-washington-statue-in-waterford/.

34   "I fortunately escaped": George Washington to John Augustine Washington, 31 May 1754, Founders Online/National Archives, https://founders.archives.gov/documents/Washington/02-01-02-0058.

36   "his Mercies": George Washington, Moncure D. Conway, Julius F. Sachse, Washington Irving, and Joseph Meredith Toner, *The Complete Works of George Washington* (Madison & Adams Press, 2017), 566.

36   a "pocket Venus": Patricia Brady, *Martha Washington: An American Life* (New York: Viking Press, 2005), 32.

37   "I am empowered by your father": Anne Hollingsworth Wharton, *Martha Washington* (New York: Charles Scribner's Sons, 1897), 22.

38   "O, ye gods": Thomas Fleming, *The Intimate Lives of the Founding Fathers* (New York: Smithsonian Books, 2009), 10.

39   "Advance preparations must have involved": Helen Bryan, *Martha Washington: First Lady of Liberty* (Hoboken, NJ: John Wiley & Sons, 2002), 195.

39   "more permanent and genuine happiness": George Washington to Armand, 10 August 1786, Founders Online/National Archives, https://founders.archives.gov/documents/Washington/04-04-02-0190.

40   "I am now I believe fixed at this seat": George Washington to Richard Washington, 20 September 1759, Founders Online/National Archives, https://founders.archives.gov/documents/Washington/02-06-02-0190.

42   "Everyone who does not agree with me": Charles River Editors, *British Legends: The Life and Legacy of King George III* (CreateSpace, 2017), 1.

43   "I recommend to my sons": Jeff Broadwater, *George Mason: Forgotten Founder* (Chapel Hill: University of North Carolina Press, 2006), 19.

Chapter Three: Breaking Point

44   "a born rebel": Ira Stohl, *Samuel Adams: A Life* (New York: Free Press, 2009), 23.

45   "taxation without representation": Ibid., 142.

45   "the Wicked Statesman": Bernard Bailyn, *The Ordeal of Thomas Hutchinson* (Cambridge: Belknap Press/Harvard University Press, 1974), 20.

46   "In the evening whilst I was at supper": John W. Tyler, ed., *The Correspondence of Thomas Hutchinson, vol. 1: 1740–1766* (Boston: Colonial Society of Massachusetts, 2014).

46   "animated with a zeal for their country": Stohl, *Samuel Adams*, 44.

46   "the strongest affection for his Majesty": Ibid., 48.

47 "The year 1765 has been the most remarkable": Diary of John Adams, "Braintree Decr. 18th 1765, Wednesday," Founders Online/National Archives, https://founders.archives .gov/documents/Adams/01-01-02-0009-0005-0001.

47 "born and tempered a wedge of steel": Pauline Maier, "Coming to Terms with Samuel Adams," *American Historical Review* 81, no. 1 (February 1976): 12–37.

48 "was due in part to his temperament": Walter Isaacson, *Benjamin Franklin: An American Life* (New York: Simon & Schuster, 2003), 226.

48 "I said when I was advised to remove": Ibid, 224.

49 "No, never, unless compelled": Excerpts from "Benjamin Franklin's Testimony to Parliament (1766)," Alpha History, https://alphahistory.com/americanrevolution/benjamin -franklins-testimony-parliament-1766/.

49 "To wear their old clothes": Ibid.

50 "Facts are stubborn things": "Adams' Argument for the Defense: 3–4 December 1770," Founders Online/National Archives, https://founders.archives.gov/documents/Adams /05-03-02-0001-0004-0016.

51 "The part I took in defense of Captain Preston": Diary of John Adams, "1773. March 5th Fryday," Founders Online/National Archives, https://founders.archives.gov/documents /Adams/01-02-02-0003-0002-0002.

51 "government is an ordinance of Heaven": Stohl, *Samuel Adams*, 62.

52 "At a time when our lordly Masters": George Washington to George Mason, 5 April 1769, Founders Online/National Archives, https://founders.archives.gov/documents /Washington/02-08-02-0132.

53 "Spirits, Wine, Cyder": George Washington from George Mason, 28 April 1769, Founders Online/National Archives, https://founders.archives.gov/documents/Washington/02 -08-02-0137.

53 "by which the revenue would lose": George Mason to George Washington, 5 April 1769, Founders Online/National Archives, https://founders.archives.gov/documents/Washington /02-08-02-0133.

53 "Mr. Speaker, the Governor commands": Freeman, *Washington*, 176.

54 "Mr. Speaker and gentlemen of the House of Burgesses": Ibid.

55 "the best that the friends to the cause": Ibid.

55 "Unlimited power has generally been destructive": Stohl, *Samuel Adams*, 107.

56 "I never did in my life know a youth": Freeman, *Washington*, 184.

57 "without uttering a word": Ibid.

58 "The next morning, after we had cleared the ships of the tea": Benjamin Bussey Thatcher, *Traits of the Tea Party: Being a Memoir of George R.T. Hewes* (New York: Harper & Brothers, 1835).

58 "The mighty realms were troubled": Oliver Wendell Holmes, "A Ballad of the Boston Tea-Party," *Atlantic* (December 16, 1873), https://www.theatlantic.com/magazine /archive/1874/02/a-ballad-of-the-boston-tea-party/631356/.

59 "the catalyst that set off the revolt": Benjamin Woods Labaree, *The Boston Tea Party* (New York: Oxford University Press, 1964), 22.

59 "There is a dignity": Harlow Giles Unger, *American Tempest: How the Boston Tea Party Sparked a Revolution* (Cambridge: Da Capo Press, 2011), 172.

59 "the cause of Boston": Ibid., 184.

59 "I am truly concerned": Isaacson, *Benjamin Franklin*, 339.

61 "The cause of Boston . . . now is and ever will be": George Washington to George William Fairfax, June 10, 1774, George Washington's Mount Vernon, https://www.mountvernon .org/library/digitalhistory/past-projects/quotes/article/in-short-the-ministry-may-rely -on-it-that-americans-will-never-be-taxd-without-their-own-consent-that-the-cause -of-boston-the-despotick-measures-in-respect-to-it-i-mean-now-is-and-ever-will-be -considerd-as-the-cause-of-america-not-that-we-approve-their-co/.

62 "I stopped one night at a tavern": David McCullough, *John Adams* (New York: Simon & Schuster, 2002), 86.

62 "to rouse the attention": Michael Cecere, "The Rise of Virginia's Independent Militia," *Journal of the American Revolution*, September 18, 2014, https://allthingsliberty.com /2014/09/the-rise-of-virginia-independent-militia/.

62 "regular uniform": Ibid.

Chapter Four: The Colonies Convene

63 "At ten the delegates all met": Diary of John Adams, 1 September 1774, Founders Online/ National Archives, https://founders.archives.gov/documents/Adams/01-02-02-0004-0006.

64 "I am well satisfied": George Washington to Robert McKenzie, 9 October 1774, Founders Online/National Archives, https://founders.archives.gov/GEWN-02-10-02-0112.

64 "Caesar had his Brutus": Freeman, *Washington*, 159.

65 "Fifty gentlemen meeting together": John Adams to Abigail Adams, 25 September 1774, Massachusetts Historical Society, https://www.masshist.org/digitaladams/archive/doc?id=L 17740925ja&hi=1&query=The%20Weather%20has%20been%20and%20held%20 so%20uncommonly%20cold%20ever%20since%20you%20left%20me&tag=text& archive=letters&rec=1125&start=1120&numRecs=1193.

65 "I am not a Virginian, but an American": Thomas Fleming, *Liberty! The American Revolution* (New York: Viking Press, 1997), 93.

67 "a generous tenderness": Journals of the Continental Congress, 1774–1789, "Joseph Galloway's Speech to the Continental Congress, September 28, 1774," Library of Congress/The American Revolution, https://memory.loc.gov/cgi-bin/query/r?ammem/hlaw:@field(DO CID+@lit(jc00120)).

68 "more blood will be spilt": George Washington to Robert McKenzie, 9 October 1774, Founders Online/National Archives, https://founders.archives.gov/GEWN-02-10-02 -0112.

69 "To a sovereign": United States Continental Congress, Petition from the General Congress . . . to the King, October 25, 1774, Gilder Lehrman Collection.

70 "Let the colonies always keep the idea": James Burke, ed., *The Speeches of the Right Honorable Edmund Burke* (Dublin: James Duffy, 1854), 576.

70 "The die is now cast": Don Higginbotham, "The War for Independence," in *The American Revolution* (Washington, DC: National Park Service), 64, https://www.nps.gov /vafo/learn/historyculture/upload/The-American-Revolution-Official-NPS-Handbook _Reduced-Size.pdf.

72 "Gentlemen may cry, Peace, Peace": Patrick Henry, "Give Me Liberty or Give Me Death," March 23, 1775, Avalon Project/Yale Law School, https://avalon.law.yale.edu /18th_century/patrick.asp.

72 "impressive and sublime": Jon Meacham, *Thomas Jefferson: The Art of Power* (New York: Random House, 2012).

73 "begged that I would immediately set off": Paul Revere to Jeremy Belknap [1798], Manuscript Collection, Massachusetts Historical Society, https://www.masshist.org/database /viewer.php?item_id=99&img_step=1&mode=transcript#page1.

73 "O! What a glorious morning": Stohl, *Samuel Adams*, 157.

74 "Never did a people rebel with so little reason": Allen French, *The Siege of Boston* (New York: Macmillan, 1911).

75 "Unhappy it is": George Washington to George William Fairfax, 31 May 1775, Founders Online/National Archives, https://founders.archives.gov/documents/Washington/02-10 -02-0281.

76 "We tremble at having an army": Charles Martyn, *The Life of Artemas Ward: The First Commander-in-Chief of the American Revolution* (New York: Artemas Ward, 1921).

76 "Greene ran his camp": Gerald M. Carbone, *Nathanael Greene: A Biography of the American Revolution* (New York: Palgrave Macmillan, 2008), 22.

78 "Tho' I am truly sensible": George Washington, "Address to the Continental Congress, 16 June 1775," Founders Online/National Archives, https://founders.archives.gov /documents/Washington/03-01-02-0001.

79 "I am now set down to write to you": George Washington to Martha Washington, 18 June 1775, Founders Online/National Archives, https://founders.archives.gov/documents /Washington/03-01-02-0003.

79 "others to wear laurels": Fleming, *The Intimate Lives*, 126.

80 "A few more such victories": Edward J. Larson, *Franklin & Washington: The Founding Partnership* (New York: William Morrow, 2020), 108.

80 "I hope I shall die": Harry Schenawolf, "Doctor Joseph Warren: Patriot Leader Killed at Bunker Hill," *Revolutionary War Journal*, October 1, 2016, https://www .revolutionarywarjournal.com/warren/.

Chapter Five: The Command

83 "The liberties of America": John Adams to Abigail Adams, June 17, 1775, Massachusetts Historical Society, https://www.masshist.org/digitaladams/archive/doc?id=L17750611ja.

84 "I am now embarked": George Washington to Burwell Bassett, 19 June 1775, Founders Online/National Archives, https://founders.archives.gov/documents/Washington/03-01 -02-0006.

84 "As he entered the confines": Washington Irving, *The Life of George Washington, vol. 1* (New York: G. P. Putnam & Co., 1858), 347.

85 "an exceedingly dirty and nasty people": Edward G. Lengel, *General George Washington: A Military Life* (New York: Random House, 2005), 193.

85 "hope that you won't consider yourself": Mark Puls, *Henry Knox: Visionary General of the American Revolution* (New York: St. Martin's Press 2008), 24.

86 "General Washington is a great addition": Ibid., 5.

86 "We found everything exactly the reverse": Worthington Chaunchey Ford, ed., *The Writings of George Washington, vol. 3* (New York and London: G. P. Putnam's Sons, 1889–1893), 14.

88 "The best general advice": George Washington to Colonel William Woodford, 10 November 1775, Founders Online/National Archives, https://founders.archives.gov /documents/Washington/03-02-02-0320.

89 "that there should be officers and soldiers": The Daily Dish, "George Washington and Guy Fawkes Day," *The Atlantic*, September 5, 2007.

90 "You will see a strange oscillation": John Adams to James Warren, 6 July 1775, Founders Online/National Archives, https://founders.archives.gov/documents/Adams/06-03-02 -0037.

90 "With respect to the few": Thomas Fleming, "The Enigma of General Howe," *American Heritage* 15, no. 2 (February 1964).

91 "Awake, arouse, Sir Billy": John Ferling, *Almost a Miracle: The American Victory in the War of Independence* (Cambridge: Oxford University Press, 2007), 189.

91 "This army . . . is truly nothing": Harry Schenawolf, "The Continental Army of the American Revolution: 'A Drunken, Canting, Lying, Hypocritical Rabble,'" *Revolutionary War Journal*, June 6, 2016, https://www.revolutionarywarjournal.com/a-drunken -canting-lying-hypocritical-rabble/.

93 "Come to me": Fleming, *The Intimate Lives*, 36.

93 "Mrs. Washington is excessive fond of the general": Ibid., 38.

94 "Everyone knew his place": George F. Scheer and Hugh F. Rankin, *Rebels & Redcoats: The American Revolution Through the Eyes of Those Who Fought and Lived It* (New York: Da Capo Press, 1987), 107.

95 "We were in high spirits": Ibid.

95 "Remember it is the fifth of March": Ibid.

96 "it is the nexus of the Northern and Southern colonies": John Adams to George Washington, 6 January 1776, Founders Online/National Archives, https://founders.archives.gov /documents/Adams/06-03-02-0200.

96 "Now if upon Long Island": Ibid.

96   "The people—why, the people are magnificent": Puhls, *Henry Knox*, 40.

97   "The unhappy fate of Thomas Hickey": George Washington, General Orders, 28 June 1776, Founders Online/National Archives, https://founders.archives.gov/documents /Washington/03-05-02-0086.

98   "That these United Colonies": Lee's Resolutions, June 7, 1776, Avalon Project/Yale Law School, https://avalon.law.yale.edu/18th_century/lee.asp.

98   "piddling genius": John Adams to James Warren, 24 July 1775, Founders Online/ National Archives, https://founders.archives.gov/documents/Adams/06-03-02-0052.

99   "were not yet ripe for bidding adieu": Thomas Jefferson, "Autobiography," Avalon Project/Yale Law School, https://avalon.law.yale.edu/19th_century/jeffauto.asp.

99   "we had been bound": Ibid., 13.

100 "To Adams independence was the only guarantee": McCullough, *John Adams*, 104.

100 "There is a tide in the affairs of men": Abigail Adams to John Adams, March 10, 1776, Massachusetts Historical Society, https://www.masshist.org/digitaladams/archive/doc?id =L17760302aa.

100 "utter the word independence": Jon Meacham, *Thomas Jefferson: The Art of Power* (New York: Random House, 2012), 150.

100 "We have every opportunity": Thomas Paine, *Common Sense* (Philadelphia: Robert Bell, 1776), https://oll.libertyfund.org/page/1776-paine-common-sense-pamphlet.

101 "I will not": John Adams to Timothy Pickering, 6 August 1822, Founders Online/ National Archives, https://founders.archives.gov/documents/Adams/99-02-02-7674.

101 "not to find out new principles": Thomas Jefferson to Henry Lee, 8 May 1825, Founders Online/National Archives, https://founders.archives.gov/documents/Jefferson/98-01-02-5212.

102 "We hold these truths to be self-evident": Declaration of Independence, America's Founding Documents/National Archives, https://www.archives.gov/founding-docs/declaration -transcript.

103 "When in the course of human events": Ibid.

104 "Future ages will scarcely believe": Jefferson, "Autobiography," 20.

105 "I shall have a great advantage": Dr. Benjamin Rush to John Adams, 20 July 1811, Founders Online/National Archives, https://founders.archives.gov/documents/Adams /99-02-02-5659.

106 "the Declaration of Independence of the United States was read": Eric Burns, *Infamous Scribblers: The Founding Fathers and the Rowdy Beginnings of American Journalism* (New York: PublicAffairs, 2006), 213.

107 "I have a letter, sir": Lengel, *General George Washington*, 234.

108 "Good God! What brave fellows": Ibid., 248.

109 "Upon the whole": Major General Nathanael Greene to George Washington, 9 November 1776, Founders Online/National Archives, https://founders.archives.gov/documents /Washington/03-07-02-0085.

111 "For several hours, the slight, boyish": Willard Sterne Randall, "Hamilton Takes Command," *Smithsonian* (January 2003), https://www.smithsonianmag.com/history /hamilton-takes-command-74722445/.

112 "If Abraham Lincoln had been president of Congress": Lengel, *General George Washington*, 150.

112 "Voltaire has remarked": Thomas Paine, *The American Crisis*, no. 1 (Philadelphia: Styner and Cist, 1776), 14, America in Class, https://americainclass.org/sources/makingrevolution /war/text2/painecrisis1776.pdf.

Chapter Six: "Victory or Death"

113 "This strength, like a snowball": George Washington to John Hancock, 20 December 1776, Founders Online/National Archives, https://founders.archives.gov/documents /Washington/03-07-02-0305.

113 "One of them by accident": Scheer and Rankin, *Rebels and Redcoats*, 211.

114 "Christmas day at night": George Washington to Colonel Joseph Reed, 23 October 1776, Founders Online/National Archives, https://founders.archives.gov/documents /Washington/03-07-02-0329.

114 "I can hardly believe that Washington": David Hackett Fischer, *Washington's Crossing* (New York: Oxford University Press, 2004).

114 "I am sorry to hear": Ibid.

114 "the fate of entire Kingdoms": Captain Johann Ewald, *Diary of the American War: A Hessian Journal* (New Haven: Yale University Press, 1979), 000.

115 "These are the times that try men's souls": Paine, *The American Crisis*, ix.

115 "deep bass voice": James Wilkinson, *Memoirs of My Own Times* (Philadelphia: Abraham Small, 1816).

116 "a part of the army": Henry Knox to Lucy Knox, December 28, 1776, Gilder Lehrman Collection, https://www.gilderlehrman.org/sites/default/files/inline-pdfs/t-02437 -00497.pdf.

117 "About day light": Fischer, *Washington's Crossing*.

118 "My brave fellows": Ibid.

118 "He was aware that his hour was come": Custis, *Recollections and Private Memoirs*, 189.

118 "a model of discipline": Fischer, *Washington's Crossing*.

119 "In this battle and that of Trenton": Sergeant R., "The Battle of Princeton," *Pennsylvania Magazine of History and Biography* 20, no. 4 (1896): 515–519.

119 "Every American friend": Henry Knox to Lucy Knox, 28 December 1776, New Jersey History Partnership, https://nj.gov/state/historical/assets/pdf/topical/war-document -december-28th-1776.pdf.

119 "more destructive to an army": George Washington to Patrick Henry, 13 April 1777, Founders Online/National Archives, https://founders.archives.gov/documents /Washington/03-09-02-0142.

120 "sterling character and clear sense of purpose": Chernow, *Alexander Hamilton*, 88.

121 "majestic figure and deportment": "George Washington and the Marquis de Lafayette," George Washington's Mount Vernon, https://www.mountvernon.org/library /digitalhistory/digital-encyclopedia/article/george-washington-and-the-marquis-de -lafayette/.

122 "Our soldiers have not yet quite the air of soldiers": Freeman, *Washington*, 348.

123 "For years after the battle": Paul Mullin, "The Plunder of Chester County During and After the Battle of Brandywine," *Westtown Gazette*, Summer Issue 2017, https://www .westtownpa.org/wp-content/uploads/2015/05/2017-Summer-The-Plunder-of-Chester -County-During-and-After-the-Battle-of-Brandywine.pdf.

123 "If Congress have not yet left Philadelphia": Alexander Hamilton to John Hancock, 18 September 1777, Founders Online/National Archives, https://founders.archives.gov /documents/Hamilton/01-01-02-0282.

124 "Congress was chased": Chernow, *Washington*, 306.

124 "At 3 this morning": Diary of John Adams, 19 September 1777, Founders Online/ National Archives, https://founders.archives.gov/documents/Adams/01-02-02-0007-0003.

124 "No, Philadelphia has captured Howe": Larson, *Franklin & Washington*, 131.

124 "The feeling that Howe lacked something essential": Robert Middlekauff, *Washington's Revolution: The Making of America's First Leader* (New York: Alfred A. Knopf, 2015), 151.

125 "He put forth several key provisions": Jane E. Calvert, "The John Dickinson Draft of the Articles of Confederation," *Journal of the Early Republic* (9 November 2020), https://thepanorama.shear.org/2020/11/09/the-john-dickinson-draft-of-the-articles-of -confederation/.

125 "firm league of friendship": Articles of Confederation, Library of Congress, https:// guides.loc.gov/articles-of-confederation.

126 "Sir William, he, as snug as flea": Francis Hopkinson, "The Battle of the Kegs," Poetrynook .com, https://www.poetrynook.com/poem/battle-kegs.

126 "Washington 'made dreadful mistakes'": David McCullough, "The Glorious Cause of America," speech at Brigham Young University, September 27, 2005, https://speeches.byu.edu/talks/david-mccullough/glorious-cause-america/.

Chapter Seven: Washington's Crucible

127 "There comes a soldier": Albigence Waldo, "Diary of Dr. Albigence Woldo, a Surgeon at Valley Forge," Albigence Waldo Papers, 1768–1793, Colonial North America at Harvard Library, http://www.let.rug.nl/usa/documents/1776-1785/albigence-waldo-from-the-diary-of-a-surgeon-at-valley-forge-1777.php.

128 "There we shall be quiet": Freeman, *Washington*, 254.

128 "between the axes": Ibid., 373.

128 "No meat!": Ibid., 372.

128 "longing, and hankering": Dr. Peter Cressy and Dr. Edward G. Lengel, *George Washington at Valley Forge*, Mountvernon.org.

129 "Sir we have only passed the Red Sea": Patrick Henry to George Washington, 20 February 1778 [Rush letter to Henry detailed], Founders Online/National Archives, https://founders.archives.gov/documents/Washington/03-13-02-0517.

130 "Heaven has been determined": George Washington to Major General Horatio Gates, 4 January 1778 [citing Conway letter to Gates], Founders Online/National Archives, https://founders.archives.gov/documents/Washington/03-13-02-0113.

130 "My enemies take an ungenerous advantage of me": George Washington to Henry Laurens, 31 January 1778, Founders Online/National Archives, https://founders.archives.gov/documents/Washington/03-13-02-0348.

130 "I know the cruelty of tongues": James R. Gaines, *For Liberty and Glory: Washington, Lafayette, and Their Revolutions* (New York: W. W. Norton & Co., 2008), 96.

130 "I thought that here almost every man": Ibid., 78.

131 "if you will give me your company": Ibid., 112.

132 "the object of my greatest ambition": Friedrich von Steuben to George Washington, 6 December 1777, Founders Online/National Archives, https://founders.archives.gov/documents/Washington/03-12-02-0519.

133 "In the midst of all our distress": Peter S. Duponceau, "Autobiographical Letters of Peter S. Duponceau," *Pennsylvania Magazine of History and Biography* 40, no. 2 (1916), 172–186.

135 "upon a signal given": Gaines, *For Liberty and Glory*, 130.

136 "left to wander like Cain": John H. Rhodehamel, ed., *The American Revolution: Writings from the War of Independence 1775-1783* (Library of America, 2001).

137 "swore that day": Lengel, *General George Washington*, 465.

138 "a cluster of ideas": Thomas Fleming, *The Strategy of Victory: How General George Washington Won the American Revolution* (Cambridge: Da Capo Press, 2017), 2.

138 "courage in the raw": James C. Rees, *George Washington's Leadership Lessons* (Hoboken, NJ: John Wiley & Sons, 2007), 28.

Chapter Eight: The Final Fight

140 "we remain unsupported": David B. Mattern, *Benjamin Lincoln and the American Revolution* (Columbia, SC: University of South Carolina Press, 1995), 88.

142 "Lincoln limped out": Ibid. 107.

142 "bagging the old fox": George Athan Billias, "The fox bagged the hunter," *New York Times*, May 3, 1970, https://www.nytimes.com/1970/05/03/archives/the-fox-bagged-the-hunter-cornwallis.html.

142 "I can give you no particular instructions": Carbone, *Nathanael Greene*, 135.

143 "nothing but a few half-starved soldiers": Ibid., 153.

143 "I arrived at this place": Ibid., 156.

143 "makes the most of my inferior force": Ibid., 157.

144 "Here is Morgan's grave": "Pension application of Dennis Trammel," http://www.revwarapps.org/r10672.pdf.

144 "Just hold up your heads, boys": Carbone, *Nathanael Greene*, 165.

144 "Hide thy face": Ibid., 171.

145 "The enemy got the ground": Carbone, *Nathanael Greene*, 182.

147 "The brightest ornament": "To the President of Congress Headquarters, Orangetown, Tuesday, September 26, 1780," https://www.historycentral.com/Revolt/washreports/092680.html.

149 "put the match": James Thacher, *An Army Doctor's American Revolution Journal 1775–1783* (New York: Dover Publications, 2019).

150 "Shell!": Puls, *Henry Knox*, 107.

150 "Listen to me and you shall hear": "The World Turned Upside Down," lyrics as transcribed in the Thomason Tracts, April 8, 1646.

151 "With what soldiers": Ewald, *Diary of the American War.*

153 "If this, then, be your treatment": Irving, *The Life of George Washington*, 628.

154 "his duty as well": George Washington, General Orders, 11 March 1783, Founders Online/National Archives, https://founders.archives.gov/documents/Washington/99-01-02-10811.

154 "By thus determining": Newburgh Address: George Washington to Officers of the Army, March 15, 1783, mountvernon.org, https://www.mountvernon.org/education/primary-source-collections/primary-source-collections/article/newburgh-address-george-washington-to-officers-of-the-army-march-15-1783/.

154 "I have not only grown gray": Freeman, *Washington*, 501.

155 "Last Thursday noon": "Goodbye to General Washington," Today in History (December 4), Library of Congress, https://www.loc.gov/item/today-in-history/december-04/.

155 "We had been assembled": Colonel Benjamin Tallmadge, *Memoir of Col. Benjamin Tallmadge* (New York: Thomas Holman, 1858), 63.

155 "I cannot come to each of you": Ibid.

155 "Such a scene of sorrow": Ibid.

Chapter Nine: The Unraveling Union

161 "I feel as a wearied traveler": Ron Chernow, *Washington: A Life* (New York: Penguin Books, 2010), 462.

162 "I am retiring": George Washington to Lafayette, 1 February 1784, Founders Online/National Archives, https://founders.archives.gov/documents/Washington/04-01-02-0064.

162 "another of the prices of being a national hero": Freeman, *Washington*, 521.

163 "No sooner did Americans stop fighting": Burns, *Infamous Scribblers*, 226.

164 "The Confederation appears to me": George Washington to James Warren, 7 October 1785, Founders Online/National Archives, https://founders.archives.gov/documents/Washington/04-03-02-0266.

165 "There are persons in this kingdom": John Adams to John Jay, 21 October 1785, Founders Online/Natioal Archives, https://founders.archives.gov/documents/Adams/06-17-02-0275.

165 "What a triumph": George Washington to John Jay, 15 August 1786, Founders Online/National Archives, https://founders.archives.gov/documents/Washington/04-04-02-0199.

166 "The vile state": Douglas Bradburn, *The Citizenship Revolution: Politics and the Creation of the American Union, 1774-1804* (Charlotteville, VA: University of Virginia Press, 2009), 65.

166 "as far remote from truth": Henry Knox to George Washington, 23 October 1786, Founders Online/National Archives, https://founders.archives.gov/documents/Washington/04-04-02-0274.

167 "Good God!": George Washington to Henry Knox, 26 December 1786, Founders Online/National Archives, https://founders.archives.gov/documents/Washington/04-04-02-0409.

167 "That she is at this moment": Ibid.

167 "Are your people getting mad?": George Washington to Benjamin Lincoln, 7 November 1786, Founders Online/National Archives, https://founders.archives.gov/documents/Washington/04-04-02-0304.

168   "Many of them appear to be absolutely so": Benjamin Lincoln to George Washington, 4 December 1786, Founders Online/National Archives, https://founders.archives.gov /documents/Washington/04-04-02-0374-0002.

168   "Both needed a political confidant": Lee Wilkins, "Madison and Jefferson: The Making of a Friendship," *Political Psychology* 12, no. 4 (Dec. 1991): 593–608, International Society of Political Psychology.

169   "the world still presents": Thomas Jefferson to James Madison, 31 August 1783, Founders Online/National Archives, https://founders.archives.gov/documents/Madison/01-07-02 -0167.

169   "As grave an error": Lynne Cheney, *James Madison: A Life Reconsidered* (New York: Penguin Group USA, 2014), 103.

169   "No money is paid": Ibid., 122.

169   "Let prejudices": George Washington to James Madison, 5 November 1786, Founders Online/National Archives, https://founders.archives.gov/documents/Madison/01-09-02 -0070.

170   "Nothing is more common": "A Letter from Phocion to the Considerate Citizens of New York," 1–27 January 1784, Founders Online/National Archives, https://founders .archives.gov/documents/Hamilton/01-03-02-0314.

170   "The world has its eye": https://founders.archives.gov/documents/Hamilton/01-03-02 -0347.

172   "By the enclosed act": Edmund Randolph to George Washington, 6 December 1786, Founders Online/National Archives, https://founders.archives.gov/documents/Washington/04-04 -02-0383.

172   "anarchy and confusion": "George Washington discusses Shays' Rebellion and the Up-coming Constitutional Convention, 1787," The Gilder Lehman Institute of American History, https://ap.gilderlehrman.org/resource/george-washington-discusses-shays%27 -rebellion-and-up#:~:text=-%20If%20government%20shrinks%2C%20or%20is,prob able%20the%20mischiefs%20will%20terminate.

172   "Randolph and Madison played Washington": Pauline Maier, *Ratification: The People Debate the Constitution, 1787–1788* (New York: Simon & Schuster 2010), 3.

173   "wish that at least a door": James Madison to George Washington, 24 December 1786, Founders Online/National Archives, https://founders.archives.gov/documents /Washington/04-04-02-0405.

173   "your presence would confer": Henry Knox to George Washington, 19 March 1787, Founders Online/National Archives, https://founders.archives.gov/documents/Washington /04-05-02-0095.

173   "the intimate companion of my youth": George Washington to Henry Knox, 27 April 1787, Founders Online/National Archives, https://founders.archives.gov/documents /Washington/04-05-02-0149.

174   "My situation is truly afflicting!": Carbone, *Nathanael Greene*, 226.

175   "Nothing but the critical situation": Freeman, *Washington*, 539.

175   "I smelt a rat": Max Farrand, *The Framing of the Constitution of the United States* (New Haven: Yale University Press, 1962), 15.

176   "After the lapse of six thousand years": Ibid., 62.

177   "If to please the people": Ibid., 66.

177   "fatal altercations": Ibid. 57.

Chapter Ten: The Scaffold of a Republic

181   "democracies have ever been spectacles": James Madison, Federalist Paper No. 10, The Federalist Papers (published in the *Independent Journal, New York Packet*, and *Daily Advertiser* between October 1787 and April 1788), https://avalon.law.yale.edu/18th _century/fed10.asp.

182   "On Sunday last": Dennis C. Kurjack, "St. Joseph and St. Mary's Churches," *Transactions of the American Philosophical Society* 43, no. 1 (1953), 199–209.

182 "He spoke more through actions": Edward J. Larson, *The Return of George Washington: Uniting the States, 1783–1789* (New York: William Morrow 2014), 120.

183 "transcendent benevolence": David O. Stewart, *The Summer of 1787: The Men Who Invented the Constitution* (New York: Simon & Schuster, 2007), 112.

184 "The House may not be precluded": Ibid., 51.

187 "national government, consisting of": James Madison, *Journal of the Federal Convention*, vols. 1 and 2.

187 "Thirteen sovereignties": George Washington to James Madison, 5 Novemeber 1786, Founders Online/National Archives, https://founders.archives.gov/documents/Madison/01-09-02-0070.

188 "an able politician": Farrand, *The Framing of the Constitution*, 34.

190 "As there is not the smallest prospect": George Washington to George Augustine Washington, 3 June 1787, Founders Online/National Archives, https://founders.archives.gov/documents/Washington/04-05-02-0197.

190 "Let our government be like that of the solar system": Cheney, *Madison*, 131.

191 "The first man put at the helm": Larson, *Franklin & Washington*, 213.

192 "The worst men": Stewart, *Summer of 1787*, 220.

192 "Whether we are to have a government": George Washington to Lafayette, 6 June 1787, Founders Online/National Archives, https://founders.archives.gov/documents/Washington/04-05-02-0200.

194 "We would sooner submit to a foreign power": A Century of Lawmaking for a New Nation: U.S. Congressional Documents and Debates, 1774-1875, Library of Congress, http://lcweb2.loc.gov/cgi-bin/query/r?ammem/hlaw:@field(DOCID+@lit(fr00191)).

194 "the people are turbulent": Stewart, *Summer of 1787*, 94.

195 "has been praised by everybody": Farrand, *Framing of the Constitution*, 89.

196 "The longer I live": Isaacson, *Benjamin Franklin*, 115.

196 "foreign aid": Bowen, *Miracle at Philadelphia*, 127.

196 "The diversity of opinions": Ibid., 550.

197 "The fate of America": Farrand, *Framing of the Constitution*, 94.

Chapter Eleven: We Have a Constitution

199 "In my passage": Alexander Hamilton to George Washington, 3 July 1787, Founders Online/National Archives, https://founders.archives.gov/documents/Hamilton/01-04-02-0110.

200 "Why did you pour that coffee": Farrand, *Framing of the Constitution*, 74.

200 "This country must be united": Ibid., 99.

201 "I *almost* despair": George Washington to Alexander Hamilton, 10 July 1787, Founders Online/National Archives, https://founders.archives.gov/documents/Washington/04-05-02-0236.

201 "that blacks be included": Farrand, *Framing of the Constitution*, 102.

202 "I cannot regard them as equal": Ibid.

203 "Upon what principle": Ibid.

203 "remember the ladies": Abigail Adams to John Adams, March 31, 1776, Massachusetts Historical Society, https://www.masshist.org/digitaladams/archive/doc?id=L17760331aa.

203 "Depend upon it": John Adams to Abigail Adams, April 14, 1776, Massachusetts Historical Society, https://www.masshist.org/digitaladams/archive/doc?id=L17760414ja.

203 "Acting before the world": https://www.consource.org/document/notes-for-a-speech-by-john-dickinson-ii-1787-7-9/.

204 "It must be kept in view": Farrand, *Framing of the Constitution*, 111.

205 "He wished the Convention might adjourn": Madison Debates, July 16, 1787, Avalon Project/Yale Law School, https://avalon.law.yale.edu/18th_century/debates_716.asp.

205 "So great is the unanimity": *Pennsylvania Packet and Daily Advertiser*, July 19, 1787, ConSource: Supplementary Records of Proceedings in Convention, https://www.consource.org/document/pennsylvania-packet-and-daily-advertiser-1787-7-19/

206 "it would be as unnatural": Farrand, *Framing of the Constitution*, 116.

206 "We seem to be entirely at a loss": Ibid., 117.

208 One day Morris was boasting: Ibid., 22.

209 "Her dignity is lowering": Lafayette to George Washington, 3 August 1787, Founders Online/National Archives, https://founders.archives.gov/documents/Washington/04-05 -02-0259.

209 "I remain in hopes": Thomas Jefferson to George Washington, 14 August 1787, Founders Online/National Archives, https://founders.archives.gov/documents/Jefferson/01-12-02 -0040.

210 "We the People": Constitution of the United States, Library of Congress, https:// constitution.congress.gov/constitution/preamble/.

211 "Who authorized them to speak": Patrick Henry at the Virginia Ratifying Convention, June 4, 1788, Bill of Rights Institute.

211 "Should all the states adopt it": Ibid.

211 "satisfied with the result": Henry Knox to George Washington, 14 September 1787, Founders Online/National Archives, https://founders.archives.gov/documents/Washington /04-05-02-0269.

211 "Mrs. Knox and myself": Ibid.

212 "I wish a disposition": George Washington to Henry Knox, 19 August 1787, Founders Online/National Archives, https://founders.archives.gov/documents/Washington/04-05 -02-0271.

212 "It was a trying and wearisome task": Farrand, *Framing of the Constitution*, 134.

215 "with the wisdom of a patient chess player": Isaacson, *Benjamin Franklin*, 457.

215 "fix an Aristocracy": Jeff Broadwater, *George Mason: Forgotten Founder*, 199.

216 "I confess that there are several": Benjamin Franklin, Madison Debates, September 17, 1787, Avalon Project/Yale Law School, https://avalon.law.yale.edu/18th_century/debates _917.asp.

217 "Met in Convention": Washington's Diary, Monday the 17th, https://washingtonpapers .org/wp-content/uploads/2013/03/3.pdf.

217 "Outside the Convention": Freeman, *Washington*, 548.

217 "little short of a miracle": George Washington to Lafayette, 18 September 1787, Founders Online/National Archives, https://founders.archives.gov/documents/Washington/04 -05-02-0309.

Chapter Twelve: The People Decide

219 "Doctor, what have we got": Larson, *Franklin & Washington*, 218.

220 "Is the Constitution": George Washington to Henry Knox, 15 October 1787, Founders Online/National Archives, https://founders.archives.gov/documents/Washington/04-05 -02-0341.

222 "I was honored": Patrick Henry to George Washington, 19 October 1787, Founders Online/ National Archives, https://founders.archives.gov/documents/Washington/04-05-02-0350.

223 "In all our deliberations": Letter of the President of the Federal Convention, Dated September 17, 1787, to the President of Congress, Transmitting the Constitution, at Avalon Project/Yale Law School, https://avalon.law.yale.edu/18th_century/translet.asp.

225 "The real wonder": James Madison, Federalist Papers no. 37, https://avalon.law.yale.edu /18th_century/fed37.asp.

225 "I have observed that your name": Gouverneur Morris to George Washington, 30 October 1787, Founders Online/National Archives, https://founders.archives.gov/documents /Washington/04-05-02-0370.

226 "It is to be lamented": Centinel, excerpt from the antifederalist "Centinel" letters, appearing in the Philadelphia *Independent Gazetteer* between October 5, 1787, and April 9, 1788.

227 "more heat": Pauline Maier, *Ratification*, 128.

228 "How many mechanics?": William V. Wells, *The Life and Public Services of Samuel Adams* (Boston: Little, Brown, 1865), 228.

230 "Mr. Chairman . . . is this a monarchy?": Arguments Against Ratification of the Constitution at the Virginia Convention (1788), https://wwnorton.com/college/history/archive/resources/documents/ch07_04.htm.

230 "What harm is there": Journal Notes of the Virginia Ratification Convention Proceedings (June 3, 1788), ConSource, Virginia Ratifacation Debates, https://www.consource.org/document/journal-notes-of-the-virginia-ratification-convention-proceedings-1788-6-3/.

230 "a relinquishment of rights": Ibid.

231 "Relaxation must have become indispensably necessary": George Washington to James Madison, 23 June 1788, Founders Online/National Archives, https://founders.archives.gov/documents/Washington/04-06-02-0312.

231 "a monster with open mouth": Chernow, *Hamilton*, 244.

231 "There ought to be a capacity": Ibid., 257.

232 "an exhilarating blend": Ibid., 265.

233 "By folly and misconduct": George Washington to Benjamin Lincoln, 29 June 1788, Founders Online/National Archives, https://founders.archives.gov/GEWN-04-06-02-0326.

234 "grow old in solitude and tranquility": Brady, *Martha Washington*, 139.

234 "We have not a single article of news": Ibid.

235 "About ten o'clock, I bade adieu": "President-Elect George Washington's Journey to the Inauguration," George Washington's Mount Vernon, https://www.mountvernon.org/george-washington/the-first-president/inauguration/.

235 "I am truly sorry": Martha Washington to John Dandridge, April 20, 1789, https://marthawashington.us/items/show/434.html.

235 "filled the doors, windows and streets": "Washington Celebrates in Philadelphia." George Washington's Mount Vernon, https://www.mountvernon.org/george-washington/the-first-president/inauguration/philadelphia/.

236 "The Defender of the Mothers": George Washington to the Ladies of Trenton, 21 April 1789, Founders Online/National Archives, https://founders.archives.gov/documents/Washington/05-02-02-0095.

236 "Welcome, mighty Chief": Richard Howell, "A sonata . . . as General Washington passed under the triumphal arch raised on the bridge at Trenton, April 21, 1789," at Martha Washington—A Life, https://marthawashington.us/items/show/117.html.

236 "Hail, thou auspicious day": "My Country 'Tis of Thee," Song Colletion, Library of Congress, https://www.loc.gov/item/ihas.200000012/.

237 "The display of boats": "President Washington's inauguration in New York City," George Washington's Mount Vernon, https://www.mountvernon.org/george-washington/the-first-president/inauguration/new-york/.

239 "No people can be bound": "President George Washington's First Inaugural Speech (1789)," Milestone Documents, National Archives, https://www.archives.gov/milestone-documents/president-george-washingtons-first-inaugural-speech.

240 "The sacred fire of liberty": Ibid.

240 "I shall again give way": Ibid.

241 "the benign Parent of the Human Race": Ibid.

241 "Time has made havoc": Fisher Ames, *Works of Fisher Ames* (Boston: Little, Brown, 1854), 34.

Chapter Thirteen: The First Term

246 "The president's title as proposed": Thomas Jefferson to James Madison, 29 July 1789, Founders Online/National Archives, https://founders.archives.gov/documents/Madison/01-12-02-0202.

246 Maclay, a witty and incisive orator: Edgar Stanton Maclay, ed., *The Journal of William Maclay, United States Senator from Pennsylvania, 1789–1791* (New York: D.A. Appleton & Company, 1890), 34.

247 "When he is at loss for expressions": Ibid., 7.

247 "for, by the time I had done breakfast": George Washington to David Stuart, 26 July 1789, Founders Online/National Archives, https://founders.archives.gov/documents/Washington/05-03-02-0180.

247 "state of the greatest confusion": George Washington to John Adams, 10 May 1789, Founders Online/National Archives: https://founders.archives.gov/documents/Washington/05-02-02-0182.

248 "Oysters and lobsters": Brady, *Martha Washington*, 142.

248 "He is polite": Abigail Adams to Mary Smith Cranch, 5 January 1790, Founders Online/National Archives, https://founders.archives.gov/documents/Adams/04-09-02-0001.

248 "a very large and painful tumor": "George Washington's Health," George Washington's Mount Vernon, https://www.mountvernon.org/george-washington/health.

249 "Cut away—deeper, deeper": John Brett Langstaff, *Doctor Bard of Hyde Park: The Famous Physician of Revolutionary Times, the Man Who Saved Washington's Life* (New York: E. P. Dutton, 1942), 170–71.

249 "so malignant": Ibid.

249 "Do not flatter me": Ibid.

250 "the defects of this Constitution": Richard E. Labunski, *James Madison and the Struggle for the Bill of Rights* (Oxford: Oxford University Press, 2016), 189.

252 "If I thought I could fulfil": Founders Online/National Archives, https://founders.archives.gov/documents/Madison/01-12-02-0126.

253 "The Constitution may be compared": Labunski, *James Madison and the Struggle*, 195.

253 "They might have declared": Cheney, *James Madison*, 198.

254 "Eleven Cooks assembled": Richard Peters to James Madison, July 20, 1789, Founders of the Bill of Rights, ConSource, https://www.consource.org/document/richard-peters-to-james-madison-1789-7-20/.

254 "nauseous": Cheney, *James Madison*, 199.

255 "I wish to have every American": Ames, *Works*, 66.

255 the Bill of Rights: https://www.archives.gov/founding-docs/bill-of-rights-transcript.

256 "a farce": Broadwater, *George Mason*, 240.

257 "And should anything occur": George Mason to George Washington, 19 June 1789, Founders Online/National Archives, https://founders.archives.gov/documents/Washington/05-03-02-0011.

258 "Suppose the President committed murder": Maclay, *The Journal of William Maclay*, 167.

259 Washington usually assembled: Lindsay M. Chervinsky, *The Cabinet: George Washington and the Creation of an American Institution* (Cambridge: Belknap Press/Harvard University Press, 2020).

260 "The treasury, Morris": Custis, *Recollections and Private Memoirs*, 350.

261 "In the selection of characters": George Washington to Thomas Jefferson, 13 October 1789, Founders Online/National Archives, https://founders.archives.gov/documents/Washington/05-04-02-0123.

262 "when I contemplate the extent of that office": Thomas Jefferson to George Washington, 15 December 1789, Founders Online/National Archives, https://founders.archives.gov/documents/Washington/05-04-02-0289.

263 "Politics were the chief topic": "Public Versus Private" (1790), *Lapham's Quarterly*, https://www.laphamsquarterly.org/swindle-fraud/public-versus-private.

263 "Hamilton was many things": Joanne B. Freeman, "Jefferson and Hamilton: Political Rivals in Washington's Cabinet," George Washington's Mount Vernon, https://www.mountvernon.org/george-washington/the-first-president/washingtons-presidential-cabinet/jefferson-and-hamilton-political-rivals/.

264 "Impressed with a conviction": George Washington to Edmund Randolph, 28 September 1789, Founders Online/National Archives, https://founders.archives.gov/documents/Washington/05-04-02-0073.

265 "I have always been persuaded": George Washington to the United States Supreme Court, 3 April 1790, Founders Online/National Archives, https://founders.archives.gov/documents/Washington/05-05-02-0201.

265 "the keystone of our political fabric": George Washington to John Jay, 5 October 1789, Founders Online/National Archives, https://founders.archives.gov/documents/Washington/05-04-02-0094.

267 "They came": Joseph J. Ellis, *Founding Brothers: The Revolutionary Generation* (New York: Knopf, 2000), 49.

268 "[The] Potomac River": George Washington to Arthur Young, 5 December 1791, Founders Online/National Archives, https://founders.archives.gov/documents/Washington/05-09-02-0153.

271 "How unfortunate": George Washington to Thomas Jefferson, 23 August 1792, Founders Online/National Archives, https://founders.archives.gov/documents/Washington/05-11-02-0009.

271 "Hamilton and myself": Thomas Jefferson to Walter Jones, 5 March 1810, Founders Online/National Archives, https://founders.archives.gov/documents/Jefferson/03-02-02-0223.

272 "North and South will hang together": Thomas Jefferson to George Washington, 23 May 1792, Founders Online/National Archives, https://founders.archives.gov/documents/Jefferson/01-23-02-0491.

273 "Your resignation would elate": Elizabeth Willing Powel to George Washington, 17 November 1792, Founders Online/National Archives, https://founders.archives.gov/documents/Washington/05-11-02-0225.

274 "This oath I am now about to take": "Second Inaugural Address of George Washington," Avalon Project/Yale Law School, https://avalon.law.yale.edu/18th_century/wash2.asp.

Chapter Fourteen: The Gift of a Peaceful Transition

276 "The duty and interest of the United States": Neutrality Proclamation, 22 April 1793, Founders Online/National Archives, https://founders.archives.gov/documents/Washington/05-12-02-0371.

277 "To my fellow citizens": Thomas Jefferson to James Madison, 9 June 1793, Founders Online/National Archives, https://founders.archives.gov/documents/Jefferson/01-26-02-0219.

277 "the constitution we have": Meacham, *Thomas Jefferson*, 276.

278 "a good riddance": Ibid.

282 "The charge against me": Alexander Hamilton, printed version of the "Reynolds Pamphlet," 1797, Founders Online/National Archives, https://founders.archives.gov/documents/Hamilton/01-21-02-0138-0002.

283 "so full of shameful concessions": Cheney, *James Madison*, 254.

285 "felicity as a people": Washington's Farewell Address to the People of the United States, United States Senate, https://www.senate.gov/artandhistory/history/resources/pdf/Washingtons_Farewell_Address.pdf.

285 "There stood the 'Father of the Country'": Custis, *Recollections and Private Memoirs*, 434.

286 "a solemn scene": John Adams to Abigail Adams, 5 March 1797, Founders Online/National Archives, https://founders.archives.gov/documents/Adams/04-12-02-0005.

286 "The President is fortunate": Meacham, *Thomas Jefferson*, 305.

286 "On one side": George Washington to Tobias Lear, 9 March 1797, Founders Online/National Archives, https://founders.archives.gov/documents/Washington/06-01-02-0017.

287 "everything in a deranged": Flora Fraser, *The Washingtons: George and Martha* (New York: Alfred A. Knopf, 2015), 341.

287 "the General and I": Martha Washington to Lucy Knox, Martha Washington—A Life, https://marthawashington.us/exhibits/show/martha-washington—a-life/the-1790s/retirement.html.

287 "Unless someone pops in": George Washington to Tobias Lear, 31 July 1797, George Washington's Mount Vernon, https://www.mountvernon.org/library/digitalhistory/past-projects/quotes/article/unless-some-one-pops-in-unexpectedly-mrs-washington-and-myself-will-do-what-i-believe-has-not-been-done-within-the-last-twenty-years-by-us-that-is-to-set-down-to-dinner-by-ourselves/.

288 "We must have your name": John Adams to George Washington, 7 July 1798, Founders Online/National Archives, https://founders.archives.gov/documents/Washington/06-02-02-0302.

288 "I cannot express": George Washington to John Adams, 13 July 1788, Founders Online/National Archives, https://founders.archives.gov/documents/Washington/06-02-02-0314.

289 "inconsistency, concealed ambition": George Washington to Jonathan Trumbull Jr., 30 August 1799, Founders Online/National Archives, https://founders.archives.gov/documents/Washington/06-04-02-0229.

290 "The unfortunate condition": David Humphreys, edited by Rosemarie Zagarri, *Life of General Washington: With George Washington's "Remarks"* (Athens: University of Georgia Press, 1991), 78.

291 "You know I never take anything": Tobias Lear II, 1799, "The Last illness and Death of General Washington," Founders Online/National Archives, https://founders.archives.gov/documents/Washington/06-04-02-0406-0002.

292 "Well! it is a debt": Ibid.

292 "Tis well": Ibid.

293 "trimmed with black": Jerry Hawn (park ranger), "The Funeral of George Washington," National Mall and Memorial Parks, National Park Service, http://npshistory.com/publications/nama/newspaper/sep-2007.pdf.

293 "First in war, first in peace": Henry Lee, "First in War, First in Peace, and First in the Hearts of His Countrymen," https://www.nlm.nih.gov/exhibition/georgewashington/education/materials/Transcript-Funeral.pdf.

Afterword: In Their Footsteps

296 "Then join hand in hand": "The Liberty Song" (1768), Dickinson College Archives and Special Collections, https://www.americanrevolution.org/war_songs/warsongs6.php.

296 "A house divided against itself": Abraham Lincoln, House Divided Speech, Illinois Republican State Convention, Springfield, Illinois, June 16, 1858, National Park Service, https://www.nps.gov/liho/learn/historyculture/housedivided.htm.

297 "Some men look": Thomas Jefferson to Samuel Kercheval on 12 July 1816, Jefferson Memorial Education Series, National Park Service, https://www.nps.gov/articles/000/jefferson-memorial-education-each-new-generation.htm.

297 "I certainly would not want a constitutional convention": "First Amendments and Freedoms," April 17, 2014, National Press Club, C-Span.

298 In 2020, the National Constitution Center: The Constitution Drafting Project, National Constitution Center, https://constitutioncenter.org/news-debate/special-projects/constitution-drafting-project.

298 "reasonable people of goodwill": Ibid.

299 the 1787 constitution "is not completely incompatible": Ibid.

299 "and we mean it": Ibid.

301 "Lifetime tenure for Justices": Ibid.

302 "Between society and society": Thomas Jefferson to James Madison, 6 September 1789, Founders Online/National Archives, https://founders.archives.gov/documents/Madison/01-12-02-0248.

304 "I have often looked": Larson, *Franklin & Washington*, 223.

INDEX

Madison, Dolley (née Payne), 169, 178, 282
Madison, James
on bank question, 270
Bill of Rights and, 223, 249–255, 256
capital and, 266–267
Congressional representation and, 202, 204, 205
on Constitution, 224, 297
Constitutional Convention and, 1–2, 9, 172–173, 175, 176, 177, 178, 184, 185–186, 189, 190
on democracy versus republic, 180–181
drafting of Constitution and, 213
executive branch and, 205–206
on factions, 296–297
Federalist Papers and, 170, 224–225
health of, 230–231
Jay Treaty and, 282–283
Jefferson and, 168–169, 262, 286, 302
Morris and, 208
national government and, 192, 194
on pay for government officials, 195
political societies and, 279–280
ratification of Constitution and, 229, 230, 232
state power and, 187
title of president and, 245
Washington and, 3, 5, 239, 240
Washington's second term and, 282
on "We the People," 211
Magaw, Robert, 109
Maier, Pauline, 173
March 11 General Orders (Washington), 153–154
Marie Antoinette, 134–135
Marshall, John, 288
Martin, Luther, 192, 204
Mason, George
absence of, 1
advice to sons from, 43
Bill of Rights and, 215, 216, 256
Congressional representation and, 202
drafting of Constitution and, 214
executive branch and, 206, 213
national government and, 192
objections from, 221–222, 223
ratification of Constitution and, 229, 230
suspension of trade and, 51–53, 54
on veto power, 191
volunteer militias and, 62
Washington and, 42, 164, 256–257

Massachusetts Compromise, 228–229
Massachusetts Government Act, 60, 66
Massachusetts Spy, 106
mathematics, Washington's interest in, 22–23
Mathews, David, 97
McClurg, James, 176
McCullough, David, 99, 126
McDaniel, Mary, 28
McHenry, James, 288, 289
McKenzie, Robert, 68
McKonkey's Ferry, 115
Middlekauff, Robert, 124
Mifflin, Thomas, 176
militias
Continental Army formation and, 79–80
formation of, 62, 66, 71, 72
start of war and, 73
training of, 87
from Virginia, 30, 31–33
Miller, David, 278
Monmouth Court House, 136–137
Monongahela, Battle of, 34–35
Monroe, James, 281–282
Morgan, Daniel, 143–144
Morris, Gouverneur
compromise and, 197, 200
Congressional representation and, 202–203
drafting of Constitution and, 210–211, 213
national government and, 188, 192
Washington and, 208, 225–226
Morris, Mary, 6, 11
Morris, Robert
anti-independence stance of, 102
Constitutional Convention and, 178
Lee and, 86
as superintendent of finance, 165
treasury and, 260
Washingtons and, 6, 236, 269
Mount Vernon
building of, 22
financial pressures of, 163
repairs to, 287
slavery and, 40–41
Washington at, 6–7, 26, 29, 39, 233–234, 287, 289–290
Washington's arrival at after war, 161
Moylan, Stephen, 93

ABOUT

MARINER BOOKS

Mariner Books traces its beginnings to 1832 when William Ticknor cofounded the Old Corner Bookstore in Boston, from which he would run the legendary firm Ticknor and Fields, publisher of Ralph Waldo Emerson, Harriet Beecher Stowe, Nathaniel Hawthorne, and Henry David Thoreau. Following Ticknor's death, Henry Oscar Houghton acquired Ticknor and Fields and, in 1880, formed Houghton Mifflin, which later merged with venerable Harcourt Publishing to form Houghton Mifflin Harcourt. HarperCollins purchased HMH's trade publishing business in 2021 and reestablished their storied lists and editorial team under the name Mariner Books.

Uniting the legacies of Houghton Mifflin, Harcourt Brace, and Ticknor and Fields, Mariner Books continues one of the great traditions in American bookselling. Our imprints have introduced an incomparable roster of enduring classics, including Hawthorne's *The Scarlet Letter*, Thoreau's *Walden*, Willa Cather's *O Pioneers!*, Virginia Woolf's *To the Lighthouse*, W.E.B. Du Bois's *Black Reconstruction*, J.R.R. Tolkien's *The Lord of the Rings*, Carson McCullers's *The Heart Is a Lonely Hunter*, Ann Petry's *The Narrows*, George Orwell's *Animal Farm* and *Nineteen Eighty-Four*, Rachel Carson's *Silent Spring*, Margaret Walker's *Jubilee*, Italo Calvino's *Invisible Cities*, Alice Walker's *The Color Purple*, Margaret Atwood's *The Handmaid's Tale*, Tim O'Brien's *The Things They Carried*, Philip Roth's *The Plot Against America*, Jhumpa Lahiri's *Interpreter of Maladies*, and many others. Today Mariner Books remains proudly committed to the craft of fine publishing established nearly two centuries ago at the Old Corner Bookstore.

MORE FROM BRET BAIER

"*To Rescue the Republic* is narrative history at its absolute finest. A fast-paced, thrilling, and enormously important book."
—Douglas Brinkley

An epic history spanning the battlegrounds of the Civil War and the violent turmoil of Reconstruction to the forgotten electoral crisis that nearly fractured a reunited nation, Bret Baier's *To Rescue the Republic* dramatically reveals Ulysses S. Grant's essential yet underappreciated role in preserving the United States during an unprecedented period of division.

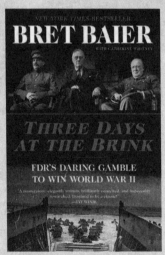

"[A] masterpiece: elegantly written, brilliantly conceived, and impeccably researched."
—Jay Winik

From the #1 bestselling author comes the gripping lost history of the Tehran Conference, where FDR, Churchill, and Stalin plotted D-Day and the Second World War's endgame.

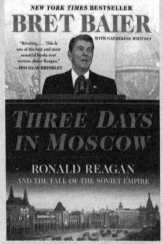

"A fascinating, thoughtful, and highly readable account of Ronald Reagan's towering contribution to his country—ending the Cold War without the firing of a shot."
—Michael Beschloss

President Reagan's dramatic battle to win the Cold War is revealed as never before by the award-winning anchor of *Special Report with Bret Baier*.

MARINER